Airlines
Worldwide

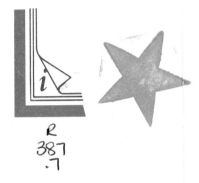

Midland Publishing

© 1994 NARA-Verlag and Midland Publishing Limited

ISBN 1 85780 021 4

First published in 1994 by
NARA-Verlag, Postfach 1241, D-85388 Allershausen, Germany
as 'Fluggesellschaften Weltweit'

First English language edition published 1994 by
Midland Publishing Limited
24 The Hollow, Earl Shilton
Leicester, LE9 7NA
England
Tel: 0455 847 256
Fax: 0455 841 805

Distributed in North America by
Specialty Press Publishers and Wholesalers
11481 Kost Dam Road
North Branch
MN 55056, USA
Tel: 800 895 4585
Fax: 612 583 2023

Printed and bound in Germany by Riess-Druck, D-83671 Benediktbeuern.

Airlines Worldwide

B. I. Hengi

Introduction

This book is an English-language version of the successful German 'Fluggesellschaften Weltweit', now in its second edition.

It aims to give an overview and illustrate 283 of the world's leading or more interesting airlines, with their history, current routes, aircraft fleet and operations.

It is not a comprehensive guide to every operator; adding together all the scheduled airlines, holiday and charter and local service operators gives an answer in the region of 5,000. This would result in a very large and expensive book.

The German edition was compiled by B. I. Hengi, edited by Josef Krauthäuser and published in January 1994. It has been ably translated by Dermot McElholm, and edited, updated and expanded by Keith Crowden so that it is as current as possible at press-time in May 1994.

Fleet quantities must be regarded as approximate only. With aircraft being delivered, retired, temporarily stored, or leased between operators every day, it is impossible to be definitive. We have also omitted some small aircraft which may be in an airline's fleet for training, communications or other purposes and are not in general passenger service. However we have done our best to ensure that the information in these pages is as up-to-date as possible and forms a valid and useful guide to the operations of the airlines described.

We hope that you will enjoy this book, and welcome your comments for future editions.

Midland Publishing
May 1994

time flies on

for C. W.

Contents

Airport Abbreviations/Codes

Europe

Aarhus (AAR)
Aberdeen (ABZ)
Adana (ADA)
Adler/Sotchi (AER)
Alicante (ALC)
Almeria (LEI)
Amsterdam (AMS)
Ancona (AOI)
Ankara (ANK)
Antalya (AYT)
Arrecife (ACE)
Athens (ATH)
Augsburg (AGB)
Avignon (AVN)
Barcelona (BCN)
Bari (BRI)
Basel/Mühlhausen (BSL/MLH)
Bastia (BIA)
Belfast (BFS)
Belgrade (BEG)
Bergamo (BGY)
Bergen (BGO)
Berlin-Schönefeld (SFX)
Berlin-Tegel (TXL)
Berlin-Tempelhof (THF)
Bern (BRN)
Bervelag (BVG)
Bilbao (BIO)
Billund (BLL)
Birmingham (BHX)
Bodo (BOO)
Bologna (BLQ)
Bordeaux (BOD)
Bratislava (BTS)
Bremen (BRE)
Brest (BES)
Bristol (BRS)
Brussels (BRU)
Bucharest-Otopeni (OTP)
Budapest (BUD)
Caen (CFR)
Cagliari (CAG)
Cardiff (CWL)
Catania (CTA)
Clermont-Ferrand (CFE)
Copenhagen (CPA)
Corfu (CFU)
Dalaman (DLM)
Dinard (DNR)
Dresden (DRS)
Dublin (DUB)
Düsseldorf (DUS)
Dortmund (DTM)
East Midlands (EMA)
Edinburgh (EDI)
Eindhoven (EIN)
Erfurt (ERF)
Esbjerg (EBJ)

Faro (FAO)
Florence (FLR)
Frankfurt (FRA)
Friedrichshafen (FDH)
Fuerteventura (FUE)
Funchal (FNC)
Gdansk (GDN)
Geneva (GVA)
Genoa (GOA)
Gerona (GRO)
Gibraltar (GIB)
Glasgow (GLA)
Gothenborg (GOT)
Graz (GRZ)
Guernsey (GCI)
Hamburg (HAM)
Hammerfest (HFT)
Hannover (HAJ)
Helsinki (HEL)
Heraklion (HER)
Hof (HOQ)
Humberside (HUY)
Ibiza (IBZ)
Innsbruck (INN)
Inverness (INV)
Isle of Man (IOM)
Istanbul (IST)
Ivalo (IVL)
Izmir (ADB)
Jersey (JER)
Jonköpping (JKG)
Kalamta (KLX)
Kaliningrad (KGD)
Katowice (KTW)
Kefalonia (EFL)
Keflavik (KEF)
Kharkov (HRK)
Kiel (KEL)
Kiev-Borispol (KBP)
Kirkenes (KKN)
Klagenfurt (KLU)
Köln/Bonn (CGN)
Kos (KGS)
Kristiansund (KSU)
Larnaca (LCA)
Las Palmas (LPA)
Leeds/Bradford (LBA)
Le Havre (LEH)
Leipzig (LEJ)
Lille (LIL)
Linz (LNZ)
Lisbon (LIS)
Liverpool (LPL)
Ljubljana (LJU)
London-Gatwick (LGW)
London-Heathrow (LHR)
London-Luton (LTN)
London-Stansted (STN)
Lvov (LWO)
Lugano (LUG)
Luxembourg (LUX)

Lyon (LYS)
Maastricht (MST)
Madrid (MAD)
Mahon (MAH)
Malaga (AGP)
Malmö-Sturup (MMX)
Malta (MLA)
Manchester (MAN)
Marseilles (MRS)
Milan-Linate (LIN)
Milan-Malpensa (MXP)
Minsk (MSQ)
Montpellier (MPL)
Moscow-Sheremetyevo (SYO)
Moscow-Domodedovo (DME)
Moscow-Vnukovo (VKO)
Munich FJS (MUC)
Münster/Osnabrück (FMO)
Murmansk (MMK)
Mykonos (JMK)
Nantes (NTE)
Naples (NAP)
Narvik (NVK)
Newcastle (NCL)
Nice (NCE)
Norrköpping (NRK)
Norwich
Nürnberg (NUE)
Odessa (ODS)
Olbia (OLB)
Oslo-Fornebu (FBU)
Oslo-Gardermoen (GEN)
Paderborn/Lippstadt (PAD)
Palermo (PMO)
Palma de Mallorca (PMI)
Paphos (PFO)
Paris-Charles de Gaulle (CDG)
Paris-Orly (ORY)
Pisa (PAS)
Porto (OPO)
Prague (PRG)
Prestwick (PIK)
Pula (PUY)
Rennes (RNS)
Reykjavik (REK)
Rhodes (RHO)
Riga (RIX)
Rome-Ciampino (CIA)
Rome-Leonardo da Vinci (FCO)
Rotterdam (RTM)
Rouen (URO)
Rovaniemi (RVN)
Saarbrücken (SCN)
Salzburg (SZG)
Samos (SMI)

Santiago de Compostella (SCQ)
Santorin (JTR)
Seville (SVQ)
Shannon (SNN)
Simferopol (SIP)
Skiathos (JSI)
Skopje (SKP)
Sofia (SOF)
Sonderborg (SGD)
Southampton (SOU)
Southend (SEN)
Split (SPU)
Stavanger (SVG)
Stockholm-Arlanda (ARN)
Stockholm-Bromma (BMA)
Strasbourg (SXB)
St. Petersburg (LED)
Stuttgart (STR)
Tallinn (TLL)
Tampere (TMP)
Teesside (MME)
Tenerife (TFS)
Thessaloniki (SKG)
Timisoara (TSR)
Tirana (TIA)
Toulouse (TLS)
Trieste (TRS)
Trondheim (TRD)
Turin (TRN)
Turku (TKU)
Valencia (VLC)
Varna (VAR)
Vasteras (VST)
Venice (VCE)
Verona (VRN)
Vienna (VIE)
Warsaw (WAW)
Westerland (GWT)
Wilna (VNO)
Zagreb (ZAG)
Zakynthos (ZTH)
Zürich (ZRH)

North America

Abilene (ABI)
Akron (CAK)
Albany (ALB)
Albuquerque (ABQ)
Amarillo (AMA)
Anchorage (ANC)
Atlanta (ATL)
Atlantic City (ACY)
Augusta (AGS)
Austin (AUS)
Bakersfield (BFL)
Baltimore (BWI)
Bangor (BGR)
Baton Rouge (BTR)

7

Beaumont/Port Arthur (BPT)
Bermuda (BDA)
Billings (BIL)
Birmingham (BHM)
Boise (BOI)
Boston (BOS)
Bozeman (BZN)
Buffalo (BUF)
Burbank (BUR)
Calgary (YYC)
Charleston (CHS)
Charlotte (CLT)
Chicago-O'Hare (ORD)
Chicago-Midway (MDW)
Churchill (YYQ)
Cincinnati (CVG)
Cleveland (CLE)
Colorado Springs (COS)
Columbus (CMH)
Corpus Christi (CRP)
Dallas/Ft. Worth (DFW)
Dallas-Love Field (DAL)
Dallas-Meacham Field (FTW)
Dayton (DAY)
Deer Lake (YDF)
Denver (DEN)
Detroit (DTW)
Des Moines (DSM)
Edmonton (YEG)
El Paso (ELP)
Eugene (EUG)
Fairbanks (FAI)
Fayetteville (FYV)
Fort Lauderdale (FLL)
Fort Myers (RSW)
Goose Bay (YYR)
Greensboro/High Point (GSO)
Halifax (YHZ)
Hamilton (YHM)
Harrisburg (MDT)
Hartford/Springfield (BDL)
Hilo (ITO)
Honolulu (HNL)
Houston-Hobby (HOU)
Houston-Intl. (IAH)
Huntsville (HSV)
Indianapolis (IND)
Inuvik (YEV)
Iqalit-Frobisher (YFB)
Jackson (JAN)
Jacksonville (JAX)
Juneau (JNU)
Kansas City (MCI)
Key West (EYW)
Knoxville (TYS)
Kuujjuaq-Ft. Chimo (YVP)
Laredo (LRD)
Las Vegas (LAS)

Lexington (LEX)
Long Beach (LGB)
Los Angeles (LAX)
Louisville (SDF)
Madison (MSN)
Memphis (MEM)
Miami (MIA)
Midland/Odessa (MAF)
Milwaukee (MKE)
Minneapolis/St. Paul (MSP)
Mobile (MOB)
Monroe (MLU)
Monterey (MRY)
Montgomery (MGM)
Montreal-Dorval (YUL)
Montreal-Mirabel (YMX)
Nashville (BNA)
New Orleans (MSY)
New York-Kennedy (JFK)
New York-La Guardia (LGA)
New York-Newark (EWR)
Norfolk (ORF)
Norman Wells (YVQ)
Oakland (OAK)
Oklahoma City (OKC)
Omaha (OMA)
Ontario (ONT)
Orange County (SNA)
Orlando (MCO)
Ottawa (YOW)
Palm Springs (PSP)
Pensacola (PNS)
Philadelphia (PHL)
Phoenix (PHX)
Pittsburgh (PIT)
Portland (PDX)
Prince George (YXS)
Prince Rupert (YPR)
Quebec (YQB)
Raleigh/Durham (RDU)
Regina (YQR)
Reno (RNO)
Resolute Bay (YRB)
Sacramento (SMF)
Saint John (YSJ)
St. Lois (STL)
Salt Lake City (SLC)
San Antonio (SAT)
San Diego (SAN)
San Francisco (SFO)
Santa Barbara (SBA)
Saskatoon (YXE)
Seattle/Tacoma (SEA)
Spokane (GEG)
Tampa/St. Petersburg (TPA)
Toronto (YYZ)
Toronto-Island
Tucson (TUS)

Tulsa (TUL)
Vancouver (YVR)
Victoria (YYJ)
Washington-Dulles (IAD)
Washington-National (DCA)
West Palm Beach (PBI)
Winnipeg (YWG)
Windsor (YOG)
Yellowknife (YZF)

South America/ Caribbean

Acapulco (ACA)
Aguadilla (BQN)
Anguilla (AXA)
Antofagasta (ANF)
Antigua (ANU)
Arequipa (AQP)
Aruba (AUA)
Asuncion (ASU)
Bahia Blanca (BHI)
Barbados (BGI)
Barcelona (BLA)
Baranquilla (BAQ)
Belem (BEL)
Belize (BZE)
Belo Horizonte (BHZ)
Bogota (BOG)
Bonaire (BON)
Brasilia (BSB)
Buenos Aires-Pistarini (EZA)
Buenos Aires-J. Newbery (AEP)
Cali (CLO)
Cancun (CUN)
Caracas (CCS)
Cartagena (CTG)
Cayenne (CAY)
Cochabamba (CBB)
Cordoba (COR)
Cozumel (CZM)
Curacao (CUR)
Cusco (CUZ)
Dominica (DOM)
Fortalezza (FOR)
Fort de France (FDF)
Freeport (FPO)
Georgetown (GEO)
Grand Cayman (GCM)
Grenada (GND)
Guadalajara (GDL)
Guatemala City (GUA)
Guayaquil (GYE)
Havana (HAV)
Holguin (HOG)
Iquassu (IGU)
Iquitos (IQT)
Kingston (KIN)

La Paz (LPB)
Lima (LIM)
Managua (MGA)
Manaus (MAO)
Mar del Plata (MDQ)
Mayaguez (MAZ)
Mazatlan (MZT)
Medellin (MDE)
Merida (MRD)
Mexico City (MEX)
Montego Bay (MBJ)
Monterrey (MTY)
Montevideo (MVD)
Montserrat (MNI)
Mount Pleasant (MPN)
Mustique (MQS)
Nassau (NAS)
Natal (NAT)
Panama City (PTY)
Paramaribo (PBM)
Pointe a Pitre (PTP)
Porlamar (PMV)
Port au Prince (PAP)
Port of Spain (POS)
Porto Alegre (POA)
Puerto Ordaz (PZO)
Puerto Plata (POP)
Puerto Vallarta (PVR)
Punta Arenas (PUQ)
Punta Cana (PUJ)
Quito (UIO)
Recife (REC)
Rio de Janeiro (GIG)
Santos Dumont (SDU)
St. Croix (STX)
St. Kitts (SKB)
St. Lucia (SLU)
St. Maarten (SXM)
St. Thomas (STT)
San Andres (ADZ)
San Jose (SJO)
San Juan (SJU)
Sand Pedro Sula (SAP)
San Salvador (SAL)
Santa Cruz (VVI)
Santiago (SCL)
Santo Domingo (SDQ)
Salvador (SSA)
Sao Pualo (GRU)
Tegucigalpa (TGU)
Tortola (EIS)
Trujillo (TRU)
Union Island (UNI)
Valencia (VLN)
Virgin Gorda (VIJ)

Asia-Pacific

Abu Dhabi (AUH)
Aden (ADE)
Adelaide (ADL)

Agra (AGR)
Aleppo (ALP)
Alice Springs (ASP)
Alma Ata (ALA)
Alor Setar (AOR)
Amman (AMM)
Amritsar (ATQ)
Anadyr (DYR)
Apia (APW)
Ashkhabad (ASB)
Auckland (AKL)
Bahrain (BAH)
Baghdad (SDA)
Baku (BAK)
Bandar Seri Begawan
  (BWN)
Bandung (BDO)
Bangalore (BLR)
Bangkok (BKK)
Beijing (BJS)
Beirut (BEI)
Bintulu (BTU)
Bishkek (FRU)
Bombay (BOM)
Bora Bora (BOB)
Brisbane (BNE)
Canberra (CBR)
Cebu (CEB)
Cheju (CJU)
Chelyabinsk (CEK)
Chiang Mai (CNX)
Chittagong (CGP)
Christchurch (CHC)
Colombo (CMB)
Dacca (DAC)
Damascus (DAM)
Darwin (DRW)
Delhi (DEL)
Denpasar (DPS)
Dohar (DOH)
Dubai (DXB)
Dushanbe (DYU)
Erevan (EVN)
Fukuoka (FUK)
Goa (GOI)
Guam (GUM)
Guangzhou (CAN)
Hanoi (HAN)
Harbin (HRB)
Hat Yai (HDY)
Ho Chi Minh City (SGN)
Honaira (HIR)
Hong Kong (HKG)
Ipoh (IPH)
Irkutsk (IKT)
Isfahan (IFN)
Islamabad (ISB)
Jakarta-Halim (HLP)
Jakarta-Soekarno (CGK)
Jeddah (JED)
Johur Bahru (JHB)

Jokjakarta (JOG)
Kabul (KBL)
Kalkutta (CCU)
Kaoshiung (KHH)
Karachi (KHI)
Kathmandu (KTM)
Khabarovsk (KHV)
Kota Bharu (KBR)
Kota Kinabalu (BKI)
Krasnojarsk (KJA)
Kuala Lumpur (KUL)
Kuching (KCH)
Kuwait (KWI)
Lae (LAE)
Lahore (LHE)
Langkawai (LGK)
Luang Prabang (LPQ)
Madras (MMA)
Magadan (GDX)
Male (MLE)
Mandalay (MDL)
Manila (MNL)
Medan (MES)
Melbourne (MEL)
Miri (MYY)
Mount Hagen (HGU)
Muscat (MCT)
Nadi (NAN)
Nagasaki (NGS)
Nagoya (NGO)
Nanjing (NKG)
Niigata (KIJ)
Norilsk (NSK)
Noumea (NOU)
Novosibirsk (OVB)
Okinawa (OKA)
Osaka (OSA)
Pago Pago (PPG)
Palembang (PLM)
Papetee (PPT)
Penang (PEN)
Perth (PER)
Phnom Penh (PNH)
Phuket (HKT)
Port Moresby (POM)
Port Vila (VLI)
Pusan (PUS)
Pyonyang (FNJ)
Rabaul (RAB)
Rarotonga (RAR)
Riyadh (RUH)
Sanaa (SAH)
Sandakan (SDK)
Semipalatinsk (PLX)
Seoul (SEL)
Shanghai (SHA)
Sharjah (SHJ)
Shenyang (SHE)
Sibu (SBW)
Singapore (SIN)
Srinagar (SXR)

Surabya (SUB)
Suva (SUV)
Sydney (SYD)
Taipei (TPE)
Sung Shan (TSA)
Tashkent (TAS)
Teheran (THR)
Tel Aviv (TLV)
Tongatapu (TBU)
Tokyo-Haneda (HND)
Tokyo-Narita (NRT)
Townsville (TSV)
Trivandrum (TRV)
Ulan Bator (ULN)
Ulan Ude (UUD)
Ulsan (USN)
Vientiane (VTE)
Vladivostok (VVO)
Wagga Wagga (WGA)
Wellington(WLG)
Wuhan (WUH)
Xiamen (XMA)
Yangon (RGN)
Zamboanga (ZAM)
Zhengzhou (CGO)

Africa

Abidjan (ABJ)
Abu Simbel (ABS)
Accra (ACC)
Addis Ababa (ADD)
Agadir (AGA)
Algiers (ALG)
Alexander Bay (ALJ)
Alexandria (ALY)
Alula (ALU)
Antananarivo (TNR)
Asmara (ASM)
Assuan (ASW)
Bangui (BGF)
Banjul (BJL)
Bamako (BKO)
Beira (BEW)
Benghazi (BEN)
Benguela (BUG)
Bissao (BXO)
Blantyre (BLZ)
Bloemfontein (BFN)
Boa Vista (BVC)
Brazzaville (BZV)
Bujumbura (BJM)
Bukoba (BKZ)
Bulawayo (BUQ)
Cabinda (CAB)
Cairo (CAI)
Casablanca (CMN)
Conarkry (CKY)
Cotonou (COO)
Dar-Es-Salaam (DAR)
Dakar (DKR)

Denis Island (DEI)
Djerba (DJE)
Djibouti (JIB)
Douala (DLA)
Durban (DUR)
Entebbe (EBB)
Freetown (FNA)
Gabarone (GBE)
Harare (HRE)
Johannesburg (JNB)
Juba (JUB)
Kananga (KGA)
Kano (KAN)
Kapstadt (CPT)
Karika (KAB)
Keetmannshoop (KMP)
Khartoum (KRT)
Kigali (KGL)
Kinshasa (FIH)
Lagos (LOS)
Libreville (LBV)
Lilongwe (LLW)
Livingstone (LVI)
Lome (LFW)
Luanda (LAD)
Luderitz (LUD)
Lusaka (LUN)
Mahe (SEZ)
Majunga (MJN)
Marrakech (RAK)
Maputo (MPM)
Maseru (MSU)
Mauritius (MRU)
Mogadishu (MGQ)
Mombasa (MBA)
Monastir (MIR)
Monrovia-Roberts (ROB)
Moroni (YVA)
Nairobi (NBO)
Ndjamena (NDJ)
Niamey (NIM)
Nouakchott (NKC)
Oran (ORN)
Ougadougou (OUA)
Port Gentil (POG)
Port Harcourt (PHC)
Port Sudan (PZU)
Praia (RAI)
Pretoria (PRY)
Rabat (RBA)
Sal (SID)
Sao Tomé (TMS)
St. Denis (RUN)
Tamanrasset (TMR)
Tangier (TNG)
Tripoli (TIP)
Victoria Falls (VFA)
Windhoek (WDH)

Photograph: de Havilland DHC-7 (Uwe Gleisberg/Munich FJS)

ADRIA AIRWAYS

Kuzmiceva 7, 61000 Ljubljana
Slovenia
Tel. 061 133 4336

Three letter code	IATA No.	ICAO Callsign
ADR	–	Adria

Adria Airways was set up in 1960. Flight operations began in March 1961 with a DC-6. Its initial fleet consisted of four ex-KLM DC-6Bs. In 1968, the airline became a part of the trading company Interexport. From then on it was called Inex Adria Airways. In 1970, new DC-9-32 aircraft flew the first scheduled flights from Ljubljana to Belgrade. From 1985 onwards, Inex also flew to Munich for the first time, as a scheduled service; there were also scheduled flights to Ljubljana. In addition to these scheduled services, charter flights are also provided for various tour operators. The airline's name changed back to Adria Airways in May 1986 when it became independent. When the first Airbus A320 was delivered in 1989, the airline took on a new colour scheme for its aircraft and reassumed its original name. Due to the civil war conditions in Yugoslavia in 1991, Adria's licence to fly was cancelled on 25th October 1991 but was returned on 16th January 1992. In 1992 Adria became the flag carrier of the independent state of Slovenia.

Routes

London, Athens, Larnaca, Djibouti, Munich, Paris, Tel Aviv as scheduled services. Charter flights from many European airports to destinations in Croatia and Slovenia; in addition, special flights carrying foreign workers.

Fleet

1 Airbus A320
5 McDonnell Douglas MD-81/82
3 McDonnell Douglas DC-9-32
2 de Havilland DHC-7

Photograph: Boeing 737-400 (author's collection)

AER LINGUS

Dublin Airport
Republic of Ireland
Tel. 01 705 2222

Three letter code	IATA No.	ICAO Callsign
EIN	53	Shamrock

In 1936, Aer Lingus Teoranta was set up for regional and European services, and Aerlinte Eireann Teoranta for international flights in 1947. The two airlines make up Aer Lingus, which is state-owned. Flights started with a de Havilland DH.84 from Dublin to Bristol. That was on 27th May 1936, and the aircraft took off from the famous Baldonnel airfield, as Dublin at that time did not have its own airport. Soon there were flights to London, Liverpool and to the Isle of Man. In 1947, seven Vickers Vikings were purchased for European services but were sold in 1948 and DC-3s became the main aircraft type in the fleet. Viscounts arrived in 1954 and enabled Aer Lingus to fly to Paris, Amsterdam, Düsseldorf, Frankfurt and Rome, and the Lockheed Constellation made flights across the Atlantic possible. From 28th April 1958 onwards, Aer Lingus flew to New York. Fokker F-27s were added in 1958. From 1st January 1960 Aer Lingus and Aerlinte were closely integrated and operated as Aer Lingus – Irish International Airlines. The Boeing 720 was introduced on the transatlantic service in December 1960. After the Boeing 720, the Boeing 747 was used from 1971 onwards. In the eighties Aer Lingus found itself in a severe crisis: numerous destinations were abandoned and excess capacities in the number of aircraft were reduced by selling or by leasing. Reorganisation took place, linked with a fleet renewal programme. Boeing 737s, first introduced in April 1969, have been the backbone of the fleet in recent years, with the 200 series latterly replaced by later models. Aer Lingus Commuter was formed in 1984 to cater for business and holiday traffic between Ireland and UK regional airports – Saab 340s and Fokker 50s are used. Boeing 747s are being replaced by Airbus A330s during 1994.

Routes

Scheduled flights to Boston and New York, to numerous cities in Britain, Amsterdam, Zürich, Frankfurt, Munich, Salzburg and charter flights to the Mediterranean region.

Fleet

3 Boeing 747-100
2 Boeing 737-300
6 Boeing 737-400
9 Boeing 737-500
6 Fokker 50
2 Boeing 767-300ER
4 Saab SF-340B
1 Airbus A330

Ordered

2 Airbus A330

Photograph: Ilyushin IL-86 (André Dietzel/Frankfurt)

AEROFLOT

Leningradsky Prospect 37, 125167 Moscow
Russia
Tel. 095 1555494

Three letter code	IATA No.	ICAO Callsign
AFL	555	Aeroflot

Aeroflot celebrated its seventieth anniversary in 1993 having been formed in March 1923 as Dobrolet, using de Havilland, Junkers and Vickers aircraft. In 1929 Dobrolet became Dobroflot when it was absorbed with a Ukranian airline and became responsible for all civil aviation activites in Russia. Dobroflot became Aeroflot in 1932. Regular international services developed only after the Second World War. Aeroflot's first supersonic passenger service was inaugurated on 1st November 1977 between Moscow and Alma Ata but was supended after several years. Aeroflot's vast fleet of over 7,500 aircraft carried

over 100,000,000 passengers for the first time in 1976, while the airline also supplied agricultural, survey, aero-medical, maintenance and training services within Russia and was also responsible for airports. In the last few years political developments in the former Soviet Union have been paralleled by changes in aviation. Since 1991, the former Aeroflot directorates became independent and established their own airlines, up to thirty or more. Newly independent republics also set up their own airlines and took over aircraft belonging to Aeroflot.
It was only in the course of 1993

that the new Aeroflot evolved in line with Western ideas, called Aeroflot-Russian International Airlines. All other services have been delegated to independent airlines.
Only a small section of the old fleet was taken over, and for the first time five Airbus A310-300s were leased although one crashed in March 1994. These were obtained by Aeroflot from July 1992 onwards especially for the routes to Japan and East Asia. Nowadays the criteria for flight operations are based much more on economic reality than social obligations.

Routes

Aeroflot-Russian International Airlines flies to around 120 destinations in Europe, America, Asia and Africa.

Fleet

27 Ilyushin IL-62M
19 Ilyushin IL-86
19 Ilyushin IL-76
 2 Ilyushin IL-96-300
 4 Airbus A310-300

 8 Tupolev Tu-134
30 Tupolev Tu-154
plus other types including Antonov An-2, An-26, An-28, Ilyushin IL-18, LET L-610, Yakovlev Yak-40 and 42

Ordered

4 Boeing 767-300ER
 Ilyushin 96-300
 Ilyushin IL-114
 Tupolev Tu-204
 (numbers not available)

Photograph: Boeing 747-200 (Josef Krauthäuser/Frankfurt)

AEROLINEAS ARGENTINAS

Paseo Colon 185, 1063 Buenos Aires
Argentina
Tel. 01 306391

Three letter code	IATA No.	ICAO Callsign
ARG	44	Argentina

Four smaller airlines merged in May 1949 at the instigation of the Argentinian Ministry of Transport to form Aerolineas Argentinas, the national airline to take over the operation of FAMA, ALFA, Aeroposta and Zonda from December 1949. The only other airline left was the Air Force-controlled LADE. Using aircraft such as DC-3s and DC-4s brought in to the airline, not only domestic destinations were served but also, from March 1950 onwards, New York. In 1959, the de Havilland Comet 4B was introduced on international routes and was used until 1966, when the first of a total of ten Boeing 707s was delivered. Boeing 737s were purchased for short-haul flights in 1969 followed by Fokker F-28s in 1975. Boeing 747s were first used regularly on the New York route in 1976, and to Europe as well from 1977 onwards. Regional routes are served by Boeing 737s, 727s and Fokker 28s, with the addition of MD-80s from the early 90s onwards. Three Airbus A310s are being acquired from Delta Airlines for use on services to the USA. Iberia has a 20% stake in Aerolineas Argentinas.

Routes

Frankfurt, Zürich, Rome, Madrid, Johannesburg, Los Angeles, Auckland, destinations in South and Central America, to Miami and New York. Dense domestic network.

Fleet

6 Boeing 747-200
8 Boeing 727-200
10 Boeing 737-200
3 Airbus A310

3 Fokker F-28
1 McDonnell Douglas MD-83
6 McDonnell Douglas MD-88

Photograph: McDonnell Douglas MD-83 (Uwe Gleisberg/Munich FJS)

AERO LLOYD

Lessingstr. 7-9, 61440 Oberursel
Germany
Tel. 06171 6404

Three letter code	IATA No.	ICAO Callsign
AEF	633	Aero Lloyd

Aero Lloyd is a private airline set up on 5th December 1980, and it started flights in March 1981 with three SE210 Caravelles. Initially it ran charter flights to the traditional regions around the Mediterranean. In addition to the Caravelle, Aero Lloyd soon also made use of three DC-9-32s, the first of which arrived in May 1982. From May 1986 onwards, there was an expansion phase with new MD-83 aircraft; from the summer on it flew new routes, and also put the first MD-87 into operation in 1988. In addition to charter flights, Aero Lloyd entered the scheduled flights business from 31st October 1988, and since then has been offering flights in Germany and to some destinations in Western Europe with the aim of undercutting the fares changed by Lufthansa. On 1st December 1989 a Munich-London Gatwick service was inaugurated. However in April 1992 Aero Lloyd withdrew from scheduled services, after Lufthansa decided to acquire a stake in Aero Lloyd. In late 1993 the last DC-9s were sold.

Routes

Charter flights are provided to all holiday destinations, altogether about forty. These depart from many airports in Germany.

Fleet

 4 McDonnell Douglas MD-87
13 McDonnell Douglas MD-83

14

Photograph: McDonnell Douglas MD-88 (author's collection)

AEROMEXICO

Paseo de la Reforma 445, CP 06500
Mexico City, Mexico
Tel. 327 207 6311

Three letter code	IATA No.	ICAO Callsign
AMX	139	Aeromexico

The original Aeromexico was established on 14th September 1934 as Aeronaves de Mexico. Pan American Airways acquired a 40% interest on 12th September 1940 but this passed to the Mexican Government when the airline was fully nationalised in 1950. Its position was strengthened with the takeovers of other Mexican airlines, including Lamsa, Aerovias Reforma and Aerolineas Mexicanas culminating in 1961 with that of Guest Aerovias, then one of the country's largest airlines. It became Aeromexico in February 1972. The present-day Aeromexico has been in operation since 1st October 1988,

after its predecessor of the same name was declared bankrupt in April 1988 by its owners, the Mexican Government and was compelled to discontinue operations. In November 1988, a consortium of Mexican business interests acquired a controlling interest in the airline and services restarted to thirty domestic destinations and five cities in the United States. Aeromexico is one of the country's two national airlines (the other being Mexicana), renamed Aerovias de Mexico, but still marketed under its former name. It acquired a subsidiary, Servicio Aereos Litoral (Aerolitoral)

in November 1990. A fleet with an increasing proportion of new aircraft ensures that Aeromexico today is able to compete again with other airlines, and the passenger figures are rising steadily. Aeromexico has a stake in Mexicana and in Aero Peru.

Routes

Around twenty destinations in Mexico, further routes to Los Angeles, Dallas, Miami, the Caribbean, Central and South America.

Fleet

5 McDonnell Douglas DC-10-15/30
18 McDonnell Douglas DC-9-32
23 McDonnell Douglas MD-82/88
3 McDonnell Douglas MD-87

4 Boeing 767-200
5 Boeing 757-200

Ordered

1 Boeing 757-200

Photograph: Douglas DC-10-10 (Patrick Lutz, Miami)

AERO PERU

Avenida Jose Pardo, 601 Lima 18
Peru
Tel. 14 478900

Three letter code	IATA No.	ICAO Callsign
PLI	210	Aeroperu

Aero Peru was set up by the Government of the Andean state on 22nd May 1973 as the new national airline. The new airline replaced Aerolinas Peruanas SA, which ceased operations on 3rd May 1971. Aero Peru brought together APSA and SATCO to form one airline. SATCO was under the administration of the Peruvian Air Force and brought three F-28 to the new airline. These aircraft were used to start operations, initially domestic services. The first Boeing 727 was acquired in May 1974. Two DC-8-50s were purchased in 1974 from the Venezuelan airline VIASA for international flights which started on 28th July 1974. From December 1978 to 1982, Aero Peru also used two Lockheed TriStars, but it was not possible to use them economically and efficiently. The privatisation of Aero Peru was completed in 1981. In 1992, Aeromexico acquired a stake in Aero Peru. The flights of these two airlines are coordinated, and Aero Peru also obtains aircraft from Aeromexico.

Routes

From Lima to Bogota, Mexico City, Buenos Aires, Caracas, Miami, Rio de Janeiro, Santiago, and in addition twenty domestic destinations such as Cuzco, Iquitos, Juanjui, Piura, Tacma, Trujillo.

Fleet

4 McDonnell Douglas DC-8-50/60
4 Boeing 727-200
2 Fokker F-28
1 McDonnell Douglas DC-10-10

Photograph: McDonnell Douglas DC-9-32

AEROPOSTAL

Torre Este, Pisos 46-48, Parque Central
Caracas 1010, Venezuela
Tel. 2 5093800

Three letter code	IATA No.	ICAO Callsign
LAV	46	Aeropostal

Aeropostal dates back to 1930 when Linea Aeropostal Venezolana was formed by the Venezuelan Government to take over the Venezuelan branch of the French company, Compagnie Générale Aéropostale which itself had been formed in 1929 to start services between France, the Caribbean and Venezuela. At first it was paft of the Ministry of Labour and Communications but in 1937 it became an autonomous government-owned corporation. By 1938 its Latécoère 28s were replaced by Lockheed Electras and Lodestars. Further expansion followed and DC-3s were acquired.

From 1953 onwards, services were provided to Lisbon, Madrid and Rome via Bermuda and the Azores. In 1957, Aeropostal expanded by taking over TACA de Venezuela and extended its flights to all of Venezuala. It used DC-3s, Martin 202s and Lockheed L-1049 Constellations. In 1961 Viasa was formed to take over the international routes opened by Avensa and Aeropostal, which were to concentrate on domestic services. After the routes were divided up after the setting up of VIASA, Aeropostal concentrated on regional flights with HS 748s and with DC-9s from 1968 onwards.

Routes

Aruba, Barbados, Curacao, Grenada, Havana, Puerte Espana, San Juan, Santo Domingo as well as over twenty domestic destinations.

Fleet

3 McDonnell Douglas MD-83
12 McDonnell Douglas DC-9-32/51

Photograph: DC-10-30 (Björn Kannengiesser/Frankfurt)

AFRICAN SAFARI AIRWAYS

Postfach 158, 4030 Basle
Switzerland
Tel. 061 3252941

Three letter code	IATA No.	ICAO Callsign
QSC	–	Zebra

This charter airline was formed on 1st August 1967 in order to carry 'club members' of the African Safari Club to Kenya. Behind the airline was the African Tourist Development Company and African Safari Lodges. Safari holidays were offered to the various East African game parks from European points. In December 1967, the first flight took place from Zürich to Mombasa with a Bristol Britannia. Six years later, the airline bought DC-8-33s from KLM and these remained until 1982 in the service of African Safari. ASA's first DC-8-63 flew on 24th March 1982, and ten years later the DC-10. When the DC-10 was introduced in early 1993, a new aircraft colour scheme was adopted.

Routes

From Basle, Frankfurt, London, Munich, Cologne and Hanover to Mombasa.

Fleet

1 McDonnell Douglas DC-8-63
1 McDonnell Douglas DC-10-30

Photograph: McDonnell Douglas DC-10-30 (author's collection)

AIR AFRIQUE

3, Ave. Joseph Anoma, 01BP 3927 Abidjan
Côte d'Ivoire
Tel. 320900

Three letter code	IATA No.	ICAO Callsign
RKA	92	Airafric

The airline was established on 28th March 1961 in co-operation with Air France, UAT (now UTA) and the former French colonies of Benin, Burkina-Faso, the Central African Republic, Chad, the Congo, the Ivory Coast, Mauritania, Niger, Senegal, Cameroon and Gabon. The first service of this multi-national airline took place in August 1961. Flights began with DC-4s and DC-6s. In the year the airline was established, a route was set up to Paris using an L-1649 Constellation. A DC-8 leased from UTA was Air Afrique's first jet aircraft on 5th January 1962. In the 1960s and 1970s, DC-8s, leased from Air France and UTA formed the basis of its fleet. Togo joined the consortium on 1st January 1968 and Cameroon withdrew in September 1971 to launch its own national airline, followed later by Gabon. In February 1973, a DC-10-30 was delivered, the airline's first widebody aircraft. The Boeing 747 was used from October 1980 to March 1984, but this aircraft turned out not to be flexible enough for Air Afrique's purposes. Airbus A310s are being increasingly used; this is obviously the ideal aircraft for Air Afrique. With the opening of a new route to Johannesburg, a return to an increase in passenger numbers was also registered in 1992.

Routes

Within the African countries which have a share in the airline, to Europe, in particular to France, and to the Middle East.

Fleet	Ordered
3 McDonnell Douglas DC-10-30	1 Airbus A310-300
3 Airbus A300B 4	
1 Antonov 12	
2 Boeing 707-300F	
4 Airbus A310-300	

Photograph: Airbus A310-200 (author's collection)

AIR ALGERIE

1, Place Maurice Audiens, Algiers
People's Democratic Republic of Algeria
Tel. 642428

Three letter code	IATA No.	ICAO Callsign
DAH	124	Air Algerie

In 1946, the Compagnie Generale de Transport Aerien was created while Algeria was still under French rule. It was merged with the Compagnie Air Transport to form the present Air Algerie on 22nd May 1953. Douglas DC-4s and Lockheed Constellations were used on routes to Paris and Marseille. Air Algerie started using the SE210 Caravelle in December 1959. In 1972 the airline was nationalised, the Caravelles were subsequently replaced by a large fleet of Boeing 727s and 737s; in 1974 the first Airbus A300B4 was taken over from TEA, before they obtained the first A310s of their own for use on routes to France.

Routes

North Africa, Europe, particularly to France, Frankfurt, Zürich and destinations in the Middle East; dense network of domestic routes.

Fleet

16 Boeing 737-200ADV
11 Boeing 727-200
 4 Airbus A310-200
 3 Boeing 767-300
 7 Fokker F-27

2 Lockheed L-100-30 Hercules

Photograph: McDonnell Douglas MD-88

AIR ARUBA

P.O. Box, Reina Beatrix
Aruba, Dutch Antilles
Tel. 23151

Three letter code	IATA No.	ICAO Callsign
ARU	276	Aruba

The regional area administration of Aruba set up Air Aruba in September 1986. Initially it worked as a ground-handling agent. With the aid of Air Holland and KLM, however, it started flights to the neighbouring islands in 1988, using NAMC YS-11s. For seasonal use a leased Boeing 757 was also used, which was replaced by the larger Boeing 767 leased since 1991. Air Aruba is active today in the business of providing scheduled flights and charters and at times also serves destinations in Europe such as Amsterdam and Cologne. The airline is using the relatively new national registration prefix 4P.

Routes

Bonaire, Buenos Aires, Caracas, Curacao, Maraicaibo, Miami, New York, St. Maarten, San Jose.

Fleet

1 Boeing 767-300ER
2 McDonnell Douglas MD-88
1 Embraer 120 Brasilia

Photograph: BAe 146-200 (author's collection)

AIR ATLANTIC

P.O. Box 9040 St. Johns, Newfoundland
A1A 2X3, Canada
Tel. 709 5700791

Three letter code	IATA No.	ICAO Callsign
ATL	–	Air Atlantic

Air Atlantic was set up as a regional airline in 1985. It began operations on 28th February 1986 with two Dash 7 aircraft as a Canadian Pacific commuter airline and is now a Canadian Airlines Partner. Its first international route was from St. Johns to Boston in August 1987. It serves around twenty destinations in the North-East of Canada today. Using the BAe 146 brought into service in 1990, Air Atlantic has in the meantime extended its services to the USA. In 1993 the airline carried around 300,000 passengers.

Routes

Boston, Churchill, Deer Lake, Frederictown, Gander, Goose Bay, Halifax, Montreal, Quebec, St. John, Stephenville, Wabush, Yarmouth.

Fleet

11 de Havilland DHC-8
 3 BAe 146-200

Photograph: de Havilland DHC-6 Twin Otter (author's collection)

AIR BC

4740 Agar Drive, Vancouver Intl. Airport
South Richmond BC, V7B 1A6, Canada
Tel. 604 2732464

Three letter code	IATA No.	ICAO Callsign
ABL	742	Aircoach

Air BC (BC stands for British Columbia) emerged in 1980 from the merger of various small airlines on Canada's western coast, including Gulf Air Aviation, Haida Airlines, Island Airlines, Pacific Coastal Airlines, Trans Provincial Airlines and West Coast Air Services.By June 1980, all the airlines had been purchased by Jim Pattison Industries and the first aircraft in the combined fleet, a Twin Otter, was rolled out in Air BC colours. The first Dash 7 arrived in 1983 and the first Dash 8 in 1986. Air Canada acquired a 85% holding in April 1987 and Air BC operates as an Air Canada Connector with an extensive regional network and services to Seattle and Portland in the USA. Its first BAe 146 was ordered in 1988. Its main hubs are at Calgary and Vancouver.

Routes

As a feeder airline for Air Canada, Air BC serves around thirty destinations in the west of Canada.

Fleet

```
 5 BAe 146-200
 4 de Havilland DHC-6
12 de Havilland DHC-8-100
 6 de Havilland DHC-8-300
 6 BAe Jetstream 31
```

Photograph: Boeing 737-400 (Josef Krauthäuser/Cologne-Bonn)

AIR BELGIUM

Vilvoordelaan 192, 1930 Zaventem
Belgium
Tel. 2 7206120

Three letter code	IATA No.	ICAO Callsign
ABB	–	Air Belgium

Air Belgium is a private charter airline set up on 3rd May 1979 as Abelag Airways. It commenced operations a month later and became Air Belgium in 1980. The main shareholder was Sun International. Its destinations were well-known regions around the Mediterranean. It used a leased Boeing 737-200. A night charter operation was also operated on behalf of DHL between Brussels and Madrid In 1988 they obtained a Boeing 737-400 of their own, followed by a Boeing 757 in 1989.

Routes

Charter flights, principally to the Mediterranean area, to North Africa, Turkey and the Canary Islands.

Fleet

1 Boeing 737-400
1 Boeing 757-200

Photograph: Boeing 757-400 (André Dietzel/Munich FJS)

AIR BERLIN

Tegel Airport, 13405 Berlin
Germany
Tel. 030 41012781

Three letter code	IATA No.	ICAO Callsign
BER	745	Air Berlin

Air Berlin USA was set up on 11th July 1978 as a wholly-owned subsidiary of the American company Leico. The first charter flights took off from Berlin in April 1979 using a fleet of US-registered Boeing 707s. As is well-known, until German unity was regained on 3rd October 1990, only airlines belonging to the victorious powers of the Second World War were allowed to fly to Berlin. Charter flights with particular departure times were provided by Air Berlin using a Boeing 707 between Berlin and Florida. However, this service, with a stopover in Brussels, was only provided from October 1980 to October 1981. Since then, Air Berlin acquired a Boeing 737-300, and has recently added 737-400s. After reunification, Air Berlin continued in the charter business. In the meantime Air Berlin has become a company under German law and is not restricted to departures from Berlin only.

Routes

Charter flights, principally to the Mediterranean area and the Canary Islands.

Fleet	Ordered
5 Boeing 737-400	1 Boeing 737-400

Photograph: Dornier 228 (DASA)

AIR BOTSWANA

P.O. Box 92, Gaborone
Botswana
Tel. 352182

Three letter code	IATA No.	ICAO Callsign
BOT	636	Botswana

Air Botswana was set up as a national airline by a presidential decree of July 1972. After Botswana National Airways (1966-1969) and Botswana Airways (1969-1972), Air Botswana took over operations on 1st August 1972 with Fokker F-27s and Britten-Norman Islanders. By 1980 a HS.748 and a Viscount comprised the fleet on scheduled services from Gaborone to Johannesburg and Lusaka and other points. The airline was a unit of the Botswana Development Corporation contracting out maintenance and flight operations control to Safair Freighters of Johannesburg. However in April 1988, it was taken over by the Botswana Government. A fleet renewal programme started in 1988, with new ATR-42s taking the place of the F-27s. In late 1989 Air Botswana also obtained its first jet, a BAe 146-100. It has formed a subsidiary, Southern Links, to develop regional business. The airline has established regional joint ventures with Air Zimbabwe and Zambia Airways.

Routes

National routes from Gabarone to Francistown, Maun, Maputo, Maseru. There are international services to Harare, Johannesburg, Windhoek and Lusaka.

Fleet

2 BAe 146-100
2 ATR-42
1 Dornier 228

Photograph: Dornier 228 (DASA)

AIR CALEDONIE

BP 212 Aerodrome de Magenta
Nouméa, New Caledonia (Nouvelle-Calédonie)
Tel. 252339

Three letter code	IATA No.	ICAO Callsign
TPC	190	Aircal

Air Calédonie started as Societe Calédonienne de Transports Aeriens (Transpac) being founded on 25th September 1955 and began operations the same month between Noumea and Lifan. The local government held 76% of the shares in this airline. In 1968 the airline took the name of Air Calédonie. In addition to its own routes, it also provides flights on behalf of UTA. Aircraft used were Cessna 310, Britten-Norman Islanders and de Havilland Twin Otters. In 1983 they carried 135,000 passengers on regional flights, and the number of passengers carried rose to over 180,000 in 1989. ATR-42s and Dorner 228s were added to the fleet from 1987 onwards, serving New Caledonia and other islands which form the Loyalty Islands.

Routes

Nouméa, Lifon, Mare, Ovre, Tiga, Huallon, Tonho, Kone, Koumac, Belep.

Fleet	Ordered
3 ATR-42	1 Dornier 328
2 Dornier 228	

Photograph: Boeing 747-400 (author's collection)

AIR CANADA

Place Air Canada Montreal, Quebec
H2Z 1X5, Canada
Tel. 514 8797766

Three letter code	IATA No.	ICAO Callsign
ACA	14	Air Canada

The Canadian government set up Trans Canada Air Lines (TCA) on 10th April, 1937, and it was administered by CNR, the Canadian Railways. On 1st September the first flights between Vancouver and Seattle started with a Lockheed 10A. Setting up a network of routes within Canada was TCA's most important concern in the following years. April 1939 saw the first flight on the Vancouver-Montreal route, and shortly afterwards TCA flew from Montreal to New York. During the Second World War, a regular connection between Canada and Scotland was created using converted Lancaster bombers. After the war, TCA flew to Düsseldorf as early as 1953 as part of the so-called emigrant flights. In addition to the DC-3, Lockheed Constellations, Canadair North Stars, Bristol 170s, Vickers Viscounts and Vickers Vanguards were in use during the prop age. On 1st April, 1960, the first jet aircraft, DC-8s, were added to the fleet. In 1964, the name Air Canada and new colours were introduced. In 1967 the first DC-9s arrived. Air Canada expanded globally and introduced the first large-capacity aircraft in 1971. Overseas flights were flown using Boeing 747s and Lockheed TriStars, with the more recent addition of the Boeing 767. It became fully privatised in 1989. The addition of the first Airbus A320 in early 1990 continued the renewal of the fleet. With around 10 million passengers in 1993, Air Canada is the leading airline in the country. A new corporate image and colour scheme is being steadily introduced in 1994. New trans-Pacific services are to start to Seoul and Osaka in 1994. It had been expected that Air Canada would be the launch customer for the DC-9X remanufacturing programme, but this is perhaps in doubt following the announcement of an order for twenty-five Airbus A319s in May 1994.

Routes

Intensive network in Canada, partly with smaller partners as feeder airlines, to the USA, the Caribbean (also charter flights); the routes to Europe were coordinated with Canadian and they were shared out in 1989. Thus ACA flies to Athens, Düsseldorf, Geneva, Lisbon, London, Madrid, Nice, Paris, Zürich, Frankfurt, Berlin.

Fleet

		Ordered
6 Boeing 747-100/200	2 Boeing 767-300ER	25 Airbus A319
3 Boeing 747-400	35 McDonnell Douglas DC-9-32	6 Airbus A340
7 Lockheed L-1011 TriStar	3 McDonnell Douglas DC-8F	4 Boeing 767-300ER
21 Boeing 767-200ER	34 Airbus A320-200	
3 Boeing 747-400		

Photograph: Boeing 727-200 (author's collection)

AIR CHARTER

4, Rue de la Couture, Sillic 318
94588 Rungis, France
Tel. 145603300

Three letter code	IATA No.	ICAO Callsign
ACF	–	Air Charter

Air Charter carries package tourists primarily to the holiday regions of the Mediterranean. It was set up on 3rd February, 1966 as Air Charter International (ACI). Flights began in July with SE 210 Caravelles taken over from Air France. In May 1979, Air Charter obtained its first Boeing 727s, and in 1988 Airbus A300B4 aircraft were acquired. When needed, Air Charter leases from or to Air France, Air Inter, EAS, Euralair. It carried around 2 million passengers in 1993. Air France has an 80% stake and Air Inter 20%. Services are flown from up to thirty-five French airports.

Routes

Charter services to the Mediterranean, North Africa and the rest of Europe.

Fleet

2 Airbus A300B4
3 Airbus A320
2 Boeing 727-200
8 Boeing 737-200
1 Boeing 737-500

Photograph: Boeing 767-200ER (Josef Krauthäuser/Hong Kong)

AIR CHINA

155 Dong-Si St. West, P.O. Box 644
Beijing, People's Republic of China
Tel. 550626

Three letter code	IATA No.	ICAO Callsign
CCA	989	Air China

Air China International was set up by the CAAC in July 1988 as an independent international division. Some aircraft carry Air China logos; however, further aircraft are leased from CAAC when needed. Air China is responsible for the international service of the People's Republic. It was formerly the Beijing – based international division of CAAC, the Civil Aviation Administration of China and was re-named Air China in July 1988. This was done at a time when the Chinese Government decided to form the airline operating divisions of CAAC into separate airlines, each with its own name, and concentrate on its role as a regulatory body. CAAC itself had been formed on 2nd November, 1949 after the creation of the People's Republic. There were new routes to Vienna from 1992 onwards, plus cargo services to Los Angeles and to Copenhagen in 1993.

Routes

Addis Ababa, Alma Ata, Bangkok, Baghdad, Belgrade, Bucharest, Frankfurt, Hong Kong, Karachi, London, Los Angeles, Manila, Melbourne, Moscow, New York, Paris, Rome, Singapore, Sydney, Toronto, Tokyo, Zürich, Vienna.

Fleet		Ordered
4 Boeing 747-200	6 Boeing 767-200ER	2 Boeing 767-300
4 Boeing 747-SP	3 Boeing 737-200	1 Boeing 747-400
7 Boeing 747-400	2 Boeing 767-300	
12 Boeing 737-300	6 Xian Y-7	
5 Boeing 707-300	4 BAe 146-100	

Photograph: Boeing 737-300 (Wolfgang Grond/Munich)

AIR COLUMBUS

Aeroporto do Funchal Santa Caterina
9100 Santa Cruz, Madeira, Portugal
Tel. 91 53334

Three letter code	IATA No.	ICAO Callsign
CNB	–	Air Columbus

Transporte Aereo Nào Regular is a joint venture of Portuguese companies and the Danish airline Sterling Airways. Sterling has a 34% share. Operations started in October 1989 with flights flown by leased Boeing 727s and flew primarily for tour operators from Germany. In 1991 another two Boeing 737-300s were added to the fleet. The home base of the airline is the Atlantic island of Madeira. After the collapse of the most important Air Columbus customers in Germany and the failure of Sterling Airways in 1993, Air Columbus is looking forward to better times again.

Routes

Charter flights from Stuttgart, Munich, Nuremberg, Paris, Zürich to Faro and other destinations in Portugal.

Fleet	Ordered
2 Boeing 737-300	3 Boeing 737-300
3 Boeing 727-200ADV	2 Boeing 757-200

Photograph: de Havilland DHC-8-300 (Uwe Gleisberg/Munich FJS)

AIR DOLOMITI

Via Aquiera 45, 34077 Trieste
Italy
Tel. 474421

Three letter code	IATA No.	ICAO Callsign
DLA	101	Dolomiti

Set up in January 1988, Air Dolomiti started operations in May 1991 with a Dash 8, on the route Trieste-Genoa. Further routes within Italy followed quickly. In November 1992 Air Dolomiti started flights abroad for the first time on the route Verona-Munich. Verona developed into a minor hub for the airline, with numerous connecting flights. Its base is the regional airport of Trieste.

Routes

Barcelona, Bari, Genoa, Florence, Munich, Trieste, Turin, Venice, Verona.

Fleet	Ordered
3 de Havilland DHC-8-300	4 ATR-42-300 2 ATR-42-500

Photograph: Boeing 737-300 (André Dietzel collection)

AIR EUROPA

Gran Via Asima 23, 07009 Palma de Mallorca
Spain
Tel. 178100

Three letter code	IATA No.	ICAO Callsign
AEA	–	Air Europa

Air Europa is the profitable remainder of the former multinational organisation Air Europe and was set up in June 1986 on the island of Majorca. The airline, registered as Air Espana SA, was, at the time it was set up in 1984, 75% owned by two Spanish banks and 25% by the British company ILG until the time of the latter's failure in 1991. It started flights on 21st November 1986 with a Boeing 737-300. The first flight was from London-Gatwick to Palma de Mallorca, which is also Air Europa's base. Air Europa and Air Europe had an identical livery and fleet, comprising Boeing 737s and 757s, and aircraft switched between the carriers to meet their individual needs at different times of the year. After the failure of its British partner, some tour organisers and banks took over its shares, enabling flights to continue. In 1991, Air Europa obtained three Boeing 757-200s for use on long-distance flights, which include services to and from Scandinavia. On 1st November 1993 Air Europa began scheduled domestic flights and shuttle services between Madrid and Barcelona from 31st January 1994 after agreeing to operate weekend flights. It is also to operate from Madrid to the Canary Islands.

Routes

Charter flights from the United Kingdom, Scandinavia and Western Europe to destinations in continental Spain, the Canaries and Majorca. Bangkok, Cancun, Delhi, Halifax, Havana, New York and Santo Domingo are some of the destinations of long-distance charter flights.

Fleet

7 Boeing 737-300
3 Boeing 757-200

Photograph: Boeing 737-200 (Uwe Gleisberg/Cairns)

AIRFAST INDONESIA

Kuningan Plaza, Suite 304 Jl HR Rasuna Sard Kar
C11-14 Jakarta, Indonesia
Tel. 21 5207696

Three letter code	IATA No.	ICAO Callsign
AFE	–	Airfast

Set up in 1971 as a joint venture between Indonesia and Australia with the objective of offering passenger and cargo charters in Southeast Asia, flights started with DC-3s. Fokker F-27s and various small aircraft for flights to the Indonesian islands were also used. The airline has been in private Indonesian ownership since 1982 and in addition to its original objectives the tasks now envisaged also include offshore flights to oilrigs, aerial photography and earth resource survey flights. Its main base is Jakarta, with a further one in Singapore.

Routes

Passenger and cargo flights within Indonesia, Singapore, Malaysia, Southeast Asia and Australia.

Fleet

3 Boeing 737-200	3 Bell 204
3 BAe HS-748	3 Bell 206
2 de Havilland DHC-6 Twin Otter	1 Bell 212
1 Douglas DC-3	2 Bell 412
1 CASA-NPTN 212	5 Sikorsky S-58

Photograph: Airbus A340 (Uwe Gleisberg/Munich FJS)

AIR FRANCE

1 Square Max Hymans, 75741 Paris
Cedex 15, France
Tel. 1 43238181

Three letter code	IATA No.	ICAO Callsign
AFR	57	Airfrans

On 30th August 1933 Air Orient, Air Union Internationale de Navigation Aérienne and Société Générale Transport Aérien merged to create the national airline Air France and bought the assets of Compagnie Generale Aéropostale. By the time of the outbreak of the Second World War, Air France had consolidated its leading position in Europe and North Africa. There were flights to all the colonies of that time, including Indochina. During the war, flights from 'free' France or from North Africa (Casablanca) were possible. After the Second World War, air transport in France was nationalised and Société Nationale Air France

was set up on 1st January 1946, followed by Compagnie Nationale Air France on 16th June when the airline was incorporated by Act of Parliament. In the beginning, the airline made use of French aircraft such as the Breguet 763, first delivered on 27th February 1953, the SE 161 and other lesser known aircraft. In 1953, the Comet was delivered, thus marking the start of jet transport. Further English aircraft, Vickers Viscounts, were employed on short and medium-distance flights, while the long-haul routes were served by DC-4 and Lockheed Constellations. 26th May 1959 saw the successful advent of the SE 210

Caravelle at Air France. Boeing 707s and Boeing 747s were used as replacements for propeller aircraft on inter-continental flights. From May 1974 Airbus A300s were also used for the first time between Paris and London, and on 21st January, 1976 the Concorde was licensed for scheduled services. The latest aircraft in the Air France fleet is the Airbus A340. Within the Air France Group are Air France, Air Inter, Air Charter and UTA. Air France also has a financial interest in Sabena. The routes and fleet of UTA, taken over in 1992, are still being integrated.

Routes

Air France has a dense network of routes throughout the world. Over 230 destinations in over 100 countries, though with emphasis on the former French colonies and to the overseas departments.

Fleet		Ordered
7 Concorde	16 Boeing 737-500	12 Boeing 737-500
37 Boeing 747-100/200	6 Boeing 737-300	15 Airbus A340-200/300
10 Boeing 727-200ADV	6 Airbus A340-200/300	9 Boeing 747-400
19 Boeing 737-200	25 Airbus A320	
8 Airbus A300	15 Boeing 747-400	
8 Boeing 767-200/300	2 Boeing 747-300	

Photograph: Fokker 100 (author's collection)

AIR GABON

P.B. 2206, Libreville
Gabon
Tel. 732197

Three letter code	IATA No.	ICAO Callsign
AGN	185	Golf November

Set up in 1951 as Compagnie Aérienne Gabonaise. In 1951 it began local services from Libreville with Beech and de Havilland aircraft. The airline was a founder member of Air Afrique and belonged to the consortium from 1961 to 1977. The airline was designated as the national carrier in 1968. In addition to its involvement in Air Afrique and international routes, the present-day Air Gabon operates independently in Gabon; it was known until 1974 as Societe Nationale Air Gabon. In 1974 it acquired its first F-28, followed by a further aircraft of this type and a Boeing 737. After leaving Air Afrique, Air Gabon then obtained a Boeing 747-200 for scheduled services to Europe in 1978. In 1988 the airline was reorganised and its network of routes tightened up. Its first Fokker 100 was acquired in 1990. The country's flag carrier, it operates an extensive network of scheduled and cargo flights and around 400,000 passengers take Air Gabon flights annually.

Routes

Abidjan, Bangui, Bitam, Cotonou, Dakar, Douala, Fougamou, Franceville, Gamba, Kinshasa, Lagos, Lambarene, Lome, Luanda, Marseille, Mekambo, Moanda, Nice, Oyem, Paris, Port Gentil, Rome.

Fleet

1 Boeing 747-200
2 Boeing 737-200
1 Fokker 100
2 Fokker F-28
1 Boeing 727-200

Photograph: ATR-42-300 (author's collection)

AIR GUADELOUPE

Aeroport du Raizet 97110 Abymes
French Guadeloupe
Tel. 903737

Three letter code	IATA No.	ICAO Callsign
AGU	–	Air Guadeloupe

Air Guadeloupe was set up by Air France and the local government of the French overseas department in 1970. It started operations with a Fairchild FH-227 for a shuttle service between Point-a-Pitre and Fort de France. The FH-227 was replaced by an ATR-42 in 1987. The delivery of the new ATR-72 provided Air Guadeloupe with a modern regional air fleet. After heavy losses in 1972, the airline applied to start insolvency proceedings; but flights continued. Its owners are the Department de Guadeloupe (46%) and Air France (45%) and it provides scheduled services from Point-a-Pitre to other islands in the Leeward Islands chain of the Lesser Antilles.

Routes

Marie-Galante, Les Saintes, La Desirade, Saint Bartholmy, Saint Martin, Saint Thomas and San Juan are important destinations in the Caribbean.

Fleet	Ordered
2 ATR-42	2 ATR-72
2 de Havilland DHC-6	
3 Dornier 228	

Photograph: Boeing 757-200 (author's collection)

AIR HOLLAND

Stationsplein Gebouw, Postbus 75116
1117 AA Schiphol-Oost, The Netherlands
Tel. 02968 84444

Three letter code	IATA No.	ICAO Callsign
AHD	–	Orange

Air Holland was formed in early 1984 by private companies and received its operating licence on 30th July that year. A Boeing 727-200 started flights on 2nd April 1985, and the second aircraft of this type followed as early as May 1985. Air Holland operates for tour operators from Amsterdam, Rotterdam, Maastricht and Eindhoven. From 1988 the 727s were replaced by four new, more modern Boeing 757s, and a further example followed in 1989 and again in 1990. Air Holland itself not only provides charter flights for tour operators but also leases the aircraft to other airlines. Air Holland Charter Bv, formerly Air Holland Nv started operations on 3rd November 1991. In 1992 Air Holland had to suspend flights for financial reasons, but after reorganisation it was able to resume charter flights in 1993.

Routes

Charter flights principally to the Mediterranean and to the Canary Islands; also, in winter to the Alps and to the Caribbean.

Fleet

2 Boeing 757-200
1 Boeing 737-300

Photograph: Boeing 747-200 (Josef Krauthäuser/Frankfurt)

AIR INDIA

A. I. Buildg. 218 Backbay Rec. Nairnam Point
Bombay 40021, India
Tel. 022 2024142

Three letter code	IATA No.	ICAO Callsign
AIC	98	Airindia

Air India can trace its history back to July 1932 when Tata Sons Ltd operated a mail service between Bombay, Madras and Karachi using de Havilland Puss Moths. Name changes followed to Tata Airlines in 1938 and to Air India on 29th July 1946. A further change came in 1948 to Air India International. Regular flights to London commenced in 1948 from Bombay via Cairo and Geneva and in 1953 all Indian air services was placed under state control and the same year Constellation flights served the Far East. Air India obtained its first Boeing 707 on 18th February, 1960, enabling Air India to provide flights to New York. In 1962 the airline's name was shortened to Air India. Its first large-capacity aircraft, a Boeing 747, was delivered in 1971. This aircraft flew on scheduled flights to London, and Frankfurt featured on Air India's flight schedule from 1973 onwards. Since the early 1980s Air India has also operated Airbus aircraft. 1989 was the year when India's flag carrier was restructured, with the aircraft also being repainted in a more 'modern' style. In late 1993 Air India obtained its first Boeing 747-400s. New services to Southern Africa and Indonesia are being introduced in 1994.

Routes

Around forty international destinations including Sydney, Perth, Singapore, Hong Kong, Tokyo, New York, Mauritius, Moscow, Rome, Frankfurt, Geneva and London.

Fleet

2 Boeing 747-300
9 Boeing 747-200
3 Airbus A300-B4
8 Airbus A310-300
2 Boeing 747-400

Ordered

2 Boeing 747-400

Photograph: Airbus A320-100 (Airbus Industrie)

AIR INTER

1 Ave. Marechal Devaux, 91550 Paray
Vieille Poste, France
Tel. 1 46751212

Three letter code	IATA No.	ICAO Callsign
ITF	279	Air Inter

Lignes Aériennes Intérieures was founded on 12th November 1954, but the first flight took place only on 17th March 1958, with a leased aircraft from Paris to Strasbourg. Air Inter operated some scheduled flights until flights were discontinued in 1958, but economic success was denied the airline. After reorganisation, Air Inter resumed operations, again with leased aircraft. The first aircraft owned by the company in 1962 were six Vickers Viscount 708s, and four Nord 262s bought from Air France. The latter also supplied 3 SE 210 Caravelles in 1965. On 16th May 1974, Air Inter took the first of a total

of ten Mercures, a French aircraft which was, however, not a success and Air Inter became the only operators of the type. This aircraft opened the route Paris-Lyon, which in the meantime has become the airline's most successful route. In October 1976, Air Inter obtained Airbus A300 large-capacity aircraft. In 1977, the company agreed with Air France to cease charter operations and received in return a 20% holding in Air Charter. Another Airbus product, the A320, was obtained by Air Inter as a launch customer as early as June 1988. The takeover of UTA on 12th January 1990 enabled Air France to

indirectly acquire a majority stake in Air Inter. Since then Air Inter, Air France and UTA have been merged into Group Air France. It is since then allowed to operate to any destination. Presently it operates some 50 permanent routes and ten seasonal ones as well as serving six permanent international routes and two seasonally. Air Inter was also a launch customer for the new twin-jet large-capacity jet aircraft, the Airbus 330, and received it in early 1994.

Routes

It connects all the important French cities with Paris, including the island of Corsica. Since 1988, Air Inter has also been flying to neighbouring countries, to cities such as Madrid, Ibiza, Rome, Athens and London.

Fleet	Ordered
9 Dassault-Breguet Mercure 100	13 Airbus A330
31 Airbus A320	8 Airbus A321
21 Airbus A300	9 Airbus A319
2 Airbus A330	

Photograph: Airbus A300B4 (author's collection)

AIR JAMAICA

72-76 Harbour Street, Kingston
Jamaica
Tel. 809 922 3460

Three letter code	IATA No.	ICAO Callsign
AJM	201	Juliett Mike

Air Jamaica was established by the government of Jamaica (66% share), together with Air Canada (40%) in October 1968. It succeeded an earlier company of the same name established with the help of BOAC & BWIA in 1962 and which had operated a Kingston-New York service with leased aircraft since 1965. Using a DC-9 leased from Air Canada, the new company started flights to Miami on 1st April 1969, and with a DC-8 to New York. From 1974 London was the only European destination in its timetable, in conjuction with British Airways, but this connection was discontinued after a few years.

Boeing 727s were acquired in late 1974 for Miami services. The DC-8 was too large for the airline's needs, and it was replaced by Airbus A300s in 1983. These are used for flights to the USA and Canada. In 1980 the airline had become fully state owned but an agreement has now been signed for privatisation which is expected to be completed by the end of June 1994.

Routes

Atlanta, Baltimore, Curacao, Grand Cayman, Miami, Kingston, New York, Philadelphia.

Fleet

5 Airbus A300B4
4 Boeing 727-200ADV

Photograph: Ilyushin IL-62M (Wilfried Salomon/Berlin)

AIR KORYO

Sunan District, Pyongyang
People's Republic of Korea
Tel. 2 37917

Three letter code	IATA No.	ICAO Callsign
KCA	120	Airkorea

Air Koryo, formerly Chosonminhang Korean Airways (CAAK) is the state airline of the Domecratic Republic of Korea (North Korea). It was formed on 12th September 1955 to succeed SOKAO, the joint Soviet – North Korean airline established in 1950, which started with Li-2s. IL-14s were used initially, later replaced by IL-18s on mainly domestic scheduled and charter services. Fleet policy was in line with the particular Soviet production of the time. Air Koryo is the new name is use since 1993.

Routes

International routes to Beijing, Berlin-Schönefeld, Khaborosk, Moscow and Sofia. Also occasional services to Prague and Tirana. Regional services to Kaesong, Wonsan, Hamhun, Kilchu, Kanggye, Chongsin and Sinuiju.

Fleet

4 Ilyushin IL-62M
4 Tupolev-154B
2 Tupolev-134 B
2 Ilyushin IL-18

8 Antonov 24
3 Ilyushin IL-76TD

Photograph: Lockheed L-1011-500 TriStar (Stefan Höllering/Zürich)

AIR LANKA

P.O. Box 670, 14 Sir Baron Jagatilaka
Mawatha, Colombo 1, Sri Lanka
Tel. 421291

Three letter code	IATA No.	ICAO Callsign
ALK	603	Airlanka

Air Lanka was set up on 10th January 1979 in order to be able to continue the business affairs of Air Ceylon, which had ceased in 1978. The airline was then 60% owned by the Sri Lankan Government and 40% with Sri Lankan businesses. Management and technical assistance was provided by Singapore Airlines. Operations started on 1st September 1979 with two leased Boeing 707s from SIA. The first TriStar owned by the airline flew from Colombo to Paris on 2nd November 1990. Zürich, Frankfurt and London followed soon after. At times there were flights with leased Boeing 747s to London-Gatwick, but the passenger volume – due to the political situation in the country – is somewhat in decline. The two Boeing 747s leased from Qantas were subsequently returned and the first L-1011 TriStar for Air Lanka went in service on 4th June 1984. The Boeing 737 is an addition to the TriStar for regional flights to India and the Maldives. A planned renewal of the long-distance fleet had to be postponed in 1993 as financing the planned Airbus A340s was not possible.

Routes

Regional network from Colombo; otherwise mainly flight to Europe, to destinations such as London, Amsterdam, Paris, Frankfurt, Vienna and Zürich.

Fleet

5 Lockheed L-1011-500
4 Lockheed L-1011
1 Boeing 737-200
2 Airbus A320-200

Photograph: Airbus A310-300 (Josef Krauthäuser/Bangkok)

AIR LIBERTE

1 rue de la Courson, Senia 128 Tiasis
94517 Rungis Cedex, France
Tel. 46862500

Three letter code	IATA No.	ICAO Callsign
LIB	718	Liberte

Air Liberté was set up in July 1987. Flights started in April 1988 with a leased MD-83, especially for Club Aquarius, one of the major tour organisers in France. From its base at Paris-Orly, Air Liberte operates passenger services to both European and Mediterranean holiday resorts from French cities in the main using its MD-83s. Two of the MD-83s are based at Monastir, Tunisia flying for Air Liberté Tunisie. For its long-haul services from Paris to Montreal and New York it used its Airbuses and it also operates charter services to the French-speaking Caribbean Islands. It opened up a scheduled service to Montreal for the first time in 1993. Otherwise the airline operates only in the charter business or leases aircraft to other airlines.

Routes

Destinations in the Mediterranean and North Africa, Réunion as well as to the Caribbean and to East Asia.

Fleet

8 McDonnell Douglas MD-83
1 Airbus A310-300
2 Airbus A300-600

Photograph: Boeing 747-200 (B. I. Hengi/Zürich)

AIR MADAGASCAR

31 Ave. de l'Independence, BP 437
Antanaraivo, Republic of Madagascar
Tel. 2 22222

Three letter code	IATA No.	ICAO Callsign
MDG	258	Madair

Air Madagascar was founded in 1961, a year after the state became independent. It was set up by the Government (51%), Air France (40%) and a predecessor company of the same name which had been in existence since 1947. Prior to 1st January 1962 it had been known as Madair. The first service was inaugurated on 20th October 1961 between Tananarive and Paris with a Douglas DC-7C operated on the airline's behalf by the French carrier Transports Aeriens Intercontinentaux (TAI). Air France's involvement in the airline was to bring in the domestic flights it had previously provided along with the corresponding aircraft. The first international route was via Djibouti and Marseille to Paris, on which Boeing 707s were employed. Over the next few years an extensive internal network was established to many points in Madagascar and to the African mainland. Further aircraft used in those early years were DC-3s and DC-4s. In 1979 the Boeing 747-200SC, its first and only large-capacity aircraft, was added to the fleet.

Routes

Paris, Zürich, Reunion, Mauritius, Kenya, Djibouti, Johannesburg, Mauritius, Réunion and to over twenty domestic destinations.

Fleet

2 Boeing 737-200
1 Boeing 747-200
3 BAe HS-748
4 de Havilland DHC-6 Twin Otter

Photograph: Dornier 228 (DASA)

AIR MALDIVES

P.O. Box 2049 Male
Maldives
Tel. 322430

Three letter code	IATA No.	ICAO Callsign
AMI	–	Maldives

Air Maldives operates domestic flights within the Maldives Republic between Male and Gan, and also serves as general sales and handling agent for various international scheduled and charter airlines. The original Air Maldives was formed in 1974 and began operations in October of that year. The airline served as the flag carrier for the Maldives until May 1977, providing services between Male and Colombo, Sri Lanka with a Convair 440, and also covering the internal route to Gan. The airline abruptly halted its Convair operations in 1977, and was succeeded in September 1977 as national flag carriers by Maldives International Airlines, operating between Male and Trivandrum (India) via Colombo from 2nd November 1977. The company had a technical and management agreement with Indian Airlines whose Boeing 737s were used on that service. The arrangement did not last and the new national carrier Maldives Airlines was set up by the Government in 1984 with three DC-8s and three Fokker F27s but it was dissolved in 1986. Air Maldives, operated by the National Travel Bureau, once again launched an air service between Male and Gan via Kaddu Island in South Maldives using a Skyvan. In late 1989 new Dorniers were added to the fleet and the airline again reorganised. The airline is to start its first jet service with a BAe 146-100 being taken on a five year lease.

Routes

Male to Gan as a regular scheduled service.

Fleet	Ordered
2 Dornier 228	1 BAe 146-100

Photograph: Boeing 727-200 (Josef Krauthäuser/Munich FJS)

AIR MALTA

Luga Airport
Republic of Malta
Tel. 824330

Three letter code	IATA No.	ICAO Callsign
AMC	643	Air Malta

Air Malta is the national airline of the island republic of Malta, and has been in existence since 30th March 1973, when it was set up by order of the government. The first service was Malta-Rome, from 1st April 1973. Air Malta used only jet aircraft from the beginning. Services were initially flown with leased British Airways Tridents, followed on 1st April 1974 by independent operations. Its network of routes was consolidated and there were regular flights, including charter flights, to London, Amsterdam, Paris, Zürich, Munich, Cairo and Tripoli. Boeing 720s were used, with the addition of Boeing 737-200s from 1978 onwards; these later replaced the 720s. With the introduction of the Airbus A320 in Spring 1990, Air Malta also adopted a new colour scheme for its fleet. Air Malta had about 1.3 million passengers in 1993. Malta Air Charter, an Air Malta subsidiary operates a Malta-Gozo-Malta link by helicopter. In spring 1994 new scheduled routes to Stockholm, Oslo and Bahrain were due to start, and four BAe RJ70s with extended range capabilities have been ordered to replace the Boeing 737-200s by March 1995.

Routes

Scheduled and charter flights to Munich, Zürich, Frankfurt, London, Rome, the Middle East, North Africa.

Fleet	Ordered
6 Boeing 737-200	4 BAe/Avro RJ 70
2 Airbus A320	
2 Boeing 737-300	
1 BAe ATP	

Photograph: McDonnell Douglas DC-8-62 (author's collection)

AIR MARSHALL ISLANDS

P.O. Box 959 Majuro
Republic of the Marshall Islands
Tel. 3373

Three letter code	IATA No.	ICAO Callsign
MRS	778	Marshallislands

In 1980 an independent state airline was established with the purpose of creating better air connections between the individual islands of the state territory and the main island of Majuro. It was known as the Airline of the Marshall Islands. The current name was adopted in 1989. The first flights were with GAF-Nomads. The most important route is from Majuro to Kwajalein, where an American missile base and airforce base is located. A leased DC-8-62 has been used recently to open up a tourist infrastructure; the intention is primarily to bring tourists from the USA to the country. The GAF-Nomads were replaced by Dornier 228s delivered in 1984 and 1985. As the flag carrier of the Government of Tuvalu twice weekly services are operated by the DC-8 between Honolulu-Majuro-Honolulu and by the HS-748 from Majuro to Suva and Nadi.

Routes

In the Pacific area, to more than twenty atolls belonging to the state territory, to Kwajalein, Kiribati, Tuvalu, to Honolulu and Los Angeles.

Fleet	Ordered
2 Dornier 228	2 Saab 2000
1 BAe HS-748	
1 McDonnell Douglas DC-8-62	

Photograph: Fokker F28-4000 (author's collection)

AIR MAURITANIE

B.P. 41, Nouakchott 174
Islamic Republic of Mauritania
Tel. 522211

Three letter code	IATA No.	ICAO Callsign
MRT	174	Air Mauritania

Air Mauritania was established in September 1962 to take over and expand the small internal network previously provided by Air France and UAT. Operations started in October 1963 with technical assistance and equipment from Spantax and the airline quickly built up its services, particularly in the important agricultural areas in the southern part of the country using Fokker F-27s. By the mid 1980's, international serives were operated to Dakar and Las Palmas in addition to an extensive domestic network. The airline was owned by the government (60%), Air Afrique (20%) and UTA (20%). UTA had been created by a merger of the two French airlines, UAT and TAI. Two Fokker F-28s have been in use since 1983.

Routes

Dakar, Las Palmas and some domestic destinations.

Fleet

2 Fokker F-28-4000
1 Pilatus Britten-Norman Islander

Photograph: Boeing 747SP (Josef Krauthäuser/Munich)

AIR MAURITIUS

Rogers House 5, President John Kennedy Street
Port Louis, Mauritius
Tel. 08-6801

Three letter code	IATA No.	ICAO Callsign
MAU	239	Airmauritius

Air Mauritius was set up on 14th June 1967 although between that date and 1972 its activities were limited to the handling of aircraft operating into and out of Mauritius. It had been formed with the Government having a 51% stake as well as holdings by British Airways and Air France. Air India also became involved. It was August 1972 when operations finally started when a Piper Navajo was leased for a flight from Port Louis to the island of Rodrigues, around 600 km away from the main island, in 1972. In 1973, a connection to Bombay was set up with the co-operation of Air India and the use of its aircraft. The same procedure was used with flights to London and with Air France to Paris. Only on 31st October 31, 1977 did Air Mauritius obtain a Boeing in its own colours. For a number of years Air Mauritius used Twin Otters on domestic services and a Boeing 707, leased from British Airways, for long-haul flights. In April 1978, Rome was included in its network, and in 1981 Durban, Johannesburg, Nairobi and Antananaraivo followed, with Jeddah and Zürich in 1983. A Boeing 747SP was leased from SAA in 1984 in order to be able to provide non-stop flights to Paris. In 1987 Munich and Singapore were included as destinations. The flights to Munich and also more recently to Frankfurt now take place several times a week. The Boeing 707s were replaced by new Boeing 767s. Five Airbus A340s have been ordered; these will be maintained by Lufthansa with whom there is also a new commercial co-operation agreement.

Routes

Madagascar, Reunion, Bombay, Durban, Johannesburg, London, Paris, Zürich, Munich, Frankfurt, Rome, Singapore.

Fleet	Ordered
3 Boeing 747SP	1 ATR-72
2 Boeing 767-200ER	5 Airbus A340-300
2 ATR-42	

Photograph: Tupolev Tu-134A (Uwe Gleisberg/Munich FJS)

AIR MOLDOVA

Airport, 277026 Kishinev
Moldavia
Tel. 2233424

Three letter code	IATA No.	ICAO Callsign
MLD	572	Moldova

The former Soviet republic of Moldavia, bordering on Romania, declared its independence in 1992 and insisted on having its own airline. As early as May 1992 it opened a regular service from Kishinev to Frankfurt, using a Tu-134A. There are also occasional charter flights to other destinations in Western Europe such as Munich and Zürich. It serves a number of destinations domestically and to cities such as Minsk, Murmansk, Sochi, St. Petersburg, Tbilisi and Volgograd in the former USSR. It continues to rely on Aeroflot for many services but is also booking more to Western Europe for assistance.

Routes

There are regular flights to Moscow, Bucharest and Frankfurt.

Fleet

9 Tupolev Tu-134A
3 Tupolev Tu-154B

Photograph: Boeing 747SP (Wolfgang Grond/Frankfurt)

AIR NAMIBIA

P.O. Box 731, Windhoek 9100
Namibia
Tel. 061 38220

Three letter code	IATA No.	ICAO Callsign
NMB	186	Namibair

Although the airline was set up as early as 1946, it was only after Namibia, the former South-West Africa, became independent that Air Namibia appeared as Namibia's national carrier. After it was formed as South West Air transport, regular flights from Windhoek to Swakopmuk began with DC-3s in 1948. Oryx Aviation was taken over in 1959 and the name changed to Suidwes Lugdiens. There was a further takeover at the end of the 60s, the charter airline Namibair Pty. Ltd. The name of this airline was adopted in 1978 as the airline provided a number of scheduled domestic feeder services to connect with SAA flights at Windhoek. It became the national airline in 1987. On 24th April, 1990, Namib Air started regular services to Frankfurt with a Boeing 747SP. The new name was adopted by Air Namibia in the course of 1991. On 6th July 1992 Air Namibia launched a weekly Boeing 747SP service between Windhoek and Heathrow via Johannesburg in competition with SAA and British Airways, flights have since been increased on the route. In 1993 a further Boeing 747SP was acquired from SAA.

Routes

From Windhoek to Swakopmuk, Grotfontein, Tsumbeli, Oshakati, Maun, Keetmanshoop, Capetown, Johannesburg, Frankfurt, London, Zambia and Botswana.

Fleet

3 Beechcraft 1900
1 Boeing 737-200
2 Boeing 747SP

Photograph: Boeing 767-200ER (Björn Kauneñglesser/Sydney)

AIR NEW ZEALAND

1 Queen Street, Auckland 1
New Zealand
Tel. 09 797515

Three letter code	IATA No.	ICAO Callsign
ANZ	86	New Zealand

The present-day Air New Zealand goes back to 1939, when Tasman Empire Airways Ltd. (TEAL) was formed as a joint British (20%), Australian (30%) and New Zealand (50%) company. Short S-30 flying boats were used for regular flights between Australia and Auckland. The flying boats were in use until 1954, and were then replaced by DC-6s. In 1961 the New Zealand Government assumed full control, TEAL entered the jet age in 1965 with the purchase of three DC-8s. In that year the name was also changed to Air New Zealand. New routes to the USA were opened up, and the domestic airline NZNAC (formed in 1945) was taken over on 1st April 1978. Larger DC-10s and Boeing 747s were added to the DC-8s, and the last DC-8 left ANZ on 1st September 1989. Frankfurt, apart from London the sole European destination, was first served on 31st October, 1987. The airline was privatised in 1988. Qantas has a 19.9% stake and Japan Air Lines 7.5%. The New Zealand public own 30% and the Government one 'Kiwi' share. Boeing 747-400s and Boeing 767-300s were added to the fleet in 1992, although some aircraft have been leased out.

Routes

Air New Zealand links nineteen domestic airports. International flights are to Australia, Singapore, Kuala Lumpur, Bali, Bangkok, Hong Kong, the Pacific area, Los Angeles, Honolulu, London.

Fleet

2 Fokker F-27
12 Boeing 737-200
8 Boeing 767-200ER
5 Boeing 747-200
3 Boeing 747-400

6 Boeing 767-300ER

Ordered

1 Boeing 747-400
3 Boeing 767-300ER
6 Boeing 737-300

Photograph: Fokker F-28 (Uwe Gleisberg/Cairns)

AIR NIUGINI

Ang House, Jacksons Airport P.O.B. 7186
7186 Boroko, Papua New Guinea
Tel. 273200

Three letter code	IATA No.	ICAO Callsign
ANG	656	Niugini

Ansett, Qantas, TAA and the government of Papua New Guinea formed Air Niugini jointly in November 1973. With eight Fokker Friendships and twelve DC-3s, the new airline took over operations from Ansett and TAA on 1st November 1973, and carried these out in Australian administered New Guinea until independence. International flights to Sydney and Singapore started in 1975; the international network of flights was extended to Honolulu using Boeing 707s. When it was set up as the national airline of Papua New Guinea, the Government held 60% of the shares, Ansett 16%, Qantas 12% and TAA 12%. In 1976, the Government bought out the Qantas and TAA holdings and in 1980 acquired the Ansett shares to make the airline wholly Government owned. It became the national airline of Papua New Guinea upon the territory's independence from Australia on 16th September 1975. A leased Airbus A300 B4 – beautifully painted – replaced the Boeing 707s in 1984. The first airline-owned Airbus A310s were delivered to Air Niugini in early 1989.

Routes

Port Moresby, Brisbane, Cairns, Hong Kong, Manila, Port Vila, Sydney, Singapore. Around twenty domestic destinations are served.

Fleet

1 Airbus A310-300
8 Fokker F-28
1 de Havilland DHC-7

Photograph: BAe 146-200 (author's collection)

AIR NOVA

1550 Bedford Highway, Bedford B4A 1EG
Nova Scotia Canada
Tel. 902 835 9900

Three letter code	IATA No.	ICAO Callsign
ARN	983	Nova

Three de Havilland DHC-8-100s were used by Air Nova when it started operations in the North-East of Canada in July 1986, having been founded in May 1986. The new airline was so successful in its early years that in addition to further DHC-8s it was also able to purchase BAe 146 jet aircraft. Air Nova is a partner of Air Canada and was one of the first airlines to enter into a relationship of this kind with Air Canada; It is now 100% owned by Air Canada, Air Nova feeds Air Canada flights at Halifax and flies to over twenty destinations in eastern Canada and the USA.

Routes

Montreal, Ottawa, Saint John, Halifax, Gander, Goose Bay, Bathurst, Deer Lake, Blanc Sablon, Boston.

Fleet

5 BAe 146-200
10 de Havilland DHC-8-100

Photograph: Boeing 767-200ER (author's collection)

AIR PACIFIC

263-269 Grantham Road, Suva
Fiji
Tel. 386444

Three letter code	IATA No.	ICAO Callsign
FJI	260	Pacific

Air Pacific, the flag carrier of Fiji, can trace its history back to 5th April 1947 when Katafanga Estates was formed. In July 1951, the company changed its name to Fiji Airways and operated its first services in September 1951, using de Havilland DH 89 Rapides. With the support of the Australian airline Qantas and in close co-operation with them, the network of routes was extended. In 1957, Qantas took over Fiji Airways as a subsidiary and subsequently opened international services on its behalf. In 1959, de Havilland Herons were added to the fleet, until in 1960 Air New Zealand and BOAC each took over a third of the company.

The fleet was renewed in 1967 with HS-748s and Britten-Norman Trislanders. The first jet aircraft was introduced in March 1972, a BAC 1-11-400. As early as 1971 the name was changed to Air Pacific, and by 1972 the government of Fiji, Kiribati, Tonga, Nauru and some private owners acquired a majority interest in the airline. By late 1978, the Fiji Government had purchased shares from Qantas, British Airways and Air New Zealand to control the majority holding. Embraer Bandeirantes were bought in 1980 for regional services. Increased demand in the passenger volume resulted in the purchase of two ATR-42s and

Boeing 767s in 1988. Qantas has a support agreement with Air Pacific.

Routes

Suva, Nandi, Tonga, Vila, Brisbane, Christchurch, West Samoa and Sydney.

Fleet	Ordered
2 Boeing 747-200	1 Boeing 737-500
1 Boeing 767-200ER	2 Boeing 767-300ER
2 ATR-42 300	

Photograph: Boeing 707-300C (author's collection)

AIR RWANDA

P.O.B. 808, Kigali
Republic of Rwanda
Tel. 75492

Three letter code	IATA No.	ICAO Callsign
RWD	178	Air Rwanda

Air Rwanda was formed as a national airline on 17th July 1975. From Kigali, the capital of the Republic of Rwanda, there are flights throughout the country and to neighbouring countries, such as Burundi, Tanzania, Uganda and Zaire. The DHC-6 Twin Otter is frequently chartered out to the International Red Cross. The Boeing 707 Freighter is used on long-haul charter flights, mainly to Belgium and Mombasa.

Routes

From Kigali to Butare, Ruhengeri, Gisengi, Bujumbura, Entebbe, cargo and charter flights also to Ostend.

Fleet

1 Boeing 707-300C
1 de Havilland DHC-6

Photograph: Boeing 767-200 (Josef Krauthäuser/Frankfurt)

AIR SEYCHELLES

P.O. Box 386, Mahe
Seychelles
Tel. 21400

Three letter code	IATA No.	ICAO Callsign
SEY	61	Seychelles

In July 1979, the government of the Seychelles bought the two domestic airlines, Air Mahe (formed in 1972) and Inter Island Airways (formed in 1976), in order to form Air Seychelles as the national airline. The routes and aircraft were taken over. Pilatus Britten-Norman Islanders and Trislanders were used for connections with the individual islands. Tourism was heavily promoted, creating a demand for international services. On 1st November 1983, Air Seychelles began scheduled flights to both London and Frankfurt with a weekly DC-10 flight, operated using an aircraft chartered from British Caledonian Airways. In November 1985, Air Seychelles took over an Airbus A300 B4 from Air France, using it for charter flights to Amsterdam, Rome and Frankfurt. In 1989, Boeing 707s replaced the Airbus temporarily until the arrival of the first Boeing 767-200. A Boeing 757-200 was added in 1993. The inter-island flights are now served by de Havilland Twin Otters.

Routes

Praslin Island, Bird Island, Denis Island, Fregate Island, Amsterdam, Paris, Rome, London, Frankfurt, Singapore, Bahrain, Nairobi and Zürich.

Fleet

1 Pilatus BN 2A Islander
4 de Havilland DHC-6
1 Boeing 767-200
1 Boeing 757-200

Photograph: Fokker F-27-500 (author's collection)

AIR SINAI

12 Kasr el Nil Street, Cairo
Egypt
Tel. 2 750600

Three letter code	IATA No.	ICAO Callsign
ASD	903	Air Sinai

Formed in early 1982, Air Sinai started a regular service to Tel Aviv, the same month as Israel completed the final phase of its negotiated return of the Sinai to Egypt. Air Sinai succeeded Nefertiti Aviation as Egypt's flag carrier on the Cairo-Tel Aviv route using Boeing 737s leased from Egyptair. Connections followed to Eilat, Sharm el Sheik, Hurgada, Santa Katharina, in other words, principally to tourist destinations. Fokker F-27s are used on domestic services. Air Sinai provides not only scheduled flights but also charter services, e.g. on behalf of Egypt Air and pilgrimage flights. The airline is a subsidiary of Egyptair.

Routes

In Egypt to Sharm el Sheik, Al Arish, Hurgada, Mesa Matruh, Ras An Nayb. Also occasional flights on behalf of Egypt Air to Munich and to other destinations in Europe.

Fleet

1 Boeing 737-200
2 Fokker F-27-500

Photograph: ATR-42 (author's collection)

AIR TAHITI

BP 314 Boulevard Pomare, Papeete
Tahiti
Tel. 422333

Three letter code	IATA No.	ICAO Callsign
VTA	135	Air Tahiti

Air Tahiti, which is partly in private ownership, was formed in 1953 to improve the connections to the individual islands which make up this French province. At that time it was called RAI (Reseau Aérien Interinsulaire) as the Government of French Oceania took over the operations of a small private airline, Air Tahiti, dating from 1950. In 1958 RAI was taken over by the French airline TAI (later UTA). On 1st January 1970 the name was changed to Air Polynesie, after UTA acquired a 62% stake in the airline. Its standard aircraft for many years were Fokker Friendships and BN Islanders, as well as Twin Otters. In January 1987, after UTA left, its name was changed to Air Tahiti. To express its independence, and when the ATR-42 was introduced in that year, the aircraft were also given the present colours. In 1992 and 1993, the larger ATR-72 was integrated into the fleet.

Routes

Air Tahiti flies to thirty-five islands in the entire archipelago, such as Bora Bora, Huahine, Maupiti, Moorea, Nuku Hiva, Hiva Oa, Raiatea, Tubuai.

Fleet	Ordered
4 ATR-42	2 ATR-72
2 ATR-72	
1 Dornier 228-200	

Photograph: Boeing 737-200ADV (author's collection)

AIR TANZANIA

P.O. Box 543 Dar-es-Salaam
Tanzania
Tel. 051 38300

Three letter code	IATA No.	ICAO Callsign
ATC	197	Tanzania

After the collapse of East African Airlines in January 1977, which had been run jointly by Kenya, Uganda and Tanzania, there were practically no air services remaining in Tanzania. Thus on March 1977 Air Tanzania was formed by the government. Fokker F-27s and a Boeing 737 were used by Air Tanzania to start flights from Dar-es-Salaam. In 1978 and '79 a further Boeing 737 and a de Havilland Twin Otter, for regional services, were acquired. The departure points for international flights are Dar-es-Salaam and Kilimanjaro International Airport and a number of African states are served.

Routes

Dar-es-Salaam, Kilimanjaro, Bujumbura, Djibouti, Dubai, Entebbe, Harare, Kigali, Mahe, Muscat and Nairobi. There are around twenty domestic destinations.

Fleet

2 Boeing 737-200ADV
3 Fokker F-27-600
3 de Havilland DHC-6 Twin Otter

Photograph: McDonnell Douglas MD-83 (Josef Krauthäuser/Long Beach)

AIRTOURS INTERNATIONAL

Wavell House, Holcombe Road, Helmshore, Rossedale, Lancashire BB4 4NB, United Kingdom. Tel. 0706 260066

Three letter code	IATA No.	ICAO Callsign
AIH/TIH	727	Kestrel/Tourjet

Set up in Manchester in 1990 by Airtours, the well-known UK tour operator, to provide it with in-house flying. Flights started in March 1991 with three MD-83s based at Manchester and two others operating out of Birmingham and Stansted. The young airline expanded quickly and acquired three further MD-83s in late 1991 for the 1992 season. In 1993 Airtours bought Aspro Holidays of Cardiff and Aspro's airline, Inter European Airways (formed in 1987) merged into Airtours International on 31st October bringing two Airbus A320s to the fleet. For the 1994 season, two Boeing 767-300s have been added for long range services to holiday destinations in the USA and the Caribbean; these services use the 'Tourjet' callsign and TIH three letter code.

Routes

Charter flights from Manchester, Birmingham, Cardiff, London-Gatwick, Glasgow, Liverpool and Newcastle to popular destinations in and around the Mediterranean, to the Caribbean and to the USA. Winter charters are flown to Geneva, Salzburg and Munich.

Fleet

6 McDonnell Douglas MD-83
2 Boeing 767-300
2 Airbus A320
2 Boeing 757-200

Photograph: Boeing 757-200 (André Dietzel/Frankfurt)

AIR TRANSAT

17380 Rue de la Paix, St. Janvier,
Quebec JON 1NO, Canada
Tel. 514 433 1011

Three letter code	IATA No.	ICAO Callsign
TSC	649	Transat

Set up in December 1986, Air Transat has become one of Canada's largest charter airlines, after Nationair ceased operations in 1992. Flights started in early 1987 with Boeing 727s. Its base is Montreal, but Air Transat also serves Toronto, Quebec City and Vancouver with flights to the United Kingdom and France, in particular. The airline obtained its first Lockheed L-1011 TriStar in late 1987 for flights to the Caribbean. In 1993 over 1 million passengers were carried for the first time.

Routes

Caribbean, Mexico, Birmingham, Belfast, Dublin, Glasgow, Frankfurt, London, Manchester, Newcastle, Shannon.

Fleet

9 Boeing 757-200
4 Lockheed L-1011 TriStar

Photograph: Airbus A320-200 (Uwe Gleisberg/Munich FJS)

AIR 2000

Oakdale, Broadfield Park, Brighton Road,
Crawley, West Sussex RH11 9RT
Tel. 0293 518966

Three letter code	IATA No.	ICAO Callsign
AMM	–	Jetset

The airline was formed in 1986 by the tour operator Owners Abroad, one of the leading British companies, for the purpose of operating intensive charter services outside London. The densely populated region in the north seemed to be perfect and Manchester was selected as the base. Commercial operations commenced with two leased Boeing 757s on 11th April, 1987. In 1988, two further Boeing 757s were obtained, one of which was based in Glasgow. Restrictive laws prevented the formation of a Canadian subsidiary (see Canada 3000). The first flights to Mombasa were in the winter season 1988/89, and after the 757s were re-equipped to the ETOPS standard there were also flights to Newark, Boston and Orlando. In October 1990, Air 2000 also received its scheduled air service licence for flights from the United Kingdom to Cyprus and services were finally launched in late 1993 from London Gatwick to Larnaca and Paphos. After regular additions to the fleet with Boeing 757s, the first two Airbus A320s came in April 1992. In addition to intensive charter flights, Air 2000 is also involved in the wetleasing business and leases its aircraft, primarily in winter to Canada 3000.

Routes

Scheduled flights from Birmingham, Glasgow, London-Gatwick, Manchester to Larnaca. From these places there are regular charter flights to the classic Mediterranean regions, to North Africa, Canada, the Caribbean, Mexico, Gambia and Kenya. In winter there are charter flights to the ski centres in the Alpine region.

Fleet

4 Airbus A320-200
15 Boeing 757-200ER

Photograph: Fokker 100 (author's collection)

AIR UK

Cross Key House, Haslett Ave., Crawley
West Sussex RH10 1HS, United Kingdom
Tel. 0293517654

Three letter code	IATA No.	ICAO Callsign
UKA	130	Ukay

British Island Airways (formed July 1976), Air Anglia (formed August 1970), Air Wales (formed July 1977) and Air Westward (formed 1976) merged on 16th January, 1980 to form the new joint airline, Air UK. The networks of routes were combined and the aircraft fleet coordinated. The carrier was a subsidiary of British Air Transport Holdings, in which British and Commonwealth Shipping Group had a 90% shareholding. The merged airline operated scheduled services to twenty-one airports in Britain and to ten international points in mainland Europe. In 1980, inclusive tour flights were also operated but that side of the business was sold to newly-formed British Island Airways, which commenced operations on 1st April 1982. Subsequently, Air UK turned over some domestic routes to Manx Airlines, in which British and Commonwealth held a shareholding. Fokker F-27s were the main type in Air UK's fleet and by the mid-1980s the airline was Britain's third largest. In 1987, KLM acquired a 14.9% stake in Air UK. It mainly serves airports on the eastern side of Britain and its main international destination is Amsterdam, where it is now the largest foreign user with over 300 movements a week. In June 1987, Air UK Leisure was formed as an autonomous sister charter airline with a fleet of Boeing 737s and operations to European holiday areas commenced in 1988.

Routes

Amsterdam, Bergen, Brussels, Edinburgh, Glasgow, London, Paris, Stavanger, Zürich and further destinations in the UK.

Fleet	Ordered
2 Shorts 360	7 Fokker 50
14 Fokker F-27	3 Fokker F-27-500
13 BAe 146-100/200/300	
5 Fokker 100	
1 Fokker 50	

Photograph: Boeing 737-400 (Uwe Gleisberg/Munich FJS)

AIR UKRAINE INTERNATIONAL

Prospekt Pere Mogy 14, 252135 Kiev
Ukraine
Tel. 2166758

Three letter code	IATA No.	ICAO Callsign
AUI	566	Air Ukraine

Formed in October 1992 as a subsidiary of Air Ukraine for international services, the still young state of Ukraine holds 88% of the ordinary shares in the airline with GPA (Guinness Peat Aviation), the leasing company owning the rest. Flights started with leased Boeing 737-400s to Western Europe. Unlike Air Ukraine, Air Ukraine International's intention is to win Western business people in particular as passengers by using modern aircraft. Air Ukraine took over all the Soviet-built aircraft of the former Aeroflot directorate in Kiev.

Routes

Amsterdam, Berlin, Brussels, Frankfurt, Kiev, London, Milan, Munich, Paris, Vienna, Zürich.

Fleet

2 Boeing 737-400

Photograph: Boeing 727-200ADV (Uwe Gleisberg/Adelaide)

AIR VANUATU

P.O. Box 148, Port Vila
Republic of Vanuatu
Tel. 23838

Three letter code	IATA No.	ICAO Callsign
AVN	218	Air Van

Air Vanuatu was set up as the national airline of the Pacific republic by Ansett Transport Industries and the government in 1981. Ansett held 40% of the shares. Flights started in September 1981 from Vila to Australia, which is where 70% of the passengers come from, using a leased Boeing 737-200 of Polynesian Airlines. Apia in Western Samoa was also served from the start of operations. In November 1987 the government acquired the remaining shares from Ansett. The airline entered a close co-operation with Australian Airlines, receiving aircraft and maintenance support from the latter. In 1989 Auckland and Adelaide were included in the network of routes. When there are capacity shortages or maintenance of the permanently leased Boeing 737-400 is imminent, the Boeing 727 is leased on a daily basis.

Routes

Port Vila, Auckland, Adelaide, Brisbane, Melbourne, Sydney, Noumea, Nadi.

Fleet

1 Boeing 737-400
1 Boeing 727-200ADV

Photograph: McDonnell Douglas DC-8-54 (author's collection)

AIR ZAIRE

B.P. 10121, Ndjili, Kinshasa
Zaire
Tel. 12 20759

Three letter code	IATA No.	ICAO Callsign
AZR	207	Air Zaire

Air Zaire is the national airline and was set up on 28th June 1961 as Air Congo by Sabena. The very dense network of routes in the former Belgian Congo was taken over in 1960 after the country became independent, including the aircraft fleet with DC-3s, DC-4s and DC-6s. A Boeing 707 was also taken over from Sabena and international services commenced from Kinshasa. In 1963 scheduled flights began between Brussels, Paris, Rome and the Republic of the Congo.The 707 was replaced in 1967 by a DC-8. In 1971 the state was renamed Zaïre, and the airline adopted a new name also. Air Zaire obtained its first large-capacity aircraft, a DC-10-30, in June 1973. It was joined a year later by a second and they were used on services to major European cities. Since 5th May 1978 Air Zaire has been a wholly-owned public enterprise. In the mid-80s the airline was completely reorganised, but it is only recovering slowly from the enormous losses of the past years.

Routes

Brussels is one of the few destinations outside Africa; in addition, Air Zaire flies to the neighbouring countries. Serves over twenty domestic points in Zaire.

Fleet

2 Boeing 737-200ADV
1 McDonnell Douglas DC-10-30

Photograph: Boeing 767-200ER (author's collection)

AIR ZIMBABWE

P.O. Box AP 1, Harare Airport
Harare, Zimbabwe
Tel. 4737011

Three letter code	IATA No.	ICAO Callsign
AZW	168	Zimbabwe

Air Zimbabwe was established on 1st September 1967 as a statutory body controlled by a board responsible to the Ministry of Transport as Air Rhodesia following the dissolution of Central African Airways Corporation. CAA had served the three territories of Southern Rhodesia, Nyasaland and Northern Rhodesia for some twenty-one years. Due to the political situation it was only possible to fly domestic routes and to neighbouring South Africa until the present government took power and the airline was renamed Air Zimbabwe Rhodesia in 1978. In April 1980, the airline took its present name when the country attained independence and became the Republic of Zimbabwe. It used DC-3s, Vickers Viscounts and Boeing 707/720. It was only after 1980 that the present Air Zimbabwe developed into an airline with flights to neighbouring countries and to Europe. A low-cost 'Sky-Coach' service was operated between Harare, Bulawayo and Johannesburg. In 1983 it took over the cargo airline Affretair; the first Boeing 767s were delivered in 1989. Joint services are operated with Qantas to Australia using Boeing 747s provided by the Australian airline.

Routes

From Harare regular services to London, Frankfurt, Athens, Nairobi, Mauritius, Australia, South Africa. Daily flights also the famous Victoria Falls.

Fleet

2 Boeing 767-200ER
4 Boeing 707-300
3 Boeing 737-200
1 BAe 146-200

Photograph: McDonnell Douglas MD-83 (author's collection)

ALASKA AIRLINES

P.O. Box 68900 Seattle
USA
Tel. 206 433 3200

Three letter code	IATA No.	ICAO Callsign
ASA	27	Alaska

Alaska Arlines traces its history back to the formation of McGhee Airways in 1932, which merged with Star Air Service in 1934. This airline then became Alaska Star Airlines in November 1943, after the airlines Pollack Flying Service, Mirow Air and Laverny Airways were taken over. These purchases placed more than 75% of the air traffic volume in Alaska under the airline's control. In 1944 the present name was adopted. In addition to scheduled services, Alaska Airlines was also particularly active in the charter business. During the time of the Berlin airlift, and later, during the Korean War, Alaska Airlines aircraft were in use. The first route from Alaska to Seattle was set up in 1951. In 1960 Convair 340s and DC-6s were acquired to replace the DC-3s previously used. On 1st February 1968, Alaska Airlines bought Cordova Airlines, and on 1st April of that year, Alaska Coastal Airlines. In allusion to the opening up of the large oilfields, the airline's first jet aircraft were also called 'golden nugget jets'. In 1970 charter flights from Fairbanks to Chabrovsk in the USSR were flown, and permission to fly to Moscow was also obtained. In the early 80s the appearance of the airline was altered: on the tail of the aircraft a smiling Eskimo appeared. Alaska Airlines became the first customer to order the new extended range MD-83 when it ordered nine aircraft in 1983. There were further purchases of airlines in 1987: Jet America and also Horizon Air which became a feeder operator for Alaska Airlines' services. The routes were extended to California and Mexico. In 1992 around 6 million passengers booked flights with Alaska Airlines, which went into the red for the first time in this year.

Routes

Anchorage, Bethel, Boise, Burbank, Fairbanks, Glacier Bay, Juneau, Kotzbue, Long Beach, Los Angeles, Oakland, Palm Springs, Phoenix, Portland, San Diego, San Francisco, San Jose, Seattle, Spokane and Tucson. Further flights to Mexico and the former Soviet Far East.

Fleet	Ordered
38 McDonnell Douglas MD-82/83	4 Boeing 737-400
19 Boeing 727-200	6 McDonnell Douglas MD-83
7 Boeing 737-200ADV	20 McDonnell Douglas MD-90
18 Boeing 737-400	

Photograph: de Havilland DHC-8 (Uwe Gleisberg/Munich FJS)

ALBANIAN AIRLINES

Pruga Kongresi i Permetit 202, Tirana
Albania

Three letter code	IATA No.	ICAO Callsign
ABW	59	Albanian

Albanian Airlines refers to itself as the new national airline of Albania. It was founded in April 1992 by the state company Albtransport and Tyrolean Airways from Innsbruck in Austria. The airline is based in Tirana and benefits from the knowledge and experience of Tyrolean. Regular scheduled flights began in May 1992, with a DHC-8 leased from Tyrolean, from Tirana to Vienna, and expansion to other European cities followed.

Routes

Tirana, Frankfurt, Istanbul, Munich, Rome, Vienna, Zürich.

Fleet

1 de Havilland DHC-8

Photograph: Boeing 747-200 (Josef Krauthäuser/Hong Kong)

ALITALIA

Piazzale Giulia Pastore 6
100144 Rome, Italy
Tel. 0654441

Three letter code	IATA No.	ICAO Callsign
AZA	55	Alitalia

Alitalia (Aerolinee Italiane Internazionali) was founded on September 16, 1946. The Italian government, BEA and some Italian companies formed the company. Operations commenced on 5th May, 1947 with Fiat 612s, SIAI Marchetti SM 95s and Lancastrians. In 1948, the first international flights, to Buenos Aires, took place. In 1950, DC-4s were acquired, and in 1953 Convair 340/440s and DC-6s. Its first jet aircraft was a DC-8 in 1960. The further development of Alitalia was preceded by its merger with LAI. Alitalia has been Italy's national airline since November 1957. Vickers Viscounts and

Caravelles for short and medium-distance flights joined the fleet. The latter were replaced from August 1967 on by DC-9s. The first Boeing 747 was delivered on 13th May 1970, and the DC-10 in February 1973. In the late seventies, Alitalia's aircraft orders caused something of a furore with the manufacturers, as Airbus A300s and DC-10s were also ordered in addition to Boeing 727s and 747s; some orders had to be cancelled, however. Since then, the tendency has become to standardise the fleet and the subsidiaries too. In November 1985 the Italian Government's stake in the airline was reduced from 99% and is

presently 89%. For its intercontinental flights Alitalia obtained 11 MD-11s from 1992 onwards. The airline has ordered forty Airbus A321s, with a further twenty on option; the first was delivered on 22nd March 1994. Alitalia is one of the largest European airlines and has stakes in other airlines including Air Europe (Itlay) 27.5%, ATI (Aero Transporte Italiani) 100% and Malev 30%.

Routes

Alitalia flies to over 100 destinations, including Basle, Cologne, Frankfurt, Geneva, Hamburg, Hanover, Munich, Nuremberg, Stuttgart, Vienna and Zürich, North and South America, Africa, the Middle East and Far East.

Fleet

Fleet		Ordered
14 Airbus A300B4	1 Airbus A321	39 Airbus A321
14 Boeing 747-200		44 McDonnell Douglas MD-82/87
34 McDonnell Douglas DC-9-32		2 MCDonnell Douglas MD-11
40 McDonnell Douglas MD-82		7 Boeing 747-400
6 McDonnell Douglas MD-11		

Photograph: Boeing 747-400 (Boeing photograph via Kauders)

ALL NIPPON AIRWAYS

3-2-5, Kasumigaseki Chiyoda-ku Tokyo 100
Japan
Tel. 035923403

Three letter code	IATA No.	ICAO Callsign
ANA	205	All Nippon

All Nippon Airways is Japan's largest airline, on the basis of the number of passengers carried. In 1989 there were over 28 million passengers, mainly on domestic flights. Formed in December 1952 as Japan Helicopter and Aeroplane Transport Company and scheduled services began in 1953. It merged in 1958 with Far East Airlines to form All Nippon Airways. The most important route at that time was Tokyo-Osaka. The network of routes was continuously extended using Convair 340s and 440s. In July 1961, two new aircraft were introduced at the same time, the Fokker F-27 and the Vickers Viscount 828. After taking over three regional airlines, Fujita in 1963, Central Japan in 1965 and Nagasaki Airlines in 1967, All Nippon grew extremely rapidly. A jet service with Boeing 727s was offered for the first time between Tokyo and Sapporo in 1964. In December 1973, the Lockheed TriStar became the first widebody aircraft to be used. The Boeing 747SR gave ANA – as it also did other Japanese airlines – a jumbo jet aircraft with particularly closely spaced seating, making it possible to carry around 500 passengers. The fleet was continually renewed, with Boeing 767s being employed from mid-1984 onwards and Airbus A320s in 1990, as well as Boeing 747-400s. International routes were opened up by ANA relatively late, from the mid-80s onwards. It launched its first scheduled international passenger service in March 1986 with flights to Guam. Services to the USA and Australia soon followed with Beijing added in 1987, Seoul (1988) and approval to serve London Gatwick from spring 1989. A Boeing 747-400D fresh from the factory was specially painted as a jubilee aircraft.

Routes

Within Japan, ANA flies to thirty-five destinations, and there are international flights to Bangkok, Beijing, Brussels, Dalian, Guam, Frankfurt, Hong Kong, London, Los Angeles, Moscow, Paris, Seoul, Saipan, Stockholm, Sydney and Washington.

Fleet

Fleet		Ordered
11 Lockheed L-1011 TriStar	16 Boeing 747-400	2 Airbus A320
9 Boeing 737-200ADV	11 NAMC YS-11A	6 Boeing 767-300
57 Boeing 767-200/300	15 Airbus A320	10 Boeing 747-400
17 Boeing 747SR		15 Boeing 777
6 Boeing 747-200		5 Airbus A340-300

Photograph: McDonnell Douglas MD-82 (author's collection)

ALM

Halo Airport, Willemstad, Curacao
Union of the Netherlands Antilles
Tel. 81322

Three letter code	IATA No.	ICAO Callsign
ALM	119	Antillean

Antilliaanse Luchtvaart Maatschappij NV, ALM Antillean Airlines for short, was set up in 1964 to replace KLM in the Caribbean whose West Indian Division had opened a service between Curacao and Aruba in January 1935. Flights started on 1st August 1964 on routes from Curacao with three Convair 340s. On 1st January 1969 96% of the shares in the airline were taken over by the government of the Netherlands Antilles. By 1971 three Douglas DC-9s were in service, acquired from KLM. Windward Island Airways International NV was bought in 1974, the rights to the routes and the aircraft also becoming the property of ALM. In October 1982 two MD-82s came from the makers and a third was leased from Continental in April 1988 and the early DC-9s were disposed of. The airline joined IATA in July 1990.

Routes

Aruba, Bogota, Bonaire, Caracas, Kingston, Medellin, Miami, New York, Port-au-Prince, Port of Spain, Santo Domingo, San Juan.

Fleet

3 McDonnell Douglas MD-82
1 Lockheed 188AF Electra
2 McDonnell Douglas DHC-8-300

Photograph: Boeing 737-400 (Boeing via Kauders/Seattle)

ALOHA AIRLINES

P.O. Box 30028 Honolulu, Hawaii
USA
Tel. 808 8364101

Three letter code	IATA No.	ICAO Callsign
AAH	327	Aloha

Aloha Airlines was set up as Trans Pacific-Airlines Ltd. on 9th June, 1946 and non-scheduled operations began in July of that year. In the first three years of its existence it was a passenger and cargo charterer in the Hawaii islands. Its first aircraft was the DC-3, as with many airlines set up at that time. The first scheduled flights started on 6th June, 1949. The airline changed its name to Aloha Airlines in 11th February 1959. Fairchild F-27s replaced the DC-3s in June 1959. In 1963 the larger Vickers Viscounts followed. Altogether, Aloha acquired three Viscounts and six F-27s. Its first jet aircraft was also a British

product. On 29th April 1966 Aloha started scheduled flights from Honolulu to Maui using BAC-1-11s. A step towards standardising the fleet was taken with the purchase and delivery of the first Boeing 737s in 1969. Due to the short flight times between destinations the Boeing 737s have very high utilisation figures. In 1987, Aloha became privately owned. With the delivery of the first Boeing 737-400s in early 1993 a new colour scheme was introduced. Since then, only Boeing 737s have been in service and more than 4.7 million passengers have used Aloha Airlines' services and it is Hawaii's largest inter-island

airline. There is a subsidiary airline, Aloha Islandair, which operates nine DHC-6 Twin Otters on local passenger schedules from Honolulu.

Routes

Honolulu, Hilo, Kohnhui, Kona, Lihue with many daily services.

Fleet	Ordered
15 Boeing 737-200 4 Boeing 737-300 2 Boeing 737-400	2 Boeing 737-400

Photograph: Airbus A320 (author's collection)

AMERICA WEST AIRLINES
4000 East Sky Harbor Blvd., Phoenix
Arizona 85034, USA
Tel. 602-8940800

Three letter code	IATA No.	ICAO Callsign
AWE	401	Cactus

America West Airlines was only formed after deregulation and was regarded as one of the most dynamic airlines in the USA. Formed in February 1981, America West started flights from Phoenix on 1st August 1983. In addition to Phoenix, Las Vegas is another major hub. Within six years, the fleet grew from three Boeing 737s at the beginning to over ninety aircraft; with the new routes and destinations the number of employees also rose. They all have a stake in America West Airlines in the form of shares. Initially, as the name indicates, the airline only operated in the western United States, but as the years passed the network of routes was extended to all the states, as well as to Canada and Hawaii. This latter route was opened in November 1989 with Boeing 747s. In 1989 AWE carried over 13.4 million passengers. Since 27th June 1991, America West has been flying under Chapter 11 bankruptcy protection with a reduced fleet and is hoping to become solvent again. Unprofitable routes are being given up and a cost reduction programme has been introduced. The America West Express commuter service was launched in October 1992, with a code-sharing agreement with Mesa airlines, serving Arizona, California, Colorado and New Mexico. 1992 was America West's most profitable year ever, and it aims to emerge from Chapter 11 protection in 1994.

Routes

Covers the USA, plus to Canada and Hawaii.

Fleet

11 Boeing 757-200
33 Boeing 737-300
23 Boeing 737-200
24 Airbus A320

Ordered

14 Boeing 737-400

Photograph: Boeing 767-200ER (author's collection)

AMERICAN AIRLINES

P.O. Box 619616 DFW Intl. Airport
Dallas, TX75261-9616, USA
Tel. 817 967 1234

Three letter code	IATA No.	ICAO Callsign
AAL	1	American

American Airlines came into being on 13th May 1934, as the successor to Aviation Corporation, which in turn had been the product of a number of smaller airlines. Before the DC-3, created according to the specifications of American Airlines, came into use, Curtiss Condors were mainly used. In 1945 AOA was taken over, an airline specialising in flights to Europe. In 1950 this airline was sold to PanAm and AA concentrated completely on the American market. American was one of America's aircraft manufacturers' most important partners in the period that followed: the DC-3, DC-7, Convair 240 and 990,

Lockheed L-188 Electra as well as the DC-10 emerged from specifications and orders placed by American. The DC-7 was used starting from November 1953 to start the transcontinental non-stop service from New York to Los Angeles. Six years later American's first jet aircraft, the Boeing 707, took over this route. BAC 1-11-400s and Boeing 727s were further aircraft in the airline's extensive fleet. 1970 saw the beginning of the era of wide-body aircraft when the Boeing 747 was taken into service, followed by DC-10s in August 1971. In that same year American took over Trans Caribbean Airways and has been

operating a dense network since then in that area. After deregulation American got larger and larger, taking over AirCal in 1987. Numerous routes were purchased from other airlines, preparing the way for for an extensive expansion of the routes to the Far East, South America and Europe. An extensive domestic commuter network serves over 170 destinations; this is run through 'American Eagle' subsidiaries and partners. In 1990 American was the largest private airline in the world with over 67 million passengers. In 1992 it had gone up to 87 million, but the present mood is one of cost-cutting and consolidation.

Routes

Over 200 cities worldwide with domestic hubs at Dallas, Chicago, Miami, Nashville, Raleigh/Durham and San Juan.

Fleet

Fleet		Ordered
241 McDonnell Douglas MD-82	30 Boeing 767-200ER	10 McDonnell Douglas MD-83
22 McDonnell Douglas MD-83	41 Boeing 767-300ER	11 Fokker 100
127 Boeing 727-200	59 McDonnell Douglas DC-10	19 Boeing 767-300ER
78 Boeing 757-200	19 McDonnell Douglas MD-11	10 McDonnell Douglas MD-11
64 Fokker 100	35 Airbus A300-600	

Photograph: Lockheed L-1011 TriStar (author's collection)

AMERICAN TRANSAIR

P.O. Box 51609 Indianapolis
Indiana 46251, USA
Tel. 317 2474000

Three letter code	IATA No.	ICAO Callsign
AMT	366	Amtran

American Transair is considered to be the largest charter airline in the United States. It was set up in Indianapolis in the state of Indiana in August 1973 and started flights with Boeing 720s for the Ambassadair Travel Club. In 1981 American Transair received permission from the FAA to operate as a charter airline and flights started in march 1981. Further Boeing 707s were acquired, followed by DC-10s and Boeing 727s in 1982. As there were no further DC-10s available on the worldwide aircraft market, they changed over to Lockheed L-1011 TriStars and had a fleet of Boeing 727s and L-1011s, replacing the Boeing 707s from 1985. The older 727s had been replaced by Boeing 757s by 1992. Today the airline, formerly a supplemental (charter) company, is a US certified air carrier with extensive domestic and international charter operations. It also has an interesting network of scheduled services including flights from Indianapolis to points in Florida and to Las Vegas and several international routes. Altogether 2.7 million passengers flew with AMT in 1993.

Routes

Scheduled services to Fort Myers, Honolulu, Maui, San Francisco. Charter flights all over the world.

Fleet

12 Lockheed L-1011 TriStar
 6 Boeing 757-200
 8 Boeing 727-200

Photograph: Boeing 727-100F (Björn Kannengiesser/Miami)

AMERIJET INTERNATIONAL

498 SW 34th Street, Fort Lauderdale, FL 33315
USA
Tel. 305 359 0077

Three letter code	IATA No.	ICAO Callsign
AJT	810	Amerijet

Amerijet International was set up in 1974 and initially provided only cargo and express goods flights. It used Learjets and Cessna 401s. In 1985 the first three Boeing 727s were acquired, and further examples followed in 1988 and 1989. A combi version of this aircraft (Boeing 727-100C) was used when the airline moved into the passenger charter business as well as our ambulance charters and cargo flights. Amerijet flies regular scheduled cargo flights for DHL and Burlington, both cargo specialists. In 1993 scheduled flights started to Guyana.

Routes

Antigua, Barbados, Cancun, Dominica, Grenada, Guyana, Merida, Mexico City, Port of Spain, St. Kitts, St. Lucia, St. Maarten, St. Vincent.

Fleet

7 Boeing 727-100 C/F
2 Cessna 410/501
3 Dassault Falcon 20C

Photograph: Airbus A320 (Björn Kannengiesser/Sydney)

ANSETT

501 Swanston Street, Melbourne
Victoria 3000, Australia
Tel. 036681211

Three letter code	IATA No.	ICAO Callsign
AAA	90	Ansett

Reginald Ansett set up his company in 1931, starting with bus and lorry journeys in Victoria. ATI Ltd. (Ansett Transport Industry) was then formed in 1936 as Ansett Airways, and the first flights were from Melbourne to Hamilton, using a Fokker Universal. Thus began the Ansett-Fokker connection which has been in existence for over fifty years. After buying up various small airlines, Ansett took over Australian National Airways (ANA) on 4th October 1957. In 1963, a controlling interest in MacRobertson Miller Airlines was acquired, now wholly-owned and until recently operated as Ansett WA. Until 1969 the new airline flew

under the logo Ansett-ANA. After the merger, aircraft such as the Vickers Viscount and the Lockheed L-188 Electra were used. The first jet aircraft was a Boeing 727, in use from 7th November 1964. Ansett also acquired DC-9s, starting in 1967. In addition to Australia, Port Moresby, at that time in Australian-administered New Guinea, was a focal point of Ansett's activities. From 1981 to 1982, Ansett altered its colour scheme and order new aircraft such as Boeing 767s and 737s. East-West Airlines was taken over by the owners of Ansett in 1987. The latest addition to the Ansett fleet is the Airbus A320.

Ansett today belongs to the Thomas-TNT group. Its subsidiary East West was fully integrated in 1993. Its first international service was to Bali in 1993 a further new routes are due to start during 1994. It is now known as Ansett Australia having previously been Ansett Airlines of Australia. Its parent company has interests in other airlines including Ansett New Zealand (100%), America West (20%) and Kendell Airlines (75%).

Routes

Dense network of routes in Australia with around fifty destinations, Bali.

Fleet		Ordered
6 Boeing 767-200	6 Fokker F 27	10 Airbus A321
4 Boeing 727-200ADV	3 BAe 146-200/300	
16 Boeing 737-300	1 DC-3	
12 Airbus A320		
3 Fokker 50		

Photograph: DC-10-30 (Wolfgang Grond/Zürich)

AOM-FRENCH AIRLINES

20 Paritalie Blvd, Pasteur 94278
Le Kremlin Bicentre Cedex, France
Tel. 146701530

Three letter code	IATA No.	ICAO Callsign
AOM	–	Air Mer

On 15th December 1988, Air Outre Mer was set up on the island of Réunion in the Indian Ocean. A service was planned to the French overseas provinces on the basis of scheduled-charter flights. Scheduled services with DC-10-30s began on 26th May 1990, initially with three weekly flights from Paris to St. Denis de la Réunion. In autumn 1990, further DC-10-30s were added to the fleet. In addition, three Dornier 228s were purchased in November 1990 for a newly created domestic service on the island of Réunion. In late 1992, it was merged with the airline Minerve, partly taking over its aircraft. The new airline was re-structured and took on a new colour scheme and revised name.

Routes

To Réunion, to the French West Indies, French Polynesia, and to another seventy destinations in over thirty countries.

Fleet

9 McDonnell Douglas DC-10-30
5 McDonnell Douglas MD-83

Ordered

3 McDonnell Douglas MD-11

Photograph: Tupolev 154M (author's collection)

ARIANA AFGHAN

P.O. Box 76 Ansari Watt, Kabul
Afghanistan
Tel. 21015

Three letter code	IATA No.	ICAO Callsign
AFG	255	Ariana

Ariana Afghan Airlines Co. Ltd was set up on 27th January 1955 as a new national airline. The Indian company Indama Corp. provided the first DC-3 aircraft and held 49% of the shares. These were taken over in 1956 by Pan American World Airways, which considerably expanded the airline. International routes to Delhi and Beirut were set up rapidly, and the Beirut route was extended via Ankara and Prague to Frankfurt. They used DC-4s and later DC-6s. London Gatwick was served by a DC-6. In 1963 its operational base was moved to Kabul from Kandahar, 1967 saw Bakhtar Afghan Airlines formed to

begin taking over Ariana's domestic services. In 1968 Ariana obtained its first jet aircraft, a Boeing 727, followed by a DC-10-30 in September 1979. After the invasion by Soviet troops over Christmas 1979, flights collapsed, the DC-10 was sold after being hit by a rocket and Soviet aircraft were added to the fleet. All operations were integrated into Bakhtar on 23rd October 1985 which became the new national carrier. However, by February 1988 it had changed back to its present title. During the ten years of the war, there were only flights to Moscow and Prague, and at times to Berlin-Schönefeld,

primarily in order to transport the injured. Flights are only expected to normalise again gradually, as the political situation is still unclear.

Routes

Kabul, Amritsar, Delhi, Tashkent, Moscow, Dubai and Prague.

Fleet

2 Tupolev Tu-154M
2 Boeing 727-100
3 Boeing 727-200
4 Antonov An-26/24
2 Yakovlev Yak-40

Photograph: DC-8-63F (Björn Kannengiesser/Miami)

ARROW AIR

P.O. Box 026062 Miami, FL 33102-6062
USA
Tel. 305 5260900

Three letter code	IATA No.	ICAO Callsign
APW	404	Big A

Arrow Airways was set up as a charter airline in late 1946 and was active as an airline until 1954. Only in 1980 was the airline reactivated by its founder George Batchelor, and it started cargo charters on 26th May 1981. A number of DC-8s were acquired for long range charters, contract services for the Military Airlift Command and later for passenger flights. July 1982 saw the first scheduled flight from Los Angeles to Montego Bay. On 18th December 1982 Arrow also flew from Tampa to London. Arrow Airways became Arrow Air in early 1983 and two DC-10s were acquired but were returned due to a cutback in operations. Reorganisation in 1984 resulted in domestic American flights being suspended; on the other hand, some routes to South America were opened. Finally, in 1985, Arrow Air withdrew completely from passenger flights. On 11th February 1986 Arrow Air filed for bankruptcy although charter cargo flights subsequently re-started using the DC-8Fs. Arrow Air made a comeback as a passenger charter airline with Boeing 727s in 1993.

Routes

Asuncion, Bogota, Buenos Aires, Caracas, Columbus, Costa Rica, Keflavik, Miami, New York, Panama, San Juan, Santiago, Shannon are regularly served with cargo flights.

Fleet

3 Boeing 727-200
7 McDonnell Douglas DC-8-62 F
4 McDonnell Douglas DC-8-63 F

Photograph: Boeing 767-300 (Josef Krauthäuser/Bangkok)

ASIANA

1 Ka Hoehuyn-Dong, Chung Ku, Seoul
Republic of Korea
Tel. 02 7588114

Three letter code	IATA No.	ICAO Callsign
AAR	988	Asiana

The economic boom in South Korea and recently the great mobility of the Koreans led to the formation of this airline. It was originally formed as Seoul Air International and started operations in December 1988, initially only on domestic routes in South Korea. Despite protests from Korean Air this restriction was soon lifted and international routes opened in 1989 with a leased Boeing 737-400, first of all abroad to Fukuoka, Nagoya and Tokyo, as well as Seoul-Pusan in Korea. In 1990 the rights to the routes to Hong Kong and Bangkok were added. Los Angeles, New York and San Francisco followed in 1992.

The fleet was further expanded with Boeing 747-400s, 737-400s and 500s. In spite of these enormous investments, the airline has not been able to make a profit.

Routes

Domestic Korean routes from Seoul, international flights to Japan, Los Angeles, New York, San Francisco.

Fleet	Ordered
15 Boeing 737-400	8 Boeing 737-400
3 Boeing 737-500	8 Boeing 767-300
7 Boeing 767-300	6 Boeing 747-400
5 Boeing 747-400	2 Boeing 767-300F

Photograph: McDonnell Douglas MD-82 (Uwe Gleisberg/Munich FJS)

ATI

Palazzo ATI, Capodichino Aeroporto
80144 Naples Italy
Tel. 081 709 1111

Three letter code	IATA No.	ICAO Callsign
ATI	–	ATI

Aero Transport Italiani (ATI) was formed on 13th December 1963 as a wholly-owned subsidiary of Alitalia. Operations started on 3rd June 1964. ATI carried out the domestic flights for Alitalia which up to 1963 had been the responsibility of Societa Aerea Mediterranea. It started operations with a Fokker F-27 in June 1964. ATI was commissioned by Libya to build up a regional service in that country. It entered the charter market in 1974. In March 1981 ATI joined Alitalia in creating the new Italian domestic airline Aermediterranea with Alitalia with an 80% stake and ATI 20%. However by the mid 1980s the airline had been merged with ATI. Today, ATI again has .a purely jet fleet, after the ATR-42 was only used for a short period on some routes. The first DC-9 was obtained in July 1969; since 1988 MD-82s have been added. In 1993, 4.9 million passengers flew with ATI, the largest Italian domestic operator. ATI has a 45% stake in Avianova.

Routes

Scheduled and charter services from England, Germany, Austria, Switzerland to Italy. Dense regional network of scheduled routes in Italy to around thirty destinations.

Fleet

  7 McDonnell Douglas DC-9-32
38 McDonnell Douglas MD-32

Photograph: BAC 1-11-500 (author's collection)

AUSTRAL

Florida 234, Piso 5, Buenos Aires 1334
Argentina
Tel. 313377777

Three letter code	IATA No.	ICAO Callsign
AUT	143	Austral

Austral was formed in June 1971 from the merger of two private airlines, Austral Compania Argentina de Transportes Aereos and Aerotransportes Litoral Argentino (ALA). Both airlines were set up in 1957 and had already been working together since 1966, when Austral acquired 30% of the shares in ALA. Thus, for example, new aircraft such as the BAC-1-11 or the NAMC-YS-11A were bought and technical services carried out jointly. Its first MD-81 was received in January 1981. Austral is today the second largest airline in Argentina and provides both scheduled and charter flights. Austral has been in the possession of the holding company Cielos del Sur since 1987. Cieles also has a stake in Aerolineas Argentinas, with Iberia, since it was privatised in 1990.

Routes

Buenos Aires, Bahia Blanca, Cordoba, Mar del Plata, Mendoza, Rosario, Tucuman, Montevideo, Rio Gallegos and Neuquen are the most important destinations in Austral's network of routes which cover over twenty-five domestic points.

Fleet

9 BAe (BAC) 1-11-500
2 McDonnell Douglas MD-81
2 McDonnell Douglas MD-83

Photograph: McDonnell Douglas MD-81 (Josef Krauthäuser/Salzburg)

AUSTRIAN AIRLINES

Postfach 50, 1107 Vienna
Austria
Tel. 0222 6835110

Three letter code	IATA No.	ICAO Callsign
AUA	257	Austrian

Austrian Airlines was set up on 30th September 1957 through a merger of Air Austria and Austrian Airways, neither of which had commenced operations. With leased Vickers Viscounts belonging to the AUA partner Fred Olsen, AUA started flights on 31st March 1958 on the route Vienna-London. A short time later, scheduled services commenced to Frankfurt, Zürich, Paris, Stuttgart and Rome.In early February 1960, AUA boughts its own Vickers Viscount 837s. In February 1963 the first Caravelle was brought into service. Domestic routes were still being served by the old faithful DC-3s, which were,

however, replaced in 1966 by HS-748s. In 1969, the AUA was reorganised, with unprofitable routes and the entire domestic flights being discontinued. The new aircraft ordered was the DC-9, and the first went into service in June 1971. With the introduction of this aircraft the airline was given a new colour scheme. Between April 1969 and March 1971 trans-Atlantic Boeing 707 scheduled flights were operated in co-operation with Sabena, the Belgian airline. Attempts to make the transition to long-distance flights failed in 1973. From 1975 onwards, DC-9-51s were ordered, and the AUA was one of

the launch customers for the MD-81. From 1988 on, the first MD-87s with extended range were added to the fleet. The third attempt to get involved in long-distance flights was successful in 1989, with the opening of scheduled flights to Tokyo and New York. These use the Airbus A310, which the AUA obtained in 1989. Among AUA's subsidiaries is Austrian Air Service, which provides regional and feeder services using Fokker 50s. Austrian is owned by the Austrian Government (51.9%), Swissair (10%), All Nippon Airways (9%) and Air France (1.5%) with the rest in public hands.

Routes

New York, Tokyo, Moscow; AUA is particularly strongly orientated towards Eastern Europe, the Middle East, Scandinavia and important destinations in Europe. There are charter services to the Mediterranean, Kenya, the Maldives and other destinations.

Fleet	Ordered
4 Airbus A310-300	7 Airbus A320
18 McDonnell Douglas MD-81/82	6 Airbus A321
5 McDonnell Douglas MD-87	2 Airbus A340
4 Fokker 50	

Photograph: Boeing 757-200 (author's collection)

AVENSA

Avda Universidad Esq. El Chorro Edif. 29
Piso 2/3 Aptdo 943 Caracas 101, Venezuela
Tel. 02455244

Three letter code	IATA No.	ICAO Callsign
AVE	128	Ave

Aerovias Venezolanas SA – Avensa for short – was set up on 13th May 1943 by Pan American and a group of Venezuelan businessmen. Freight flights started in December 1943 with Ford Trimotors and Stinson Reliants ferrying much needed supplies to the growing oil industry in the Carteru part of the country; passenger services started in May 1944 with Lockheed 10As. After the Second World War, DC-3s were added to the fleet. In 1953, Convair 340s were ordered in 1953 in order to set up a connection to Miami in 1955. By 1960 Avensa had developed a substantial domestic route network plus a regional

international system to Miami, New Orleans, Aruba and Jamaica. However in 1961, the then international services of Avensa and LAV (Aeropostal) were merged to from VIASA, in which Avensa has a 45% holding. The first jet aircraft, a Caravelle, was received in 1964, as was the larger Convair 580 turboprop. In 1976, Pan Am sold its 30% shareholding to the Venezuelan government with the other 70% held by private interests. Now the airline is wholly-owned owned by the Veneuelan government. Boeing 727s were added to the fleet, and in 1989 a fleet renewal programme was

initiated with the arrival of the first Boeing 757s and Boeing 737-300s.

Routes

Regional and national scheduled services to over thirty destinations in Venezuela and neighbouring countries.

Fleet

2 Boeing 757-200
5 Boeing 727-200ADV
1 Boeing 727-100
5 McDonnell Douglas DC-9-31/51
2 Boeing 737-200ADV

1 Boeing 737-300
1 Convair 580

Photograph: Fokker F-27-600 (author's collection)

AVIACO

Maudes 51, 28003 Madrid
Spain
Tel. 1 554 3600

Three letter code	IATA No.	ICAO Callsign
AYC	110	Aviaco

Aviacion y Comercio SA, or Aviaco for short, was founded on 18th February 1948 by a group of Bilbao businessmen to operate all-cargo flights. Bristol 170 Freighters were used to transport agricultural produce from Spain to Northern Europe. As this business was not very profitable, they applied to run passenger flights. 1950 marked the first service from Bilbao, the headquarters of the company, via Madrid to Barcelona; there were further domestic flights to the Canary Islands, the Balearic Islands and to Morocco, which was still Spanish at that time. The first international route was from Bilbao to Marseilles via Palma. They used SE 161 Languedocs, Convair 440s, DC-3s, DC-6s and Constellations. As early as the mid-50s charters were being flown from Britain to Spain. Iberia bought 65% of the shares in Aviaco in 1960. Using an ATL-98 Carvair in 1964 Aviaco opened a 'ferry service' for cars and their occupants from Barcelona to Palma de Mallorca. After the first Caravelle, bought in 1960 from Sabena, a number of other Caravelles were bought from Iberia, taking the place of the older generation of propeller aircraft. DC-8s and DC-9-32s were also bought, replacing the Caravelles in the early 80s, and since 1990 modern MD-83s have been in use. Deliveries of its order for thirteen MD-88s commenced in August 1991, the first of the model to enter service in Europe. The company now operates as a subsidiary of Iberia, from whom it is gradually taking over more domestic routes.

Routes

Dense regional network in Spain, on the Balearic Islands and the Canary Islands. Charter flights throughout Europe.

Fleet

8 Fokker F-27-600
13 McDonnell Douglas MD-88
22 McDonnell Douglas DC-9-32/34

Photograph: Boeing 747-200 (author's collection)

AVIANCA COLOMBIA

Av. Eldorado Piso 4, Bogota
Columbia
Tel. 1 4139511

Three letter code	IATA No.	ICAO Callsign
AVA	134	Avianca

Avianca is one of the world's oldest airlines, tracing its history back for 75 years and claims to be the first airline in the Americas. The Sociedad Colombo-Alemanos de Transportes Aereos (SCADTA) was formed on 5th December 1919, and started flights from the port of Barranquilla on 12th September 1920. Initially, Junkers F-13s were used for the route to Puerto Berrio. Destinations in neighbouring Ecuador and Venezuela were served with Junkers W34s. In 1930 Pan American acquired a 80% majority interest in SCADTA, took over the international flights itself and exchanged the German aircraft

for American ones. SCADTA and SCAO were merged in 1940 to form Avianca. On 14th June, 1940 SCADTA became Aerovias Nacionales de Colombia (Avianca) and merged with Servico Aereo Colombiano, which has operated a small network since its foundation in 1933. In 1947 Avianca flew to Miami and two years later to New York as well using DC-4s. This aircraft was also used for flights to Europe, to Paris and Lisbon. On 17th April 1953, Hamburg was added to the network of destinations, and in the following year Frankfurt, using Lockheed Constellations. Jet aircraft were first used for international

routes in 1962, Boeing 707s and 720s. Avianca was the first South American airline to purchase Boeing 727s and the first went into service in April 1966. In 1970, all the aircraft were painted in the colours still used today. The first Boeing 747s were delivered in November 1976; since 1988, Avianca has been using new ones, plus Boeing 767s. Avianca has been in Columbian ownership since 1978 after Pan American sold its shareholding. It is now 97.2% owned by private Colombian interests and 2.8% by the government. Its home base is the airport of Eldorado in Bogota.

Routes

Dense domestic network, international flights to destinations in the Caribbean, United States and Europe.

Fleet		Ordered
2 Boeing 767-200ER	6 Fokker 50	4 Fokker 50
3 Boeing 707-300	10 McDonnell Douglas MD-83	
7 Boeing 727-200	2 Boeing 757-200	
1 Boeing 747-200		

Photograph: ATR-42 (Uwe Gleisberg/Munich FJS)

AVIANOVA

Via Carlo Veniziano 58, 00148 Rome
Italy
Tel. 66551489

Three letter code	IATA No.	ICAO Callsign
NOV	–	Avianova

After Meridiana (see page 207) sold its stake in Avianova to ATI in 1993, this airline is now also owned by the Alitalia group, a fact which also becomes clear from the colours of the ATR-42 aircraft. Up until the time the airline was sold, these aircraft still bore the red and blue colours of of the original Avianova. It was set up as a regional airline in Olbia, Sardinia, in December 1986 and started flights in August 1987 with three ATR-42s.

The Alitalia group acquired a stake in Avianova as early as 1989 and further ATR-42s were taken over from ATI. The headquarters was also moved to Rome in 1989. After the merger of Alisarda and Universair to form Meridiana, the latter finally sold its shares.

Routes

Bastia, Florence, Geneva, Cologne, Milan, Marseille, Munich, Nuremberg, Olbia, Perugia, Pisa, Stuttgart, Tirana, Venice, Vienna, plus charter flights.

Fleet

11 ATR-42-300

Photograph: Boeing 737-300 (author's collection)

AVIATECA

Avienda Hincapie, Aeroporto La Aurora
Guatemala City, Guatemala
Tel. 63227

Three letter code	IATA No.	ICAO Callsign
GUG	240	Aviateca

On 14th March in 1945 the airline Empresa Guatemalteca de Aviacion SA (Aviateca) was set up by the government, to take over the operations of PAA-financed Aerovias de Guatemala SA which had been founded in 1939. DC-3s were used to continue operations. DC-6Bs were added to the fleet in 1961, thus making it possible to extend the network of routes to Miami, New Orleans and other destinations. Its first jet aircraft was a leased BAC 1-11 in 1970. In 1974 the airline was renamed Aerolinas de Guatemala and 2 Boeing 727s were added to the aircraft fleet. The company was privatised in 1989.

Since 1989, Aviateca has been flying with leased modern Boeing 737-300s.

Routes

Miami, Managua, Mexico City, New Orleans and further destinations in the Caribbean.

Fleet

4 Boeing 737-300s
4 Boeing 737-200

Photograph: de Havilland DHC-8-300 (author's collection)

BAHAMASAIR

P.O. Box N-4881 Nassau
Bahamas
Tel. 809 327 8451

Three letter code	IATA No.	ICAO Callsign
BHS	111	Bahamas

Bahamasair was established on 18th June, 1973, just prior to Bahamian independence from Britain, and immediately took over the domestic and international routes of Out Island Airways and the domestic routes of Flamingo Airlines to become the national airline. Among the aircraft used were HS-748s and BAC 1-11s. Bahamasair's main route is the connection from Nassau and Freetown to Miami in Florida. The Bahamian Government assumed full control of the airline in 1979. Since 1990 they have been replacing the older HS-748s by DHC-8s and starting a fleet renewal programme which intends the use of turboprop aircraft only.

Routes

Service between the islands, to the USA and to other Caribbean islands.

Fleet

7 de Havilland DHC-8-300
3 BAe HS-748
3 Cessna 402
1 Beech 200

Photograph: McDonnell Douglas MD-82 (Gottfried Auer/Salzburg)

BALAIR CTA

Postfach, 1215 Geneva Airport
Switzerland
Tel. 22 799 2020

Three letter code	IATA No.	ICAO Callsign
BBB	–	Balair

Balair taking its name from its home base, Basle, was set up as a flying school in 1953, but it soon had the idea of starting up charter flights. The involvement of Swissair made it possible in 1957. A Vickers Viking was used for charter flights to Italy. In 1959 Balair obtained its first DC-4, and in December 1961 a DC-6. Balair's DC-6 became moderately famous for its numerous special missions in Biafra and in other Red Cross missions. A DC-9 joined the fleet in 1970, and in January 1979 the first widebody aircraft, a DC-10-30. Its first Airbus A310 was introduced in 1985. In the late 80s modern MD-80s were then acquired. Aircraft have been switched over the years from Swissair on short-term lease, when required, to meet demand. In late 1991 Balair decided to paint the fleet in more modern colours, which were then changed again after the merger with CTA (Compagnie de Transport Aérien) from January 1993. Swissair is the major shareholder with a 57% interest.

Routes

Charter flights to the area around the Mediterranean, to Africa, the Far East and to the USA.

Fleet

4 Airbus A310-300
3 McDonnell Douglas MD-82
4 McDonnell Douglas MD-87
1 Fokker F-27-400

Photograph: Boeing 737-500 (Albert Kuhbandner/Munich FJS)

BALKAN

Vrajdebna Airport Sofia
Bulgaria
Tel. 02661690

Three letter code	IATA No.	ICAO Callsign
LAZ	169	Balkan

The formation of Balkan-Burgarian Air Transport goes back to 29th June 1947, when BVS-Bulgarske Vazdusne Solstenie was set up. This airline only served a few domestic destinations up to 1949. In 1949, the involvement of the Soviet Union led to the creation of a new company, TABSO, 50/50 owned by Bulgaria and Russia. The first international service, between Sofia and Budapest was operated on 12th September 1949. Lisunov Li-2s and Ilyushin IL-14s served Paris, Frankfurt and Moscow. In 1954, the Soviet share in TABSO passed into the ownership of the Bulgarian state. The four-engined IL-18 came into service in 1962; this aircraft is still familiar to many holidaymakers to the shores of the Black Sea, as it was particularly used for charter flights. 1968 saw the change of name to the one we know today, and also the acquisition of the first Tupolev Tu-134; then, in 1972, came the larger Tu-154. In 1987 the fleet was given a modern colour scheme, to the surprise of many, and in autumn 1990 it even acquired its first Western aircraft, a Boeing 737. The fleet and the service are being increasingly brought up to the Western level; Airbus 320s and further Boeing aircraft are in use. In the last few years Balkan has shed its non-airline functions and become an autonomous body within the Bulgarian Civil Aviation Corporation.

Routes

Abu Dhabi, Accra, Addis Ababa, Algiers, Amsterdam, Athens, Baghdad, Bangkok, Beirut, Berlin, Bratislava, Budapest, Casablanca, Colombo, Damascus, Dubai, Frankfurt, Harare, Helsinki, Istanbul, Copenhagen, Lagos, Lisbon, London, Moscow, Munich, Singapore, Vienna, Zürich, and some fifteen domestic destinations.

Fleet

4 Yakovlev Yak-40	3 Antonov An-12
14 Antonov An-24	4 Airbus A320-200
9 Tupolev Tu-134	3 Boeing 737-500
6 Ilyushin IL-18	2 Boeing 767-200
22 Tupolev Tu-154	

Photograph: Tupolev Tu-134B (Frank Schorr/Frankfurt)

BALTIC INTERNATIONAL

4 Pils Street, Riga 226050
Latvia
Tel. 220446

Three letter code	IATA No.	ICAO Callsign
BIA	610	Baltic International

Baltic International was set up in 1992. Scheduled flights started with a service to Frankfurt using aircraft from its major shareholder Latvian Airlines (itself based on the former Latvian division of Aeroflot), the balance being owned by Houston-based, Baltic International. The independent subsidiary flies to neighbouring western countries. In addition to Tu-134s, a DC-9-15 was also used which came on loan to the fleet in 1993, but was returned in early 1994.

Routes

From Riga to Frankfurt, Hamburg, Düsseldorf, London Gatwick and further destinations in Western Europe.

Fleet

3 Tupolev Tu-134B

Photograph: de Havilland DHC-8-100 (Josef Krauthäuser/Bangkok)

BANGKOK AIRWAYS

144 Sukhumvit Road, Bangkok 10110
Thailand
Tel. 2538352

Three letter code	IATA No.	ICAO Callsign
BKP	–	Bangkok Air

Set up in 1985 by the owner of Sahokol Air, an air-taxi company which had been formed in 1968 to operate between Bangkok and the tourist resorts of Samui Island and other points, Bangkok Airways started scheduled operations with an Embraer-110 in January 1986. In addition, a Piper PA-31 Navajo was used. An order for to Saab 340A was announced in September 1986 but did not come to fruition. In 1989 and 1990 de Havilland DHC-8s were added to the fleet. Its home base is the Don Muang Domestic Airport in Bangkok. At times Fokker 100s were used on routes to Phnom Penh. Some Shorts aircraft were taken over from Thai for use on domestic services. From November 1993, a new Bangkok-Chiang Mai-Mandalay service began.

Routes

From Bangkok to tourist resorts in southern Thailand such as Kaabi, Surim and others.

Fleet

5 de Havilland DHC-8-300
1 de Havilland DHC-8-100
1 Shorts 330
2 Shorts 360

1 Embraer-EMB 110

Photograph: Ilyushin IL-76 MD (André Dietzel/Munich FJS)

BELAIR

30 Tankovaya, 220004 Minsk
Republic of Byelorussia
Tel. 237346

Three letter code	IATA No.	ICAO Callsign
BLI	–	Air Belarus

Belair is the first private airline in Belarus and was set up in 1992. It is based in Minsk and operates regional routes from there with Yakovlev Yak-40s. However, its main business is operating cargo flights, the only way in this country to earn money or foreign currency from flying. Thus Belair flies charter flights for other airlines, including Western airlines, to Western Europe. Belair should not be confused with Belavia (Belarussian Airlines) which is a state-owned carrier and follows on from the former Aeroflot division in the Republic of Belarus/Byellorussia.

Routes

Regional routes and charter flights.

Fleet

6 Yakovlev Yak-40
1 Tupolev Tu-134A
2 Ilyushin IL-76 MD

Photograph: BAe ATP (author's collection)

BIMAN BANGLADESH

Biman Bangladesh Building,
Motijheel, Dhaka, Bangladesh
Tel. 255901

Three letter code	IATA No.	ICAO Callsign
BBC	997	Bangladesh

After independence, a new state airline was set up on 4th January 1972 to represent the state of Bangladesh (formerly East Pakistan) to the outside world when it split from Pakistan. Flights started on 4th February 1972 with scheduled services to Chittagong and several other domestic points using a DC-3 leased from the Bangladesh Air Force. DC-3s were soon replaced by F-27s. The first international flights were between Dhaka and Calcutta. A weekly charter service between Dacca and London on 9th March 1972 with a leased Boeing 707. In January 1973, scheduled flights to London started with leased Boeing 707s. Two Fokker F-28s were added to the fleet in 1981; the Boeing 707s were taken out of service when the DC-10-30s arrived from Singapore Airlines in 1983. In August 1990, the first BAe ATP arrived, thus introducing the renewal of the regional fleet. Now scheduled international services take place to twenty-eight destinations.

Routes

Domestic destinations of Chittagong, Syltet, Jessone and Soidyen are served from Dhaka; internationally the network stretches from London via Frankfurt and the Middle East to Singapore.

Fleet

6 McDonnell Douglas DC-10-30
2 Fokker F-28-4000
2 BAe ATP

Photograph: CASA CN-235-10 (author's collection)

BINTER CANARIAS

Avenida Alcado Ramirez Betancourt 8
35080 Las Palmas, Spain
Tel. 28 380366

Three letter code	IATA No.	ICAO Callsign
IBB	138	Canaria

In January 1988, Iberia, Spain's
state airline, set up Binter Canarias
in order to reorganise regional
Spanish flights to the Canary
Islands from mainland Spain,
previously operated by Aviaco. The
brief hops to the islands were
uneconomical for the Iberia jets, and
so in mid-1988 Binter Canarias
started flights with a CASA CN-235.
That same year, another aircraft was
acquired, and two further aircraft in
spring 1989, followed by the first
ATR-42s in the autumn of that year.
These latter were only used for a
short period, and were replaced by
the larger ATR-72s.

Routes

Binter Canarias runs scheduled flights within the Canary Islands, i.e. Lanzarote, Tenerife, Gran Canaria,
Fuerteventura and Las Palmas.

Fleet

5 CASA CN-235-10
7 ATR-72

Photograph: Douglas DC-8-61 (Uwe Gleisberg/Munich FJS)

BIRGENAIR

Cumhureyet Caddeshi 111, Bingul Ham Kat 4
Elmaday 80230 Istanbul, Turkey
Tel. 0212 2401150

Three letter code	IATA No.	ICAO Callsign
BHY	–	Birgenair

The owner of this charter airline, which has been in existence since 1988, is the Birgen Cetin charter group, an influential Turkish company. They use a DC-8-61 which previously belonged to Spantax. This completely overhauled aircraft is the only one in Europe and is used, like the Boeing 737 and 757, for flights to destinations in Turkey. Birgenair is linked with the tour operator Öger Tours. In the peak season aircraft are leased, and in winter Birgenair flies subcharters for other companies using the Boeing 757.

Routes

Charter flights to Turkey from many European destinations.

Fleet

1 Boeing 737-300
1 Boeing 757-200
1 McDonnell Douglas DC-8-61

Photograph: Boeing 737-200ADV (Josef Krauthäuser/Frankfurt)

BRAATHENS SAFE

Oksenoeyveien 3, 1330 Oslo
Norway
Tel. 47 2597000

Three letter code	IATA No.	ICAO Callsign
BRA	154	Braathens

Ludvig G. Braathen, a Norwegian shipowner, formed his airline, Braathens South-America and Far East Air Transport, on 26th March 1946, and started flight operations with Douglas DC-4s. As can be seen from the name, the airline operated charter flights to South America and Hong Kong. On 5th August 1949 a scheduled service from Oslo via Amsterdam-Cairo-Basra-Karachi-Bombay-Calcutta-Bangkok to Hong Kong was introduced. It was only in April 1954 that SAS took over this route. As early as 1952 a network was also built up in Norway, first with de Havilland Herons, and later (1958) with Fokker F-27s. The first

jet aircraft, Boeing 737s came in 1969; the F-27s and Douglas DC-6s were replaced by Fokker F-28s. In 1984 Braathens obtained its first widebody aircraft, the Boeing 767; however, this aircraft was sold again because it was not being fully used. The introduction of the new Boeing 737-400/500 generation provides Braathens with a very modern fleet and it is disposing of its series-200 aircraft as more series-500 aircraft are delivered. Braathens added an Oslo-London Gatwick scheduled service to its network in 1992.

Routes

Domestic services in Norway with route Oslo-Trondheim-Stavanger which is served several times daily. Charter flights throughout Europe.

Fleet

9 Boeing 737-200
6 Boeing 737-400
16 Boeing 737-500

Ordered

6 Boeing 737-500

Photograph: Boeing 737-300 (Björn Kannengiesser/Salzburg)

BRITANNIA

Luton Airport, Bedfordshire LU2 9ND
United Kingdom
Tel. 0582 424155

Three letter code	IATA No.	ICAO Callsign
BAL	754	Britannia

From modest beginnings, Britannia grew into the largest charter airline in the world. On 1st December 1961, Euravia (London) was set up, and it started flight operations on 5th May 1962 with an L-1049 Constellation under contract to Universal Sky Tours, then the principal shareholder. When a Bristol Britannia 102 was commissioned on 6th December 1964, the present name of the airline was also adopted. The Thomson Organisation, one of the major tour operators, took over the airline on 26th April 1965, and Boeing 707s were used for charter flights to Hong Kong, Kuala Lumpur and other faraway destinations. Its first Boeing 737 was put into service in 1968, the first European airline to operate the type. But Britannia withdrew from the long-distance business between 1973 and 1985, as the Boeing 737 was unsuitable. The first Boeing 767 was delivered in February 1984, and in 1988 Orion Airways was bought when Thomson's acquired its parent company, Horizon Travel and six Boeing 737-300s were taken over. By 1989, Britannia had thirty-four Boeing 737s in service but by 1992 this number had been reduced to twenty and its last 737 was disposed of in 1994 as it has increased its fleet of Boeing 757s and 767s. Over 7.5 million passengers were carried in 1994, making it the largest international carrier at eight UK airports.

Routes

Worldwide charter flights to the Caribbean, Australia, New Zealand, USA, in Europe to the summer and winter holiday resort areas and North Africa.

Fleet	Ordered
10 Boeing 767-200ER 16 Boeing 757-200	3 Boeing 757-200

Photograph: BAe/Aerospatiale Concorde (author's collection)

BRITISH AIRWAYS

P.O. Box 10 London-Heathrow Airport
Hounslow, Middx. TW6 2JA, United Kingdom
Tel. 081 759-5511

Three letter code	IATA No.	ICAO Callsign
BAW	125	Speedbird

British Airways is the result of the merger of BEA and BOAC, following a government decision bringing together British aviation interests under government control. British Airways came into being on 1st April 1972. Up until 1974, BEA and BOAC were still to all appearances operating separately; the merger became visible on the aircraft in 1974, since which time the airline has been flying as BA. BOAC had been formed in 1940 to take over the undertaking of Imperial Airways, formed in 1924, and another company called British Airways. BEA was established under the Civil Aviation Act of 1946 as a separate corporation to serve routes in Britain and Europe. In January 1976 British Airways inaugurated, jointly with Air France, the world's first supersonic passenger services using the Concorde to Washington. In 1988, the second largest private airline, British Caledonian, was taken over, after British Airways had been partly privatised in 1984 and the airline given a new image. In 1992 and 1993 British Airways featured more in the headlines than any other airline. First it acquired a stake in US Air, then in the Australian airline Qantas and finally in the French airline TAT and Deutsche BA. Dan Air was taken over for the symbolic amount of one pound sterling. BA set up its own 'profit centres' in 1993, forming the regional airlines BA Manchester and BA Birmingham. The airline also owns Caledonian Airways, a charter subsidiary based at Gatwick, and Brymon Airways, operating principally from West Country airports in BA colours. Likewise, 'franchise' services are operated in BA colours by CityFlyer from Gatwick, MaerskAir from Birmingham, and by TAT in France and Deutsche BA in Germany (to whom BA gave up its internal German services). The Scottish airline Loganair is about to introduce a similar franchise deal.

Routes

Worldwide to over 160 destinations from its principal base at Heathrow, and from Gatwick and other UK airports.

Fleet

Fleet		Ordered
10 Airbus A320	20 Boeing 767-300	15 Boeing 747-400
7 AS/BAe Concorde	10 Lockheed L-1011 TriStar	13 Boeing 747-400
24 Boeing 737-200	8 McDonnell Douglas DC-10-30	15 Boeing 777-200
2 Boeing 737-300	26 Boeing 747-400	20 Canadair Regionaljet
37 Boeing 737-400	32 Boeing 747-100/200	
40 Boeing 757-200		

Photograph: BAe Jetstream 61/ATP (Heinz Kolper/East Midlands)

BRITISH MIDLAND

Donington Hall, Castle Donington, Derbyshire
DE7 2SB, United Kingdom
Tel. 0332 854000

Three letter code	IATA No.	ICAO Callsign
BMA	236	Midland

BMA was origininly formed in 1938 as Derby Air Schools, a flying school which provided pilot and navigator training for the RAF during the Second World War. It was registered as Derby Aviation in 1948 and local services started on 16th February 1949 using a DH Rapide. The name British Midland Airways was adopted in July 1964. Scheduled services were offered from Derby, Birmingham and Manchester. It made use of DC-3s, Handley Page Heralds, BAC-1-11s, Vickers Viscounts and Boeing 707s. In 1965 the airline moved base from Derby to the new East Midlands Airport. In addition to charter and scheduled services, BMA also offered aircraft leasing in the 70s. It was bought in 1968 by an investment group Minster Assets, and in 1978 under its present managing director Michael Bishop it again became privately owned, since which time it has been flourishing. Manx, formed in 1982, was a joint venture between British Midland and British and Commonwealth (owners of Air UK) and Loganair became a subsidiary of BMA in December 1983. British Midland is a main shareholder in Manx Airlines and Loganair. The holding company for these three airlines is the Airlines of Britain Group formed in March 1987, in which SAS also has a 24.9% stake. This stake was increased to 35% in March 1992, rising to 40% in 1994. In 1985 the colours of the aircraft were also changed. A replacement of the DC-9 fleet is planned for the period 1994-1996; careful expansion is taking place and new routes are being opened. Frankfurt was its latest scheduled service from London Heathrow in March 1993 with some routes (and aircraft) taken over from SAS added in 1994. British Midland is Heathrow's second largest scheduled service operator.

Routes

Amsterdam, Brussels, Belfast, Birmingham, Dublin, Edinburgh, Frankfurt, Glasgow, Jersey, Leeds/Bradford, Liverpool, Luton, Nice, Palma de Mallorca, Teeside.

Fleet

Fleet		Ordered
2 BAe ATP/Jetstream 61	1 Fokker 100	3 Fokker 100
7 Boeing 737-300		3 Fokker 70
6 Boeing 737-400		8 Boeing 737-500
3 Boeing 737-500		
13 McDonnell Douglas DC-9 15/32/41		

Photograph: BAe BAC-1-11-500 (André Dietzel/Munich FJS)

BRITISH WORLD AIRLINES

Viscount House, Southend Airport,
Essex SS2 6YL, United Kingdom
Tel. 0702 354435

Three letter code	IATA No.	ICAO Callsign
BAF	762	British World

British United Air Ferries Ltd was set up in Southend in January 1963. It was the result of a merger between Silver City Airways (formed in 1948) and Channel Air Bridge (established as Air Charter in 1954). The airline became famous for its ferry services with Carvair aircraft. The cars were loaded onto them through a large front door, while the passengers also boarded and flew from England to France, Belgium and Holland. Handley Page Heralds were used for charter flights, to which larger Vickers Viscounts were added. In September 1967 the airline changed its name to British Air Ferries. BAF was purchased by the Keegan

family in 1971 and sold to Jadepoint in March 1983. In the 1980s it was involved in worldwide aircraft leasing, contract and flight support, and tour group charter activities. It had stopped flying its own scheduled service in 1978 but continued such services in the 1980s for British Caledonian, Air UK and British Midland using its own aircraft, mainly Viscounts. It also operated the Virgin Atlantic Gatwick-Maastricht service. In the late 1980s it had financial problems but came out of administration, a form of bankruptcy protection in May 1989 and was then acquired by Mostjet. The present name was adopted in

1993. New names also involve different colours, and so the British World aircraft were also given an attractive new scheme. The operational base is primarily London-Stansted, with a further base at Aberdeen. British World's activities are extensive, for example flying scheduled services on behalf of other airlines, charter flights, cargo services, supply flights. It opened a scheduled service of its own in 1993 between Stansted and Bucharest using BAe 1-11s but the route was suspended in early 1994 following a change in company policy on future operations.

Routes

Charter flights in Britain and Europe. Cargo flights on behalf of the Post Office and other companies in the country.

Fleet	Ordered
8 BAe BAC 1-11-500	3 Dornier 328
3 BAe 146-300	
10 Vickers Viscount 800	

Photograph: Lockheed L-1011 TriStar 500 (author's collection)

BWIA INTERNATIONAL

Administration Building, Piarco Intl. Airport
Trinidad
Tel. 809 669 3000

Three letter code	IATA No.	ICAO Callsign
BWA	106	West Indian

Set up on November 1939, daily flights started on 17th November 1940 with a Lockheed Lodestar between Trinidad and Barbados. It had been founded as one of the TACA Group of Central American airlines as British West Indian Airways. Two more Lodestars were added to the fleet in 1942, and charter flights for US Army personnel were also started. In 1947, BWIA was sold to BSAA and remained a subsidiary of this airline. But this was not to have much future, for a new airline was set up with the old name, 'BWIA' in 1948. Five Vickers Vikings was used to serve practically all the islands in the Caribbean. In June 1949, BSAA was merged with BOAC, so that BWIA was now a subsidiary of the latter and took over flights and aircraft from it. Four Vickers Viscounts were added to the fleet in 1955, and in 1960 leased Bristol Britannias were first used to fly to London, via New York. In November 1961 the government of Trinidad and Tobago bought back 90% of the shares in BWIA from BOAC and the remaining 10% in 1967. BWIA used Boeing 727s for the first time on the Miami route in 1965, replacing the Vickers Viscounts. On 14th December 1968, Boeing 707s were first used on the route to New York. Flights to London-Heathrow started in 1975. On 1st January 1980 Trinidad and Tobago Airways Corporation (BWIA International Airways) was formed as the national airline of the Caribbean, through the merger of BWIA and Trinidad and Tobago Air Services, which has been itself formed in 1974. The first L-1011 TriStar reached Trinidad on 29th January 1980, with a further example in August 1980. Regional services are flown with a modern fleet of MD-83s, and there is a co-operation agreement with Delta Airlines. It is planned to privatise the airline shortly.

Routes

Scheduled services to sixteen destinations in the Caribbean, from Trinidad, Tobago, Aruba, Curacao and Martinique to Miami and New York. In Europe, London, Stockholm, Frankfurt and Zürich are served. In addition, there are charter flights from destinations in the USA to Trinidad-Tobago and Europe.

Fleet

4 Lockheed L-1011-500 TriStar
9 McDonnell Douglas MD-83

Photograph: Lockheed L-1011 TriStar (author's collection)

CALEDONIAN AIRWAYS

Caledonian House, Crawley
West Sussex RH6 0LF, United Kingdom
Tel. 0293 668280

Three letter code	IATA No.	ICAO Callsign
CKT	885	Caledonian

British Airways bought the traditional airline British Caledonian in 1987. The charter activities of British Caledonian and the British Airways subsidiary British Airtours were combined and Caledonian was set up in late 1987. British Airtours had been set up by British Airways in 1969 and used a fleet of Boeing 737s and TriStars. British Caledonian had been created on 30th November, 1970 when a previous Caledonian Airways (formed in 1961) took over British United Airways and was known as Caledonian/BUA until September 1972. The new Caledonian is owned 100% by British Airways. The fleet consisted initially of TriStars and Boeing 737s, but some Boeing 757s were taken over from the parent company in 1988. The fleet was expanded to the present level to cope with additional business following the collapse of Air Europe and Dan Air. At peak periods further aircraft can be leased from British Airways. The airline is based at Gatwick Airport.

Routes

From London and other British cities to the Mediterranean, the USA, Canada, Kenya, Bangkok. Also winter charters to Salzburg, Zürich, Geneva and Munich.

Fleet

6 Boeing 757-200ER
5 Lockheed L-1011 TriStar
1 McDonnell Douglas DC-10-30

Photograph: Boeing 747-200 (author's collection)

CAMEROON AIRLINES

3, Ave. du General de Gaulle, BP 4092
Douala, Cameroon
Tel. 422525

Three letter code	IATA No.	ICAO Callsign
UYC	604	Camair

Cameroon Airlines was set up on 26th July 1971 by the Cameroon Government in order to be able to withdraw from the multinational airline Air Afrique and its interest in the consortium ended on 2nd September 1971. It began its own flight operations, between Douala and Yaonde, with Boeing 737s on 1st November 1971. A Boeing 707 was acquired for long-distance flights, which was then replaced by a Boeing 747. The two main shareholders are the Cameroon Government (75%) and Air France (25%). A Douala-Johannesburg service started in February 1994.

Routes

From Douala to Paris, London. Regional flights mainly to West Africa and domestic routes.

Fleet

1 Boeing 747-200
3 Boeing 737-200
1 BAe 748

Photograph: Boeing 757-200 (Björn Kannengiesser/Fort Lauderdale)

CANADA 3000 AIRLINES

27 Fasken Drive, Toronto, Ontario M9W 1K6
Canada
Tel. 416 6740257

Three letter code	IATA No.	ICAO Callsign
CMM	570	Elite

Founded in 1988 as Air 2000 Airline Ltd, a subsidiary of the British airline Air 2000, the Canadian Ministry of Transport suspended its licence a few days before flight operations were due to commence. The reason was massive objections on the part of other airlines from Canada. Consequently, local investors took over the British shares, and logically enough the name was changed to the present one. Flight operations started in 1989 using Boeing 757s leased from Air 2000. The airline is based in Toronto, but Canada 3000 also operates from Vancouver on the west coast, Calgary and other cities. In addition to regular charter flights, the airline also leases aircraft outside the season. In 1992, for the first time, over 1 million passengers were carried. The first Airbus A320 was delivered on 29th May 1993, giving Canada 3000 one of the most modern and up-to-date fleets. Air 2000 continued to supply Boeing 757s to Canada 3000 on lease each winter in an arrangement which benefits both airlines.

Routes

Acapulco, Amsterdam, Antigua, Barbados, Belfast, Birmingham, Cancun, Costa Rica, Dublin, Düsseldorf, Edinburgh, Fort Lauderdale, Glasgow, Honolulu, Nassau, London, Paris and many destinations in the Caribbean.

Fleet

4 Airbus A320
7 Boeing 757-200

Photograph: McDonnell Douglas DC-10-30 (Josef Krauthäuser/Bangkok)

CANADIAN AIRLINES

Scotia Center 2800, 700-2nd Street SW
Calgary, Alberta T2P 2W2, Canada
Tel. 403 294 2000

Three letter code	IATA No.	ICAO Callsign
CDN	18	Canadian

Canadian Airlines International was only set up in January1988 on a legal basis but it had been formed the previous January and the name came into use in March 1987 and officially on 26th April. Prior to that, the former Canadian Pacific Airlines had been taken over by the slightly smaller Pacific Western Airlines. The parent company of the new airline was Pacific Western Airlines Corporation, based in Calgary. Canadian Pacific had been formed in 1942 as an amalgam of ten small operations and international services began in 1949 with flights to Australia by Canadair 4s. Pacific Western had been formed in July 1945 as Central British Columbia Airways. Before the merger Canadian Pacific was Canada's second largest airline and PWA one of the country's largest regional carriers. In order to strengthen its position with regard to Air Canada, the largest private Canadian airline, Wardair, was taken over in 1989. Canadian acquired its first Boeing 707 in 1988, and in 1990 Boeing 747-400. Also, the Airbus A320 was put into service. Canadian has operated regular services to Frankfurt and Munich since 1988. There is close co-operation with American Airlines and AA would also like to have a share in Canadian, after obtaining government approval. Canadian has formed the largest network of commuter services in Canada, operating under the 'Canadian Partner' logo. Carriers participating under this alliance include Air Atlantiic, Calm Air, Ontario Epress, Norcan Air and Time Air. Canadian's latest international route is to Beijing from May 1994.

Routes

Manchester, London, Paris, Amsterdam, Copenhagen, Frankfurt, Munich, Milan and Rome in Europe, Buenos Aires, Santiago, Lima, Rio de Janeiro in South America, also Sydney, Auckland, Nadi, Bangkok, Hong Kong, Nagoya, Tokyo and over fifty destinations in Canada. A total of about 160 destinations in 17 countries.

Fleet		Ordered
60 Boeing 737-200ADV	17 Airbus A320	10 Airbus A320
12 Boeing 767-300ER		6 Boeing 767-300ER
3 Boeing 747-400		
8 McDonnell Douglas DC-10-30		

Photograph: Boeing 747-200C (Josef Krauthäuser/Hong Kong)

CARGOLUX

Luxembourg Airport P.O. Box 591
2015 Luxembourg, Luxembourg
Tel. 42111

Three letter code	IATA No.	ICAO Callsign
CLX	172	Cargolux

Cargolux Airlines International SA Europe's largest scheduled all-cargo airline was set up on 4th March 1970. The shareholders were Luxair SA, the Icelandic airline Loftleidir and the Swedish shipping company Salenia AB. Flight operations began in May 1970 with a Canadair CL-44. Altogether 5 CL-44s were used, replaced in 1971 by a DC-8-61. In 1973 the first Boeing 747-200C was acquired. After the Salenia and Loftleidir shares had been taken over by Luxair in the late 70s, Lufthansa joined Luxair as a shareholder, thus becoming a shareholder of Cargolux as well. In 1987 Cargolux (45%) and Luxair (55%) formed a passenger-carrying company, Lionair, with two Boeing 747-100s with seating for 505 passengers. They were leased out for charters worldwide and were well known on Manchester-Barbados flights during 1988. Both were up for sale by 1990. The first Boeing 747-400F in the world, a cargo aircraft of the latest generation, was delivered in November 1993.

Routes

Worldwide cargo service scheduled and charter.

Fleet	Ordered
5 Boeing 747-200C/F 2 Boeing 747-400F	3 Boeing 747-400F

Photograph: Boeing 727-200ADV (author's collection)

CARNIVAL AIR LINES

1815 Griffith Road, Dania, Florida 33004-2213
USA
Tel. 305 7644476

Three letter code	IATA No.	ICAO Callsign
CAA	521	Carnival Air

Carnival Air Lines is a company belonging to Carnival Cruise Lines in Fort Lauderdale, Florida. Formed in 1988, the company bought the aircraft and services of Pacific Interstate Airlines, the present name was adopted in 1989. Carnival Air Lines flies a feeder service to the cruise liners in the Caribbean from various airports in the USA. An agreement with Iberia has been in place since 1992, under which Carnival operates scheduled services from Miami to Chicago, Los Angeles, New Orleans and Houston. Over a million passengers were carried in 1992.

Routes

Charter flight operations, mainly to the Caribbean. Scheduled flights from Miami as a partner of Iberia.

Fleet

7 Boeing 727-200
2 Airbus A300
4 Boeing 737-200
3 Boeing 737-400

Photograph: Lockheed L-1011 TriStar (Josef Krauthäuser/Hong Kong)

CATHAY PACIFIC

Swire House, 9 Connaught Road
Hong Kong
Tel. 5 7475000

Three letter code	IATA No.	ICAO Callsign
CPA	160	Cathay

Cathay Pacific Airways Ltd. was set up on 24th September 1946, and started setting up a connection from Shanghai via Hong Kong and other stopovers to Sydney using a DC-3. In 1948, the Swire Group bought its way into the airline, acquiring 45% of the capital. A small fleet of DC-3 and Catalina amphibians began to fly a regional network from the Crown Colony, with routes increasing as DC-6's were acquired in the early 1950s. The BOAC subsidiary, Hong Kong Airways, was taken over in 1959. In April 1959, Lockheed L-188 Electras were acquired, and three years later Convair 880s as well. Boeing 707s

were added to the fleet, until the decision was made to acquire the first widebody aircraft, the Lockheed TriStar. These aircraft opened up new routes in the Middle East. In order, as a British airline to be able to fly to London as well, Boeing 747s were bought, and the first of these was employed on the route to London on 17th July 1980. By 1980 the Swire Group, through its company Cathay Holdings, had increased its shareholding to 70%, helped by the purchase of 15% from British Airways Associated Companies. The rest of the shares are owned by the Hong Kong and Shanghai Banking Corporation and

the China International Trust and Investment Corporation. In addition to London, there were direct flights to Frankfurt in 1984, which were quickly changed to non-stop flights after the Boeing 747-300 had been introduced. Cathay's fleet replacement continues steadily with the introduction of the Boeing 747-400 and large orders for aircraft of the latest generation.

Routes

Amsterdam, Frankfurt, London, Paris, Rome and Zürich in Europe, Abu Dhabi, Bahrain, Vancouver, San Francisco, Los Angeles, Sydney, Auckland, Tokyo, Seoul, Bali, Bombay, Bangkok, Singapore, Manila and further destinations in South-East Asia.

Fleet	Ordered
18 Lockheed L-1011 TriStar	2 Boeing 747-400
3 Boeing 747-200F	10 Airbus A330-300
8 Boeing 747-200	10 Airbus A340
6 Boeing 747-300	11 Boeing 777-200
17 Boeing 747-400	

Photograph: Boeing 737-400 (author's collection)

CAYMAN AIRWAYS

P.O. Box 1101 Georgetown
Grand Cayman, British West Indies
Tel. 809 949 8200

Three letter code	IATA No.	ICAO Callsign
CAY	378	Cayman

Cayman Airways Ltd was formed in July 1968 to take over the affairs of Cayman Brac Airways Ltd, which in turn had been set up by the Costa Rican airline LACSA. LACSA owned 49% of the shares in Cayman Airways until December 1977 when the airline came under the control of the government of Cayman. Flight operations to Jamaica and Miami started with BAC 1-11s. Britten-Norman Trislanders flew the service between the islands of Grand Cayman, Brac and Little Cayman. Boeing 727-200s replaced the BAC 1-11s, and also a DC-8 which had been in service up to the mid-70s. In 1989 the first leased Boeing 737-400s were added to the fleet as a replacement for the Boeing 727s.

Routes

Caribbean islands, Miami, Montego Bay, Atlanta, Houston, Tampa.

Fleet

1 Boeing 737-400
3 Boeing 737-200ADV

Photograph: Boeing 737-500 (Frank Schorr/Düsseldorf)

CESKOSLOVENSKE-CSA

Revolucni 1, 1100 Prague
Czech Republic
Tel. 4 481 5108

Three letter code	IATA No.	ICAO Callsign
CSA	64	CSA Lines

CSA was formed on 19th July 1923 and began operations on 28th October 1923 for the provision of postal, cargo and passenger transport services. The first flight, with a Hansa Brandenburg Aero A-14, was from Prague to Bratislava. On 30th July 1930 the service, which had previously been solely domestic, was expanded and became an international service with the inclusion of the route Prague-Bratislava-Vienna-Zagreb. Routes to Rumania and the Soviet Union followed. In the mid-30s CSA was a leading European airline. CSA had to suspend its independent flight operations from 15th March 1939 following the partitioning of the country on the eve of the Second World War and 15th September 1946 when the present company was formed. All its aircraft were seized by the German occupying power and given to Lufthansa. Reconstruction began in 1946 with DC-3s. With the political changes in 1948 came the influence of Soviet technology, and CSA flew with IL-12s and IL-14s; Tu-104As were also used from 9th December 1957 onwards. CSA flew this aircraft as far as Jakarta. IL-12s were replaced by IL-18s and a scheduled service to Havana was started. CSA started using IL-62s for long-distance flights in 1969, with services to New York and Montreal starting in 1970. Tu-134As were used for a long time for the European routes; from April 1988 the more modern Tu 154Ms were used. The drastic political change in 1989 allowed the airline to order western aircraft again for the first time in forty years. Airbus A310-300s were ordered and delivered in 1990 to replace the IL-62s. The fleet is being continuously replaced and brought up to western standards with further aircraft. Following the partition of the former Czechoslovakia, a new colour scheme is being adopted.

Routes

Domestic network to five cities. In addition, CSA flies from Prague to fifty destinations on four continents.

Fleet

5 Tupolev Tu-134A	5 Boeing 737-500
4 Tupolev Tu-154M	4 ATR-72
2 Airbus A310-300	8 IL-62

Photograph: Airbus A300-600 (Josef Krauthäuser/Hong Kong)

CHINA AIRLINES

131, Nanking East Rd., Taipei 104
Republic of China
Tel. 02 7152626

Three letter code	IATA No.	ICAO Callsign
CAL	297	Cal

On 16th December, 1959, some former members of the national Chinese air force set up CAL. PBY Catalina flying boats were initially used for charter flights. Domestic scheduled flights were also operated using DC-3s and Curtiss C-46s. In 1965 the airline became the official flag carrier of the Republic of China. Lockheed Constellations were used to start a scheduled connection to Saigon in December 1966, primarily in order to transport members of the US Armed Forces and cargo to Vietnam. Connections to Hong Kong and Tokyo also came into existence in 1967 using two new

Boeing 727s. 1970 saw the first trans-Pacific flight to San Francisco, via Tokyo and Honolulu. CAL obtained its first jumbo jet aircraft, a Boeing 747, in 1975. The 747 was followed in June by Airbus A300s for regional services in 1982 when a Boeing 767 was also delivered making China Airlines the first airline in the world to operate the A300 and B767 together. It was the first airline in Asia to purchase the latter type. In 1983 a route to Amsterdam was set up, the only destination in Europe for many years. This situation is for political reasons, however. MD-11s and Boeing 747-400s have been added to the fleet or have been

used to replace older aircraft. Frankfurt was added to its routes in 1993. The major shareholder is the China Aviation Development Foundation.

Routes

From Taipei to Dallas, San Francisco, New York, Los Angeles, Honolulu, to Japan, South Korea, Manila, Singapore, Djakarta, Hong Kong, Bangkok, Dharan, Amsterdam and Frankfurt.

Fleet

5 Boeing 747-400	4 McDonnell Douglas MD-11
4 Boeing 747SP	6 Airbus A300 B4
4 Boeing 747-200B	6 Airbus A300-600
3 Boeing 747-200F	
3 Boeing 737-200	

Photograph: Airbus A300-600 (Josef Krauthäuser/Hong Kong)

CHINA EASTERN

Hong Qiao Airport,
200335 Shanghai, People's Republic of China
Tel. 21 2558899

Three letter code	IATA No.	ICAO Callsign
CES	781	China Eastern

In May 1988 China Eastern separated from CAAC, which had previously had air traffic under its sole control and initially shared ten MD-82s with China Northern Airlines acquired from CAAC. Since then it has assumed responsibility for its flights from Shanghai. China Eastern has developed continuously and has also been expanding considerably internationally. MD-11s delivered in 1992/93 allowed routes to be flown to Bahrain, Brussels, Chicago, Madrid, Los Angeles and Seattle. There have been cargo flights with an MD-11F to Zürich and Frankfurt in Europe and Seattle and Chicago in the USA.

Routes

Fukuoka, Hong Kong, Osaka, Tokyo, Bahrain, Chicago, Madrid, Los Angeles, Seattle. A dense network of routes is operated within the People's Republic, the departure airport being Shanghai.

Fleet

2 Airbus A310
3 Airbus A300-600
3 Antonov 24
3 BAe 146-100
5 McDonnell Douglas MD-11

11 MD-82 (made under licence in China)
 4 Shorts 360
10 Xian Y-7
10 Fokker 100

Ordered

4 Airbus A300-600
6 Airbus A340-300
6 Airbus A330-200

Photograph: BAe 146-100 (Uwe Gleisberg/Hong Kong)

CHINA NORTHWEST AIRLINES

Laodong Nanlu, Xiguan Airport,
710082 Xioan, Shaanxi,
People's Republic of China, Tel. 29 742022

Three letter code	IATA No.	ICAO Callsign
CNW	783	China Northwest

The former CAAC regional direction of Xian has been flying under the name of China Northwest Airlines since 1989 and has been given the task of operating regional scheduled and charter flights. The fleet taken over from CAAC was based in Lanzou and Xiguan and still consisted of Soviet-built aircraft, mainly Tupolev 154s. However, these are being gradually added to and replaced by Western aircraft. Thus in 1990/91, BAe 146s were delivered for regional services as a replacement for the An-24. In the following year Airbus 300-600s and A310s were brought into service.

Routes

Dense regional network with around seventy destinations, several flights daily to Beijing, Shanghai and Hong Kong.

Fleet	Ordered
2 Antonov An-24	3 Airbus A300-600
11 BAe 146-100/300	
10 Tupolev Tu-154	
2 Airbus A310	
6 Airbus A300-600	

Photograph: Boeing 767-300 (Uwe Gleisberg/Hong Kong)

CHINA SOUTHERN

155 Dongsi Street West, 510405 Guangzhou
People's Republic of China
Tel. 20 6678901

Three letter code	IATA No.	ICAO Callsign
CSN	784	China Southern

This airline also came into existence in 1989 after the reorganisation of Chinese airlines and the CAAC. The third largest Chinese international airline, based in Guangzhou, is growing and undergoing an enormous boom, increasing at annual rates of over 40%. In two years more than $600 million was invested in the fleet and its replacement. From 1990, Boeing 737s, 757s and more recently 767s were in continual use on all routes. Apart from some small aircraft, the fleet consists only of aircraft manufactured in the West.

Routes

Bangkok, Beijing, Changsa, Guangzhou, Hanoi, Hefei, Hong Kong, Jakarta, Kuala Lumpur, Kunming, Manila, Nanning, Penang, Qindo, Shantou, Shasai, Surabaya, Xiamen, Yichang, Zhanjiang and many other destinations.

Fleet		Ordered
7 Boeing 737-200	5 Pilatus BN-2 Islander	6 Boeing 777
8 Boeing 737-300	4 Saab SF 340	6 Airbus A340
10 Boeing 737-500	3 Shorts 360	
15 Boeing 757-200	5 Yunshi Y7	
3 Boeing 767-300		

Photograph: Boeing 737-300 (Josef Krauthäuser/Hong Kong)

CHINA SOUTHWEST AIRLINES

Shuangliu Airport, 610202 Chengdu, Sichuan
People's Republic of China
Tel. 298804

Three letter code	IATA No.	ICAO Callsign
CXN	785	China Southwest

A further airline which has been separated from the CAAC is China Southwest, which was also set up to run its own flight operations in 1989. Initially the main airliner types used were the Antonov 24 and Boeing 707s and Tupolev 154s. Since 1992 Boeing 737s and 757s have been increasingly used to meet passenger demand. It is based in Sichuan. Scheduled and charter flights take off from here to around seventy regional airports and to Hong Kong. It also has a Lhasa to Kathmandu service.

Routes

In the south-west of the People's Republic; the airline flies to Hong Kong from Shuangliu, and from Lhasa to Katmandu.

Fleet

4 Boeing 707-300	4 Harbin Y-12
6 Boeing 757-200	5 Xian Y-7
17 Boeing 737-300	
3 Antonov 24	
4 Tupolev 154M	

Photograph: Douglas DC-3 (author's collection)

CLASSIC AIR

Postfach, 8058 Zürich Airport
Switzerland
Tel. 01 8143085

Three letter code	IATA No.	ICAO Callsign
CLC	–	Classicair

On 7th November 1985, exactly fifty years after the maiden flight of the DC-3, Classic Air was set up in Grenchen. The aim of this airline is to operate classic Douglas DC-3 aircraft and provide exclusive charter flights. After the first aircraft had been thoroughly overhauled, Classic Air started flight operations in 1986. The number of 'oldie' fans is increasing from year to year. A second DC-3 has been in operation since 1987.

In 1993, over 16,000 passengers either went on sightseeing flights or on trips lasting several days with the DC-3.

Routes

Inclusive tours and charter flights in Europe.

Fleet

2 Douglas DC-3

Photograph: Boeing 737-200 (author's collection)

COPA PANAMA

Apartado Postal 1572, Avenida Justo
Arosomena y Celle 230 Panama City, Panama
Tel. 254117

Three letter code	IATA No.	ICAO Callsign
CMP	230	Copa

The Compania Panameña de Aviacion SA – COPA – was formed on 21st June 1944. As was the case with many other South and Central American airlines, Pan American Airways set up COPA, together with businesspeople from Panama, Pan American provided 32% of the capital. Scheduled services to neighbouring countries commenced on 15th August 1947 with DC-3s. A Convair CV 240 was added to the fleet in 1952. Up until the time when jet aircraft came into use, an HS-748 and a Lockheed L-188 were in the service of COPA. International services had been introduced from 1965 and in 1981 COPA discontinued scheduled Panamanian domestic services. In 1971 Pan American withdrew its from Copa Panama and sold its shares. New services were started to Mexico City in October 1991 and to Cali, Montego Bay and San Juan (Puerto Rico) in 1992.

Routes

Panama, Costa Rica, El Salvador, Guatemala, Nicaragua, Jamaica, Haiti and Miami.

Fleet

4 Boeing 737-200
1 Boeing 737-100

Photograph: Boeing 757-200 (Josef Krauthäuser/Frankfurt)

CONDOR FLUGDIENST

Hans-Böckler-Str. 7, 63263 Neu-Isenburg
Germany
Tel. 06102 2451

Three letter code	IATA No.	ICAO Callsign
CFG	–	Condor

Condor is the traditional charter-flight subsidiary of the German Lufthansa. Set up in 1955 as Deutsche Flugdienst GmbH, German Federal Railways, two shipping companies and Lufthansa were shareholders in DF. The first aircraft were Vickers Vikings. After DF's considerable initial successes, it suffered a setback in 1959 and was completely taken over by Lufthansa with the aid of the state, thus averting the threat of bankruptcy. In October 1961, Lufthansa bought the Condor Luftreederei (formed in 1957) from the Oetker group and merged it with the DF to form the new Condor Flugdienst GmbH. Vickers Viscounts were bought in 1961 and two Fokker F-27s in 1963; in 1965 the first Boeing 727 entered service. Condor had a purely jet fleet as early as 1968. Condor obtained a Boeing 747-100 in 1971, plus another in 1972. These aircraft opened up new routes to Bangkok and to the USA. In the late 70s, the first oil crisis resulted in excess capacity being reduced. From then on, the smaller DC-10-30 replaced the jumbo on long-distance flights. Boeing 737-300s and Airbus A310s have been in use since 1987. In 1989 the Boeing 757 in the Condor colours was first spotted at Europe's airports, the 757s replacing the 727s. In order to be able to meet the rising demand, but also to be able to operate scheduled flights for Lufthansa, the fleet is being expanded. Condor flies nowadays to the CIS states and to Taipei. It is now one of the world's largest charter airlines operating an all-jet fleet out of Frankfurt, Düsseldorf, Munich and Stuttgart and a number of other German cities.

Routes

Charter flights to the USA, Caribbean, Middle East and Far East, India, Nepal and destinations in the Mediterranean, the Canary Islands, North Africa and Kenya. To the former Soviet republics and to Taipei.

Fleet	Ordered
3 DC-10-30	8 Boeing 767-300ER
5 Boeing 737-300	
17 Boeing 757-200	
5 Boeing 767-300ER	
1 Boeing 747-400	

Photograph: BAe Jetstream 31 (author's collection)

CONTACT AIR

Postfach 230442, 70599 Stuttgart
Germany
Tel. 0711 797690

Three letter code	IATA No.	ICAO Callsign
KIS	–	Contactair

Contactair was set up in 1969 and worked as a non-scheduled air carrier, operating among other things ambulance flights and charter flights. It has been serving some routes from Stuttgart, Münster and Hamburg for DLT for some years now, using BAe Jetstream 31s. In 1989 Contactair obtained a de Havilland DHC-8 leased from Tyrolean; since then the airline has also acquired its own DHC-8s and has continued to expand its fleet – some operate in Lufthansa CityLine colours.

Routes

Scheduled flights on behalf of DLT/Lufthansa and others to various regional destinations.

Fleet	Ordered
2 BAe Jetstream 31	1 de Havilland DHC-8-300
2 de Havilland DHC-8-100	
5 de Havilland DHC-8-300	

Photograph: BAe 146-200 (British Aerospace)

CONTI-FLUG

Theodor-Heuss-Ring 200, 50688 Cologne
Germany
Tel. 0221 120222

Three letter code	IATA No.	ICAO Callsign
EPC	798	Conti

The Cologne company, set up in 1964, initially operated business flights, ambulance flights and other charter flights. In the 1980s it was operating a BAe 125 and international executive charters were undertaken in Condor's colour scheme. In 1992 Conti Flug obtained the contract for a daily scheduled service from Hamburg to Toulouse on behalf of Airbus Industrie. BAe 146s were acquired for this purpose, and for a further service from Berlin to London City Airport. It thus became the third operator using the BAe 146 at London City in October 1992. In addition to scheduled flights, these aircraft are also used for weekend charter flights. In late 1993 a service from Berlin-Tempelhof to Riga was started; Conti Flug is aiming at further route expansions.

Routes

Hamburg, Berlin, London City Airport, Riga, Toulouse, Venice.

Fleet

2 BAe 146-200
2 Beechcraft King Air 200
3 Canadair Challenger

Photograph: Airbus A300 (author's collection)

CONTINENTAL

2929 Allen Parkway, Houston
Texas 77210, USA
Tel. 713 834 5000

Three letter code	IATA No.	ICAO Callsign
COA	5	Continental

Continental can trace its history back to 15th July 1934 as the southwest division of Varney Speed Lines when its first service operated; its name was changed to Varney Air Transport on 17th December 1934. This airline changed its name in 1937 to Continental Air Lines. A network of routes was established using various Lockheed aircraft, mainly in the western United States. After the Second World War, Convair 240s, DC-6s and DC-7Bs were employed. Pioneer Airlines was taken over in 1954. Boeing 707s started the 'golden jet' flights on 8th June 1959. During the Vietnam War, lucrative charter flights to Vietnam and Thailand were operated. As early as the 60s there were group charter flights to Europe. The first jumbo jet aircraft, a Boeing 747, flew for the first time on 18th May 1970; the DC-10 followed two years later. In October 1981, Texas International acquired a stake in Continental, and the merger of the two companies followed in October 1982 under the name of Continental. 1983 brought enormous financial problems and collapse under Chapter 11 bankruptcy protection in September 1983. More than half of the staff were made redundant, many aircraft grounded and routes discontinued.

It emerged from Chapter 11 protection in 1986. In February 1987, the parent company bought up PeoplExpress, New York Air and Frontier, and these airlines were also merged with Continental. The airline's operations doubled as a result, with considerable difficulties during the consolidation. Over 40 million passengers flew Continental in 1990 but the airline placed itself once again under Chapter 11 in December 1990, until May 1993, at which time a new colour scheme was adopted. An extensive network of feeder services is operated by partner airlines under the name 'Continental Express'.

Routes

Continental has a dense network of scheduled routes in America, it flies to Canada, Mexico, the South Pacific, to Manila, Guam, Hong Kong, Taipei. To Paris, Madrid, London and Frankfurt in Europe.

Fleet

Fleet		Ordered
35 McDonnell Douglas DC-9-32	38 Boeing 737-100/200	31 Boeing 737-300
65 McDonnell Douglas MD-81/82/83	76 Boeing 737-300	20 Boeing 757-200
20 McDonnell Douglas DC-10-10/30	101 Boeing 727-200/200ADV	12 Boeing 767
8 Boeing 747-200	23 Airbus A300B4	5 Boeing 777
3 Boeing 757-200		

Photograph: Boeing 747-100 (André Dietzel/Munich FJS)

CORSAIR

24 rue Saarinen, Silic 221,
94528 Rungis Silic Cedex, France
Tel. 149794980

Three letter code	IATA No.	ICAO Callsign
CRL	–	Corsair

Formed in 1981 as Corse-Air International, Corsair started operations on 1st July 1981 and acquired four SE 210 Caravelles. There were charter flights from Paris and Ajaccio within Europe and to North Africa. A characteristic feature of the fleet was a striking head with a headband on the tail of the aircraft. The first Boeing 737s were obtained in 1987, marking the start of a fleet replacement programme. In 1990 a Boeing 747 followed. There were alterations to the airline's name and to the colours of the aircraft in 1991, after a leading French tour operator acquired a stake in the airline.

Routes

Charter flights to North America, within Europe, North Africa and to the French overseas territories.

Fleet

2 Boeing 737-400
2 Boeing 747-100
1 Boeing 747-200

Photograph: Airbus A320-200 (André Dietzel/Munich FJS)

CRETAN AIRLINES

18 Athinas 713 Heraklion, Crete
Greece
Tel. 288108

Three letter code	IATA No.	ICAO Callsign
KRT	–	Cretan

Set up in 1982 by businessmen and local tour operators in Crete, Cretan Airlines started flights in April 1993. Leased aircraft are used for flights mainly from German airports to Crete and to further destinations in Greece. An expansion of the services to Austria, Switzerland and other countries is planned for 1994/95. Cretan Airlines also offers domestic flights in Greece.

Routes

Athens, Düsseldorf, Hamburg, Heraklion, Munich, Thessaloniki.

Fleet	Ordered
2 Airbus A320-200	2 Dornier 328

Photograph: Boeing 737-200ADV (Wolfgang Grond/Zürich)

CROATIA AIRLINES

Savska Cesta 41, 41000 Zagreb
Croatia
Tel. 4161311

Three letter code	IATA No.	ICAO Callsign
CTN	831	Croatia

After the collapse of Yugoslavia, the Republic of Croatia was formed in the north of the country with Zagreb as the capital. The national airline formed in 1989 was initially called Zagal – Zagreb Airlines using Cessna and Piper aircraft, but took the present name in 1990. The scheduled services formerly belonging to JAT were taken over using DC-9s from Adria Airways and operations commenced on 5th May 1991 between Zagreb and Split Due to the UN embargo and the continued fighting, the airspace over the country was closed from September 1990 until 1st April 1992. After it was reopened, Croatian Airlines expanded its flights and has been operating since then with ex-Lufthansa Boeing 737-200s. ATR-42s also came into use in 1993. On 15th May 1993 a twice weekly 737 service started between Manchester and Pula.

Routes

Amsterdam, Berlin, Brac, Düsseldorf, Frankfurt, Istanbul, London, Manchester, Milan, Moscow, Munich, Paris, Pula, Rome, Stuttgart, Vienna, Zagreb, Zürich.

Fleet

2 ATR-42-300
6 Boeing 737-200ADV

Photograph: BAe/Avro RJ 85 (author's collection)

CROSSAIR

Postfach, 4002 Basle Airport
Switzerland
Tel. 061-3252525

Three letter code	IATA No.	ICAO Callsign
CRX	724	Crossair

Crossair started a charter service from Zürich to Nuremberg with a Swearingen Metro II on 2nd July 1979. A predecessor had originally been in existence since 14th February 1975 called Business Flyers Basle. This airline operated as a non-scheduled air carrier. When scheduled services started, the name Crossair was used, a name by now well known beyond the borders of the Swiss Confederacy. Crossair had further rights to scheduled routes for Innsbruck and Klagenfurt. Under the guidance of their President Moritz Suter, Crossair made great contributions to European regional services. Crossair provided pioneer crews and ideas for the Saab SF-340 regional aircraft, for which the airline was a launch customer with an order for five aircraft in October 1980 after it had ordered Metro IIIs earlier in the year for delivery starting in 1981. In July 1982, Crossair confirmed an earlier option for five more Saab 340s into a firm order. In Switzerland, Crossair opened up new services from Basle, Berne and Lugano over the years. On 15th June 1984 a Crossair Saab 340 entered service on the Basle-Paris route which it had taken over on behalf of Swissair. Crossair's achievements were rewarded with many awards, eg that of 'Commuter Airline of the Year'. In 1990, over 1 million passengers were carried for the first time, and at the same time the Fokker 50 and its first jet aircraft, the BAe 146, were introduced. On 30th March 1992, a BAe 146 service between Zürich and London City commenced. The airline, in which Swissair has a 59.8% young stake, is a launch customer for the Saab 2000 50-seat regional airliner with twenty ordered and options on a further twenty-five. This will be introduced in the later part of 1994 after some delivery delays.

Routes

From Basle, Zürich, Geneva, Berne and Lugano Crossair operates scheduled services to Italy, France, Germany, Belgium, the UK and the Netherlands. In addition,there are also flights on behalf of Swissair and Lufthansa.

Fleet	Ordered
5 Fokker 50	20 Saab 2000
15 Saab SF-340 A/B	
3 BAe 146-200	
4 BAe/Avro RJ 85	

Photograph: Ilyushin IL-62M (author's collection)

CUBANA

23-64 Vedado Havana 4
Republic of Cuba
Tel. 774911

Three letter code	IATA No.	ICAO Callsign
CUB	136	Cubana

Cubana had been formed originally on 8th October 1929 as Compania Nacional Cubana de Aviacion Curtiss by the Curtiss Aviation Group and started operations on 30th October 1930 using a Ford 4-AT-E. On 6th May 1932, the carrier was purchased by Pan American and the name 'Curtiss' was removed from its title. In 1945 the word 'Nacional' was also removed and Cuban interests took a 46% shareholding. It first international service under it own name took place on 15th May, 1946 to Miami flown by a DC-3. Cubans gained a 52% interest in 1948 and Pan American sold its remaining shares

in 1954. For the past few years socialist Cuba has been opening its doors to western tourists, after tourism had been discovered as a way of earning foreign currency. Since that time, Cubana IL-62s are occasionally to be seen at European airports. The Empresa Consolidada Cubana de Aviacion was established by the Cuban government in 1959 when its predecessor, Compania Cubana de Aviacion SA was taken over, reorganised and merged with smaller airlines. At that time the fleet consisted of English and American aircraft such as Constellations, Britannias and Viscounts and the

majority were offered for sale in 1961. After the USA's economic blockade, only Soviet-built aircraft were used and IL-14s, IL-18s, An-12s and An-24s arrived between 1961 and 1967. In 1974 Cubana's first pure jet, an IL-62, arrived and went into service in November between Havana and Madrid. It is only now, after the collapse of the 'Warsaw Pact', that more services have been introduced to the West. The acquisition of six Fokker F-27s from Aviaco in 1994 is another sign of the easing of relations with the non-communist world.

Routes

Dense domestic network, the Caribbean, Central America and some destinations in Europe such as Cologne, Prague, Basle, Berlin, Moscow and Paris, Frankfurt and Munich.

Fleet		Ordered
4 Yakovlev Yak- 42	8 Tupolev Tu-154 B-2/M	5 Ilyushin IL-96-300
10 Yakovlev Yak-40	13 Ilyushin IL-62M	
12 Antonov An-24	1 McDonnell Douglas DC-10-30	
25 Antonov An-26	8 Fokker F-27-600	
2 Ilyushin IL-76 MD		

Photograph: Airbus A320-200 (Josef Krauthäuser/Frankfurt)

CYPRUS AIRWAYS

21 Alkeou Street Engomi, Box 1903
Nicosia, Cyprus
Tel. 2443054

Three letter code	IATA No.	ICAO Callsign
CYP	48	Cyprus

Cyprus Airways was set up on 24th September 1947 by British European Airways, Cypriot business people and the government. British registered DC-3s were used to start flight operations to Athens on 18th April 1948. There were further routes to Haifa, Istanbul, Rome, Beirut and Cairo. Vickers Viscounts opened the London route in the fifties after BEA, on behalf of Cyprus Airways, began the world's first sustained turboprop passenger service on 18th April 1953 when a Viscount flew the London Heathrow-Nicosia route. Cyprus became an independent nation in August 1960 and BEA signed a deal with Cyprus Airways in 1961 to operate its services, initially for a five year period, with BEA aircraft. The arrangement finally ended in late 1969. Its first jet aircraft were two Hawker-Siddeley Tridents bought in November 1969 from BEA. In July 1974 Cyprus Airways had to close down operations, as Turkish troops had occupied Nicosia Airport and a Trident was destroyed in fighting. The first Boeing 707 took off on 8th February 1975 from the new base at Larnaca airfield in the south of Cyprus. In the same year the first Airbus A310 arrived, and at the end of 1989 the new Airbus A320 was delivered. In March 1992 Cyprus Airways created a wholly-owned subsidiary Eurocypria Airlines to operate charter flights from Europe to Larnaca and Paphos using three Airbus A320s.

Routes

Scheduled and charter services from Larnaca to many cities in Europe and the Middle East.

Fleet

3 BAe BAC 1-11-500
4 Airbus A310-200/300
8 Airbus A320-200

Photograph: L-1011 TriStar (Josef Krauthäuser/Los Angeles)

DELTA AIR LINES

Hartsfield Atlanta Airport
Georgia 30320, USA
Tel. 404 715 2600

Three letter code	IATA No.	ICAO Callsign
DAL	6	Delta

Delta Air Lines is not only one of the major airlines in the United States, it is also one of the oldest of all. Huff Daland set up the firm of the same name in 1924 to spray cotton fields in the American South. Its headquarters was in Monroe, Louisiana in the Mississippi Delta. The name Delta Air Services was taken in 1928 in reference to this area. A Travelair was used on its first scheduled passenger service on 17th June 1929 from Dallas to Jackson. The company was sold to the Aviation Corporation in 1930 and became Delta Air Corporation. In 1940, there were already ten Lockheed Electras and five DC-3s in the fleet. A further name change came in 1945 to the present title. In 1953 Delta merged with Chicago and Southern Airlines and for a short time was known as Delta C&S Air Lines. Northeast Airlines was taken over in 1972, and finally Western Airlines was acquired in April 1987 to become the third-largest US carrier. These mergers and takeovers meant that the network of routes was continually expanded. In 1959 DC-8s, in 1960 Convair 880s and in 1965 DC-9s came into service. Delta was a launch customer with all of these aircraft. Boeing 747s were in service from 1970-77, plus DC-10s from 1972-75. However, the airline eventually settled on the Lockheed TriStar. In 1978 flights started across the Atlantic to London, and a year later Frankfurt was on the schedule, followed in 1986 by Stuttgart and Munich. In November 1991, Pan Am with its rich tradition was bought up and all the routes and aircraft were integrated. In 1992 over 86 million passengers flew with Delta Air Lines. Several partner airlines operate feeder services into Delta hubs under the name 'Delta Connection', with Delta flight numbers and aircraft livery. A code sharing agreement with Virgin Atlantic was made in April 1994 for transatlantic routes.

Routes

About 180 US domestic destinations from main hubs at Atlanta, Cincinnati, Dallas/Fort Worth, Salt Lake City, Orlando and Los Angeles, and to over thirty countries interantionally.

Fleet

153 Boeing 727-200ADV
58 Boeing 737-200
15 Boeing 727-300
85 Boeing 757-200
15 Boeing 767-200
41 Boeing 767-300ER

30 Airbus A310
124 McDonnell Douglas MD-88
39 Lockheed L-1011-200 TriStar
17 Lockheed L-1011-500 TriStar
15 McDonnell Douglas MD-11

Ordered

55 Boeing 737-300
26 McDonnell Douglas MD-90
3 Boeing 757-200
3 Boeing 767-300
2 McDonnell Douglas MD-11

Photograph: Boeing 737-300 (Uwe Gleisberg/Munich)

DEUTSCHE BA

Löwental Airport, 88046 Friedrichshafen
Germany (Munich from 1994)
Tel. 07541 3080

Three letter code	IATA No.	ICAO Callsign
DEL	–	Speedway

Delta Air from Friedrichshafen was set up by the Scholpp transport group in Stuttgart in March 1978 and started flights between Friedrichshafen and Stuttgart with a DHC-6 Twin Otter in April 1978, as well as Friedrichshafen-Zürich. In 1982 a Swearingen Metro III was added to the fleet. A second Metro III was added in 1984 as well as a Dornier 228, the latter being used on the route Friedrichshafen-Oberpfaffenhofen. In 1985 Delta Air was converted into a private limited company, with the involvement of the Swiss airline Crossair. In May 1987 it was given the status of a scheduled airline and since then has been flying some routes with SF-340s, added to the fleet in 1986, on behalf of the German airline Lufthansa. In March 1992 three German banks bought 51% of the shares and British Airways the remaining 49% stake in Delta Air and the name was changed to Deutsche BA on 5th May 1992. The new scheduled airline used not only SF 340s but also Boeing 737-300s. In the course of '92/'93 it started scheduled services to Moscow, Ankara and other destinations. Its future headquarters will be Munich.

Routes

Friedrichshafen, Frankfurt, Cologne, Zürich, Munich, Geneva, Moscow and Ankara. Further destinations such as Hamburg, Bremen, Münster, Berlin, Prague, Klagenfurt, Brussels, Paris are served on behalf of other airlines. Charter flights primarily from Berlin to Mediterranean destinations.

Fleet	Ordered
1 Dornier 228	5 Saab 2000
9 Saab SF-340	3 Fokker 100
7 Boeing 737-300	

Photograph: Boeing 727-100 (author's collection)

DOMINICANA DE AVIACION

P.O. Box 1415 Santo Domingo
Dominican Republic
Tel. 809 532 6269

Three letter code	IATA No.	ICAO Callsign
DOA	113	Dominicana

Compania Dominicana de Aviacion was formed on 5th May 1944, by a Dominican businessman and the company's first president, who subscribed 60% of the capital, with the assistance of Pan American (40%). The first service opened on 5th July 1944 from the capital Ciudad Trujilo (now Santo Domingo) to two local towns. Flights started with Stinson Reliants and a Ford Trimotor. In 1947 Dominicana obtained two DC-3s from US Air Force stocks. In 1972, the first Boeing 727 replaced the DC-6 delivered in the early fifties. These aircraft were used from then on by Dominicana for charter and cargo flights. In the mid-80s, all the airline's shares were transferred to a government corporation as it operated with a Boeing 707, three Boeing 727s and a leased Boeing 747, plus a DC-6A freighter.

Routes

Caracas, Curacao, Miami, New York, San Juan are the most important destinations.

Fleet

3 Boeing 727-200/100
1 Boeing 707-300
1 Douglas DC-6A

Photograph: Airbus A320 (Uwe Gleisberg/Hong Kong)

DRAGONAIR

12 F Tower 6 Hong Kong City
33 Kanton Road Kowloon, Hong Kong
Tel. 37383388

Three letter code	IATA No.	ICAO Callsign
HDA	43	Loongair

Dragonair became active in April 1985, mainly in order to serve destinations in the People's Republic of China from Hong Kong. The airlne started flight operations with two Boeing 737-200ADV although during the first year of operations much of the time the aircraft were grounded due to opposition from Cathay Pacific. However over the next few years some scheduled routes were awarded to Dragonair and several more Boeing 737s were leased as the network of scheduled routes was expanded.Dragonair was a wholly-owned subsidiary of Hong Kong Macau International

Investments until late 1989. China International Trust and Investment and the Swire Group now own some 89% of the shares. Since 1989, destinations outside the People's Republic of China are also being served and a charter department has been set up. In mid-1990 a Lockheed L-1011 TriStar was acquired from Cathay Pacific. When the first Airbus A320 was delivered in late 1992, a new aircraft colour scheme was adopted.

Routes

Beijing, Dalian, Dhaka, Guilin, Hangzhon, Haikon, Hiroshima, Kagoshima, Kota Kinabalu, Nanjing, Phuket, Sendai, Xiamen and Xian are served from Hong Kong.

Fleet	Ordered
2 Lockheed L-1011 TriStar	1 Airbus A320
6 Airbus A320-200	2 Airbus A330

Photograph: BAe 146-100 (Josef Krauthäuser/Bangkok)

DRUK AIR

P.O. Box 209 Thimpu,
Kingdom of Bhutan
Tel. 22825

Three letter code	IATA No.	ICAO Callsign
DRK	787	Druk

Druk Air was established on 1st April 1981 by decree of the King of Bhutan. After the infrastructure for air traffic had been created, a Dornier 228 started operations with a flight to Calcutta on 12th February, 1983. In mid-1983 a second aircraft of the same type was acquired. Charters were flown for the Indian domestic carrier, Vayudoot, on routes in eastern India. When a BAe 146 was delivered, the airline entered the jet age. Druk Air intends to expand its network using this aircraft. The first new service point was Bangkok. The BAe 146 is also available to the King of Bhutan for personal flights. The English equivalent of Druk Air is Royal Bhutan Airlines, and this is painted on the aircraft.

Routes

Some destinations in India, Bangkok, Dhaka and Kathmandu.

Fleet

1 Dornier 228
2 BAe 146-100

Photograph: Boeing 737-200 (author's collection)

EGYPT AIR

International Airport, Cairo
Egypt
Tel. 23902444

Three letter code	IATA No.	ICAO Callsign
EGY	77	Egyptair

Misr Airwork was founded on 7th June 1932 and services started in July 1933 with de Havilland Dragons. In 1949 the then wholly-owned Egyptian-owned operation was renamed Misrair. Following a political union between Egypt and Syria in February 1958, Misrair was re-named United Arab Airlines and in December 1958, Syrian Airways was merged into UAA. However, in September 1961 Syria withdrew from the amalgamation. The UAA used Comet 4Bs and Vickers Viscounts. Egypt carried on the airline under the name of UAA. In 1964 Misrair was revived as a domestic airline, and both airlines were brought together on 10th October 1971 to form the new Egypt Air. For political reasons UAA/Egypt Air also flew Soviet aircraft in the sixties and seventies including An-24s, IL-18s, IL-62s and Tu-154s. In April 1975 the airline switched to Airbus A300s and Boeing 737s. Boeing 707s followed for long-distance routes, and later Boeing 747s as well. In November 1980, Egyptair was financially re-organised and the share capital is now held equally by the National Bank of Egypt and Misr Insurance. An extensive fleet replacement began with Boeing 767s and Airbus A300-600s in 1989. The intention is that by the mid-nineties only these aircraft and Airbus A320/321s will be in use.

Routes

Egypt Air's network extends from Los Angeles and New York in the USA to Tokyo. Altogether there are flights to sixty destinations, including Vienna, Geneva, Zürich, Munich, Berlin, Frankfurt and Düsseldorf.

Fleet

2 Boeing 747-300
5 Boeing 767-200/300ER
9 Airbus A300-600
3 Airbus A300B4

7 Airbus A320-200
4 Boeing 737-200ADV
5 Boeing 737-500
6 Boeing 707

Ordered

6 Airbus A321
3 Airbus A340
3 Boeing 777

Photograph: Boeing 767-200 (author's collection)

EL AL ISRAEL AIRLINES

P.O. Box 41 Ben Gurion Airport
70100 Tel Aviv, Israel
Tel. 03 9716111

Three letter code	IATA No.	ICAO Callsign
ELY	114	El Al

El Al took the initiative after the founding of the State of Israel with aircraft belonging to the Israeli Air Force and started building up services. These were and are vital for the state of Israel, which is surrounded by potential enemies. The aircraft used after the airline was set up on 15th November 1948 were transports, Curtiss C-46 and DC-4s (C-54s). Operations began on 31st July 1949. The first flights were to Rome and Paris. London was served from 1949. A regular service to New York was established as early as 1950 using Lockheed Constellations. Bristol Britannias were acquired in 1957 and the

changeover to jet aircraft began in 1960, initially with leased Boeing 707s. The backbone of the El Al fleet for many years was Boeing 707s/720s. In 1971 the first Boeing 747 arrived; in 1983 Boeing 767s replaced 707s, followed in 1987 by Boeing 757s. El Al's was the first airline to use the twin engined Boeing 767 on trans-atlantic flights when it started a Montreal-Tel Aviv service in 1984. In the mid-80s, El Al was restructured, as the danger of economic collapse threatened. After the peace treaty with the PLO and further easing of tension in the Middle East, El Al is also awaiting a regional boost and opportunities to

fly to new destinations in this region.

Routes

Scheduled flights to the USA, Canada, South Africa, Kenya, Amsterdam, London, Brussels, Cologne, Munich, Zürich, Geneva, Vienna, Frankfurt, Rome and further destinations in Europe.

Fleet		Ordered
7 Boeing 747-200 1 Boeing 747F 4 Boeing 767-200 7 Boeing 757-200	2 Boeing 737-200ADV	2 Boeing 747-400

Photograph: Airbus A310-300 (Josef Krauthäuser/Frankfurt)

EMIRATES

P.O. Box 686 Dubai
United Arab Emirates
Tel. 4-228151

Three letter code	IATA No.	ICAO Callsign
UAE	176	Emirates

The independent state airline was formed in 1985 with the support of the Sheikh of the United Emirates and operations commenced on 25th October 1985 with a flight between Dubai and Karachi. Emirates had been formed by the Dubai Government under a management agreement with Pakistan International airlines and initially used a leased PIA Boeing 737 and Airbus A300. The first services were to India and Pakistan, followed by Dacca, Colombo and Cairo in 1986. 1987 saw the first flights to London, Frankfurt and Istanbul. In 1992 Emirates expanded its services with new scheduled flights to Djakarta, Paris, Rome and Zürich. Emirates now serves over thirty destinations worldwide with scheduled services and in planning route consolidation to the Far East, Europe and the Middle East in 1994/95.

Routes

Gulf region, Pakistan, India, Ceylon, Egypt, Singapore, the Philippines, Thailand and Frankfurt, London Manchester, Paris, Rome and Zürich in Europe.

Fleet	Ordered
5 Airbus A300-600	7 Boeing 777
8 Airbus A310-300	
3 Boeing 727-200	

Photograph: Tupolev Tu-134A (Martin Bach/Amsterdam)

ESTONIAN AIR

Lennujaama 2, EE 0011 Tallinn
Estonia
Tel. 421142

Three letter code	IATA No.	ICAO Callsign
ELL	960	Estonian

Estonian Air was set up by the government of the newly formed state of Estonia on 1st December, 1991 and declared to be the country's flag carrier. Estonian Air started the first scheduled service to Helsinki with Tu-134s in the same month. Further routes, especially to Scandinavia, were established in quick succession. In the long term the intention is to privatise the airline and equip it with Western aircraft.

Routes

Amsterdam, Frankfurt, Hamburg, Helsinki, Copenhagen, Kiev, Minsk, Moscow, Stockholm, Vilnius.

Fleet

4 Yakovlev Yak-40
12 Tupolev Tu-134 A

Photograph: Boeing 767-200ER (Jörg Thiel/Frankfurt)

ETHIOPIAN AIRLINES

P.O. Box 1755, Bole Airport, Addis Ababa
Democratic People's Republic of Ethiopia
Tel. 1612222

Three letter code	IATA No.	ICAO Callsign
ETH	71	Ethiopian

Ethiopian Airlines was set up on 26th December 1945 by proclamation of the emperor of the time, Haile Selassie to develop international Services and to establish connections from the capital to communities in isolated mountainous regions, where little or no surface transport existed. Scheduled flights started on 8th April 1946 with five DC-3s. The first service was between Addis Ababa and Cairo. A management contract was concluded with the American airline TWA assuring long-term support. DC-6Bs were used to operate regular flights to the first European destination, Frankfurt in June 1958 followed by Athens, Rome, Paris and London. Boeing 720 jet aircraft were introduced in 1962, followed by further Boeing 707s and 720s. Its first Boeing 727 arrived in December 1981. Boeing 767s replaced the 707s and 757s supplanted the 727s, and the DC-3s were largely replaced by the first modern ATR-42s in 1989. The airline's slogan is 'Bringing Africa Together' which is especially opposite to the extensive African network centred on Addis Ababa.

Routes

More than forty domestic destinations, thirty destinations in Africa, to Athens, Bombay, Beijing, Aden, Abu Dhabi, Berlin, Jeddah, Frankfurt, London and Rome.

Fleet

1 Boeing 707-300C
3 Boeing 767-200ER
1 Boeing 757-200F
4 Boeing 757-200ER
1 Boeing 737-200ADV

2 ATR-42
5 DHC-6 Twin Otter
1 DHC-5 Buffalo
2 Lockheed L-382 Hercules

Photograph: Boeing 737-300 (Josef Krauthäuser/Munich)

EUROBERLIN

Kleiststr. 23-26, 10623 Berlin
Germany
Tel. 030 88752601

Three letter code	IATA No.	ICAO Callsign
EEB	770	Eurober

A subsidiary of Air France (51%) and Lufthansa AG (49%). In order to find a way to counter the overpowering competition of the American airlines in flights to and from Berlin – before reunification – the two airlines set up Euroberlin France, a company under French law with headquarters in Berlin, on 9th September 1968 with Luton-based Monarch Airlines contracted to supply its fleet of Boeing 737-300s, four of which were initially supplied. Flight operations started with leased Boeing 737-300s on 7th November 1988. 600,000 passengers flew with this airline in 1989. After Germany regained its air sovereignty in Berlin as well, there was no immediate need for Euroberlin any more. Since October 1990 Euroberlin has been flying mainly on behalf of Lufthansa to Berlin, but it is also increasingly flying charter flights. After the leasing contracts for the aircraft expire, it is intended to dissolve Euroberlin.

Routes

From Berlin several times daily to Cologne, Munich, Frankfurt and Stuttgart.

Fleet

6 Boeing 737-300

Photograph: ATR-72 (Uwe Gleisberg/Munich FJS)

EUROWINGS

Flughafenstrasse 100, 90411 Nuremberg
Germany
Tel. 0911 36560

Three letter code	IATA No.	ICAO Callsign
EWG	104	Eurowings

NFD and RFG were merged on 1st January 1993 to form Eurowings. After the majority shareholder, Albrecht Knauf, had insisted on a concentration and division of tasks of the two airlines, the result was a joint operation. At the same time the aircraft were also given a new corporate image. NFD and RFG operated extensive regional services from Dortmund and Nuremberg, in both cases with ATRs, Metroliners and Do 228s. Nuernberger Flugdienst (NFD) had been formed in 1975 and undertook scheduled commuter services, express carto flights, charter and ambulance services. Commuter services started on 1st April, 1980. RFG Regionflug, founded in 1956, and based at Dortmund and Paderborn had undertaken similar work to NFD. An all-cargo BAe 146-200 QT is operated for TNT. In addition to its own scheduled services, Eurowings also flies for Lufthansa and Swissair, plus it operates charter flights.

Routes

Dense German network of routes and to Amsterdam, Budapest, Brussels, London, Lyon, Milan, Prague, Vienna and Zürich.

Fleet	Ordered
18 ATR-42	4 ATR-72
12 ATR-72	
1 BAe 146	

Photograph: Boeing 747-400 (Björn Kannengiesser/Vienna)

EVA AIR

376 Hsin-nan Road, Sec 1 Luchu,
Taoyuan Hsien, Taiwan, Republic of China
Tel. 3515151

Three letter code	IATA No.	ICAO Callsign
EVA	695	Eavaair

In March 1989 Evergreen, the largest container shipping line in the world, set up its own airline. But state-imposed conditions, quarrels concerning the airline's name (confusion with the names of other companies) and new aircraft that were not immediately available prevented them from starting flights straightaway. Finally, EVA Air, provided with US$370 million, started flights on 1st July 1991. It used Boeing 767-300ERs on routes to Bangkok, Manila, Hong Kong and Seoul. It has been serving Vienna since November 1991, and London since April 1993. There are also important connections to the USA since the carrier's first trans-Pacific service, from Taipei to Los Angeles, started in December 1992. A charter service is operated to the Republic of Maldives. EVA Air is growing rapidly and is becoming one of the top Taiwanese airlines, with an impressively modern fleet.

Routes

Bangkok, Ho Chi Minh City, Jakarta, Hong Kong, Kaoshing, Kuala Lumpur, Los Angeles, London, Manila, Maldives, New York, Penang, Seattle, Seoul, Singapore, Taipei, Vienna.

Fleet	Ordered
5 Boeing 767-300ER 7 Boeing 747-400	14 McDonnell Douglas MD-11 4 Boeing 767

Photograph: Boeing 747-100 (author's collection)

EVERGREEN INTERNATIONAL

3850 Three Mile Lane, Mc Minnville, OR 97128-9496, USA
Tel. 503 472 0011

Three letter code	IATA No.	ICAO Callsign
EIA	494	Evergreen

Evergreen International Airlines is a division of Evergreen Aviation. This holding company also owns one of the largest helicopter companies in the USA, Evergreen Helicopter, and also the famous Marana Airpark in Arizona, where aircraft are parked when temporarily not in use. The airline was set upon 28th November 1975 when Evergreen Helicopters acquired the operator's certificate from Johnson Flying Service. Operating as Johnson International, the company was founded as early as 1924 and was awarded one of the first supplemental certificates in 1957. Evergreen operates a domestic American cargo service as a subcontractor of UPS and other companies, but it also has its own cargo routes. In addition, aircraft are wetleased, i.e. with crew, to other airlines. The airline itself also operates scheduled charter flights and works for the US Army in troop transportation.

Routes

Regular cargo flights from Hong Kong to New York and on worldwide cargo charters and contract services.

Fleet

11 Boeing 727F
13 Boeing 747
 3 McDonnell Douglas DC-8-63/75
 8 McDonnell Douglas DC-9-15/30

Ordered

2 McDonnell Douglas MD-90

Photograph: McDonnell Douglas DC-10-30 (author's collection)

EXPRESS ONE

3890 West Northwest Highway, Suite 700, Dallas
TX 75220, USA
Tel. 214 902 2500

Three letter code	IATA No.	ICAO Callsign
LHN	–	Longhorn

Express One is a US supplemental air carrier and a subsidiary of Wikert and Wikert. The airline began in 1975 as Jet East International with air taxi services from Dallas Love-Field Airport, using Beech King Airs and Learjets moving more into the 'airline' business from 1980. It also flew five Boeing 727s on behalf of UPS, the well-known 'parcel flyer'. Its name was changed to Express One in 1989, and it had contracts with Emery and DHL, also carriers. It used five further Boeing 727s also for passenger flights on a charter basis, adding DC-9s to these in 1991/92. Express One made it across the Atlantic for the first time in July 1993 using leased DC-10s for charter flights to Frankfurt.

Routes

Charter flights within the USA, Canada, to the Caribbean, Latin and South America, Europe. Cargo flights within the USA.

Fleet

5 Boeing 727-100
7 Boeing 727-100F
7 Boeing 727-200ADV
3 McDonnell Douglas DC-10-30
4 McDonnell Douglas DC-9-31

Photograph: Lockheed L-1011 TriStar (author's collection)

FAUCETT PERU

P.O. Box 1429 Lima 100
Peru
Tel. 14 463424

Three letter code	IATA No.	ICAO Callsign
CPF	163	Faucett

Elmer J. Faucett, an American citizen and pilot, set up the Compania de Aviacion Faucett SA on 15th September 1928. A true flying pioneer, he established a connection from Talara in the north to Arequipa in the south via Lima. He used Stinson Detroiters. Stinson designed the F-19 specially for Faucett's needs. Aircraft were produced by Faucett under licence and used in flight operations. In addition to aircraft operations, the airports in many places in Peru were laid out or expanded by Faucett. In 1938 Aerovias Peru was taken over; after the Second World War, DC-3s and DC-4s were bought, followed in 1960 by DC-6s and in April 1968 the first jet aircraft, a Boeing 727. BAC 1-11s were added to the fleet; the first was delivered in 1971. Aeronaves del Peru, a cargo airline has been the main shareholder in Faucett since 1982. In 1984 the main international service to Miami by DC-8 was discontinued for some time or only flown as far as the Cayman Islands due to political differences with the USA. Mainly cargo is carried with a somewhat aged fleet; the passenger figures have been on the decline for years on exclusively domestic routes.

Routes

Arequipa, Ayachucho, Chiclayo, Chimbote, Cusco, Iquitos, Julica, Miami, Piura, Pucallpa, Porto Maldonado, Rioja, Tacna, Talara, Tarapoto, Tumbes, Yurimagues.

Fleet

2 Boeing 727-200
4 Boeing 737-100/200
4 McDonnell Douglas DC-8-50
1 Lockheed L-1011 TriStar

Photograph: McDonnell Douglas MD-11 (Björn Kannengiesser/Fort Lauderdale)

FEDERAL EXPRESS

P.O. Box 727, Memphis TN 38194-2424
USA
Tel. 901-3693600

Three letter code	IATA No.	ICAO Callsign
FDX	23	Express

Frederick W. Smith, the present chairman, set up Federal Express in June 1971, and it started flight operations on 17th April 1973 using Dassault Falcon 20s. Up to sixty of these aircraft were in use. In 1978 Fed Ex, as it is abbreviated, was floated on the stock exchange and became a joint-stock company. The Fed Ex system revolutionised the entire cargo market twenty years ago and has found a lot of imitators since then. The shipments are distributed from a central hub in Memphis with US regional sorting centres at Newark, Oakland, Los Angeles and Indianapolis using the hub-and-spoke distribution system which it invented. After air cargo deregulation in November 1977, Fed Ex was also able to operate larger aircraft. They bought Boeing 727s in large numbers, and later DC-10s and Boeing 747s as well. Brussels, which is a sorting centre for the European market, and London Stansted have been in the network since 1986.

In 1989 Flying Tiger Line, which had been established and well-known for many years, was bought and its DC-8s and Boeing 747s were integrated. Although only express shipments were transported at the beginning, other cargo shipments are also tranported, making more than 2 million shipments a day; Federal Express is thus the largest air freight carrier in the world. The company has also invested in newly-built cargo aircraft, rather than conversions of tired passenger aircraft. The first of twenty-five Airbus A300-600F on order was to be handed over on 27th April 1994; there is an option on a further twenty-five.

Routes

Federal Express serves over 100 cities in the USA, and around 180 countries around the world.

Fleet

160 Boeing 727-100/200
 10 Boeing 747-100/200F
 27 McDonnell Douglas DC-10s

 13 McDonnell Douglas MD-11s
220 Cessna Caravan
 32 Fokker F-27

Ordered

 10 Airbus A310
 25 Airbus A300-600F
100 Cessna Caravan

Photograph: McDonnell Douglas DC-10-30 (author's collection)

FINNAIR

Mannerheimintie 102, 00250 Helsinki
Finland
Tel. 90 410411

Three letter code	IATA No.	ICAO Callsign
FIN	105	Finnair

Set up on 9th October 1923 as Aero OY, the German company Junkers also had a 50% stake in this airline. The first flight was from Helsinki to Tallinn on 20th March 1924 with a Junkers F-13, the most advanced passenger aircraft of that time. In the years to 1936, seaplanes were used exclusively until the first airports were built in Finland. In the next few years there were further flights from Berlin to Paris. Aero OY had to discontinue operations on 21st September 1944, and they remained suspended until the spring of 1945. Eight C-47s were bought from the USAAF in early 1945. The first flights were to

Stockholm and Copenhagen. Düsseldorf was added to the network of routes in 1951. Convair 340/440s replaced the C-47s (DC-3s). A new connection with Moscow in 1956 was one of the highlights, followed by Frankfurt, Cologne, Basle and Geneva in 1957. The Caravelle was introduced in 1960, and Finnair started to change over to jet aircraft. KarAir, a private Finnish airline, founded in 1957 to continue the operations of Karhumaki airways which started in 1951, was taken over in 1962. DC-8s were ordered for new long-distance flights to the USA, and the first arrived in 1969. They were also

used for charter flights to the Mediterranean. In 1968 the name Finnair was adopted as the sole valid designation of the airline. DC-10-30s were delivered from 4th February 1975. These were used primarily for flights to the American west coast, to Tokyo and New York. For medium-distance flights, the Caravelles were replaced by DC-9s. The first MD-11 was acquired in December 1990. For reasons of cost, KarAir, which had previously operated independently, was integrated in 1993. A subsidiary, Finnaviation, operates six Saab 340s on domestic services.

Routes

Los Angeles, New York, Toronto, Tokyo, Singapore, Bangkok, Beijing, Moscow, Prague, Warsaw, Leningrad, Hamburg, Berlin, Frankfurt, Vienna, Zürich, Geneva, Stuttgart and Munich are important Finnair destinations; there are also many destinations in Scandinavia.

Fleet

17 McDonnell Douglas DC-9-41/51
3 McDonnell Douglas MD-87
14 McDonnell Douglas MD-82/83
5 McDonnell Douglas DC-10-30
4 McDonnell Douglas MD-11

2 Airbus A300B4
5 ATR-72

Photograph: Boeing 727-100 (Josef Krauthäuser/Ottawa)

FIRST AIR – BRADLEY AIR SERVICES

Carp Airport, Carp Ontario KOA 1LO
Canada
Tel. 613 839 3340

Three letter code	IATA No.	ICAO Callsign
BAR	245	Bradley

Bradley Air Services is Canada's largest independent regional carrier and provides scheduled charter and cargo flights from various points in Canada. The scheduled flights go under the name of First Air. Bradley Air Services was set up in 1954 having originally started as Bradley Flying School in 1946 and started flight operations with DC-3s the same year. Main bases are at Carp and at Resolute Bay, Hall Beach and Frobisher Bay, all in the Northwest Territories where it undertakes specialist Arctic charter work. First Air's home airport is in Ottawa, from where there are flights to the USA and to Greenland. The first scheduled services were flown in the 1970's by DC-3s followed by HS748s in the 1980s. Its first Boeing 727 was acquired in 1986 and was introduced on Frobisher Bay – Ottawa services.

Routes

Boston, New York, Godthab, Cambridge Bay, Halifax, Montreal, Ottawa and other destinations, particularly in the north of Canada.

Fleet

4 Boeing 727-100
9 BAe HS-748
5 de Havilland DHC-6 Twin Otter

Photograph: Dornier 228 (author's collection)

FORMOSA AIRLINES

87 Jung Kiang Road, Taipei 10428
Republic of China (Taiwan)
Tel. 02 5084183

Three letter code	IATA No.	ICAO Callsign
FOR	–	Formosa

Formosa Airlines, which is in private ownership, has been in existence since 1966 as an agricultural concern although in the 1970s a DC-6B was employed on charter work. At this time the airline was known as Yung Shing Airlines. In 1978 a group of businessmen took control to develop a variety of air work. Domestic flights started with Britten-Norman Islanders. Two Dornier 228s came into operation in 1983, and a further three followed in 1985. In 1987 the name was changed to the present Formosa Airlines and an order for two Saab 340s was placed in December 1987 and both were delivered in 1988.

Today Formosa operates the largest commuter network in Taiwan. Almost 380,000 passengers were carried by Formosa Airlines in 1993.

Routes

Dense regional network of scheduled routes in the Republic of China, plus charter flights to tourist destinations on the island.

Fleet	Ordered
3 Saab SF-340	5 Dornier 328
6 Dornier 228	
3 Pilatus-Britten-Norman Islander	

Photograph: Boeing 737-400 (Josef Krauthäuser/Vienna)

FUTURA

Calle Jesus 4, 07003 Palma de Mallorca
Spain
Tel. 71755196

Three letter code	IATA No.	ICAO Callsign
FUA	–	Futura

Futura International Airways was set up in 1989 as a joint venture between Aer Lingus (25%) and Spanish investors based at Palma with the objective of providing package tours from Ireland to Spain. In February 1990, flights started from Dublin to Palma de Mallorca with two Boeing 737-300s leased from Guinness-Peat Aviation (GPA). Other airports such as Basle, Düsseldorf, Manchester, Munich and Vienna followed quickly. Larger Boeing 737-400s were acquired in 1991 and 1992. Ownership is now split 85% Aer Lingus, 15% Belton Air.

Routes

Charter flights from Ireland, Britain, Germany, Austria and Switzerland to Spain, especially Majorca and the Canary Islands.

Fleet

2 Boeing 737-300
6 Boeing 737-400

Photograph: McDonnell Douglas MD-11 (Josef Krauthäuser/Munich FJS)

GARUDA INDONESIA

Jalan Merdeka Selatan 13, Jakarta 10110
Indonesia
Tel. 213801901

Three letter code	IATA No.	ICAO Callsign
GIA	126	Indonesia

26th January 1949 is the official date when Garuda was founded. On this day, a DC-3 flew from Calcutta to Rangoon registered under the name of 'Indonesian Airways'. It was the first civil aircraft of the new Republic of Indonesia, but could not fly in Indonesia for political reasons. It was only after the official declaration of independence at the end of 1949 that the airline was also installed by the government in Indonesia; however, at the beginning it needed the assistance of KLM. Garuda Indonesian Airways was set up on 31st March 1950 by the government and KLM, as the successor to the post-war Inter-Island Division of KLM

and the pre-war KNILM, and to succeed Indonesian Airways. The airline was nationalised in March 1954. In addition to DC-3s, Convair 240/340s were in use, plus Lockheed L-188 Electras from 1961 onwards. In 1963, De Kroonduif, an airline in the Indonesian part of New Guinea, was taken over. Convair CV 990s were Garuda's first jet aircraft to fly to Amsterdam, in 1965. These aircraft were replaced in 1968 by DC-8s. Sydney was served for the first time in 1969, via Bali, and DC-10s were also bought in that year, with some Fokker F-27s for domestic services. These were, however, taken out of service in

1971 and sold, due to the purchase of F-28s. Large-capacity aircraft were added to the Garuda fleet in the form of DC-10-30s in 1973, initially leased from KLM. In early 1980 the airline put Boeing 747s into service and flew with them to Frankfurt. In the late 80s, on the occasion of the airline's fortieth anniversary, the entire fleet was repainted in new attractive colours. Starting with the summer schedule in 1992, after the delivery of the MD-11s, Garuda opened up a weekly Medan-Jakarta-Munich flight and Madrid and Berlin were added to the network in 1993.

Routes

Amsterdam, Brussels, Frankfurt, Zürich, Vienna, Rome, London, Paris, Munich, Madrid and Berlin in Europe, Cairo, Jeddah, Riyadh, Abu Dhabi, Singapore, Kuala Lumpur, Hong Kong, Manila, Taipei, Tokyo, Los Angeles, Darwin, Perth, Sydney, Melbourne and over thirty destinations in Indonesia are served by Garuda.

Fleet		Ordered
8 Boeing 747-200	34 Fokker F-28	3 McDonnell Douglas MD-11
8 Boeing 737-300	12 Airbus A300-600	16 Boeing 737-400
9 Airbus A300 B4	9 McDonnell Douglas MD-11	9 Boeing 747-400
6 McDonnell Douglas DC-10-30		12 Fokker 100
18 McDonnell Douglas DC-9-32		

Photograph: Boeing 737-200 (Josef Krauthäuser/Salzburg)

GB AIRWAYS

Ian Stewart Centre, Gatwick Airport,
West Sussex RH6 0PB, United Kingdom
Tel. 0293 664239

Three letter code	IATA No.	ICAO Callsign
GBL	171	Gibair

The airline was formed as Gibraltar Airways as early as 1930 by M. H. Bland Ltd the Gibraltar Shipping Line. A Saro flying boat was used for flights from Gibraltar to Tangiers. In 1932 activities ceased and the airline only started flight operations again on 30th August 1947 with a Gibraltar-Tangier DC-3 service after being reformed on 15th May 1947 and BEA had acquired a stake. The Gibraltar-Tangier route is the shortest intercontinental routre in the world with a 15 minute flying time between Europe and Africa. The airline, renamed Gibair, started using Vickers Viscounts in 1953. Due to political tensions with Spain in the late 60s involving the return of Gibraltar, Gibair was the only British airline to maintain flights. The present name was adopted on 1st November 1981. After the merger of BOAC and BEA to form British Airways, their shares in GB Airways were reduced to 49% with the other 51% owned by the Bland Group. It used Boeing 737s leased from British Airways. As well as scheduled flights, a large number of charter links are provided from London-Gatwick and Manchester.

Routes

London, Manchester, Gibraltar, Madeira, Sevilla, Valencia, Casablanca, Freetown, Funchal, Salzburg, Tangiers.

Fleet

5 Boeing 737-200

Photograph: Boeing 737-300 (Uwe Gleisberg/Munich)

GERMANIA

Cologne-Bonn Airport, 51147 Cologne
Germany
Tel. 02203 402182

Three letter code	IATA No.	ICAO Callsign
GMI	–	Germania

In 1986, exactly ten years after it had been set up, the SAT (Special Air Transport) airline changed its name to Germania. Operations with jet aircraft had begun in September 1978 with three former LTU Caravelle 10Rs. The first SAT aircraft was an F-27. As well as the Caravelles, the airline owned two Boeing 727s, but these were only flown in Germania's colours after the airline had been renamed. The Caravelles were replaced from 1989 onwards and the first Boeing 737-300s were bought. Germania flies subcharters today for other airlines and for various tour operators flying out of Germany to various Mediterranean destinations. Some of Germania's aircraft flew in DFD colours. Germania has a considerable number of flights from Berlin. Among other things, scheduled services from Berlin to Heringsdorf/Baltic Sea have been introduced. six further Boeing 737-300s have been in use since spring 1992, and the colour scheme of the fleet was altered.

Routes

Charter flights to the Mediterranean, to North Africa, the Canary Islands, Turkey.

Fleet

12 Boeing 737-300

Photograph: McDonnell Douglas DC-10-30 (author's collection)

GHANA AIRWAYS

P.O. Box 1636, Accra
Ghana
Tel. 664856

Three letter code	IATA No.	ICAO Callsign
GHA	237	Ghana

With the support of BOAC, the government of Ghana set up the national airline on 4th July 1958 with the government having a 60% stake and BOAC 40% to take over the operations of West African Airways Corporation in the British colony formerly known as the Gold Coast. Soon, on 16th July a scheduled service to London began, using Boeing 377 Stratocruisers leased from BOAC. Domestic services were taken over from WAAC on 1st October 1958. The Stratocruisers were later replaced by Bristol Britannias. On 14th February 1961 Ghana took over sole control of the airline. Soviet IL-18s were bought as part of a further expansion. As these were not particularly economical to use, all eight aircraft were returned to the manufacturer after a period of time. Ghana Airways' first jet aircraft was a Vickers VC-10. In 1983 the Douglas DC-10 arrived and was used for long distance flights, and regional routes were flown with Fokker F-28s and and DC-9s. There are plans to introduce services to Jeddah and New York.

Routes

Abidjan, Banjul, Conakry, Dakar, Freetown, Harare, Kuassi, Lagos, Las Palmas, Lome, Monrovia, London, Düsseldorf.

Fleet

1 McDonnell Douglas DC-10-30
1 McDonnell Douglas DC-9-51
2 Fokker F-28

Photograph: Tupolev Tu-154M (author's collection)

GREENAIR

Cumhuriyet Caddeshi 279, Adli Han, Kat 4 Harbiye, Istanbul Turkey
Tel. 1434190

Three letter code	IATA No.	ICAO Callsign
GRN	–	Greenair

The boom in tourism to Turkey in the late 80s and the legal possibilities opened up made the creation of new airlines feasible. Greenair was set up in early 1990 and flies with Soviet-made aircraft leased from Aeroflot which has an interest in the airline. For the time being only charter flights were planned and at a later date scheduled services were proposed from Istanbul to Moscow. Greenair's base is Istanbul Airport. However by early 1993 its aircraft had returned to Aeroflot.

Routes

Frankfurt, Nuremberg, Berlin, Paris, London, Milan to destinations in Turkey.

Fleet

3 Tupolev Tu 154M

Photograph: Boeing 767-300ER (author's collection)

GULF AIR

P.O. Box 138 Manama
Bahrain
Tel. 231166

Three letter code	IATA No.	ICAO Callsign
GFA	72	Gulfair

Gulf Air is the national carrier of the Gulf state co-operation of Bahrain, Qatar, the United Arab Emirates and Oman. This airline was set up as Gulf Aviation on 24th March 1950, with flights in the region using Avro Ansons starting on 5th July 1970. De Havilland Dove and Heron aircraft followed and DC-3s and F-27s were added to the fleet, partly under British sponsorship. These were replaced from 1969 onwards with BAC 1-11s. 1970 saw the start of regular flights to London with leased Vickers VC 10s. On 1st April 1974 the four states took Gulf Aviation over, giving the airline a new legal status and the present name of Gulf

Air. Boeing 737s replaced the BAC 1-11s from 1977. For long-distance flights, Gulf Air used Lockheed L-1011 TriStars starting in 1976. Fleet replacement and expansion started with the arrival of the first Boeing 767-300ERs. In the long term these are intended to replace the older TriStars. However, the Gulf War led to this programme being suspended for the time being, and it was only resumed in 1993 with the delivery of Airbus A320s. One of the four states, United Arab Emirates comprises a number of states and most do not recognise Gulf Air as their official carrier. One, Dubai set up its own official airline, Emirates,

in 1985 and Gulf Air then ceased services to Dubai.

Routes

From six airports in the Gulf, regular flights to London, Paris and Frankfurt, Hong Kong, Manila, Sydney, Bangkok, Bombay, Colombo, Nairobi, Dar es Salaam, Cairo, Singapore.

Fleet	Ordered
8 Boeing 737-200	6 Boeing 777
18 Boeing 767-300ER	4 Airbus A320
8 Lockheed L-1011 TriStar	12 Airbus A321
8 Airbus A320	6 Airbus A340-300

Photograph: Boeing 727-200 (author's collection)

HAITI TRANS AIR

BP 2526 Port-au-Prince
Haiti
Tel. 39584

Three letter code	IATA No.	ICAO Callsign
HTC	362	Haiti Transair

Haiti Trans Air started scheduled and charter flights in 1987 to the Caribbean and the USA using a leased Boeing 727. A further aircraft was acquired in 1988. From its home airport, Port-au-Prince, there are passenger and cargo flights to Miami and San Juan. In spite of the difficult political situation, HTC has developed positively, allowing the airline to acquire a DC-8 in 1992.

Routes

Pointe-A-Pitre, Port-au-Prince, Miami, San Juan

Fleet

2 Boeing 727-200
1 McDonnell Douglas DC-8-61

Photograph: de Havilland DHC-8-100 (author's collection)

HAMBURG AIRLINES

Building 175, Airport, 22415 Hamburg
Germany
Tel. 040 50752902

Three letter code	IATA No.	ICAO Callsign
HAS	99	Hamburg Air

Hamburg Airlines was set up on 15th April 1988 in order to take over Hanse Express, which had gone bankrupt. Hanse Express had been founded as Hadag Air on 1st March 1974 and was known as Holiday Express until August 1986 when its final name was adopted. In addition to the route rights, two Dornier 228s were also taken over by the new airline. In September 1988 the first DHC-8 was leased in order to be able to overcome capacity bottlenecks. New routes to Amsterdam and Rotterdam, as well as to London-Gatwick were opened. After the reunification of Germany, Hamburg Airlines was also active in the new federal states. Scheduled services were expanded in early summer 1990 with the use of Fokker 100s for charter flights. In 1992 the airline was sold in its entirety to Saarland Airlines. After the collapse of a tour operator – Saarland Airlines got into financial difficulties – Hamburg Airlines also had to apply to open insolvency proceedings in autumn 1993. Flights are continuing and there are hopes of consolidation after a new partner had been found, resulting in a change to the legal form of the company's organisation.

Routes

From Hamburg to Rotterdam, Amsterdam, London, Brussels, Berlin, Dresden, Leipzig.

Fleet

3 de Havilland DHC-8-100
3 de Havilland DHC-8-300

Photograph: Airbus A310-200 (Josef Krauthäuser/Munich FJS)

HAPAG-LLOYD FLUG

Postfach 420240, 30662 Hanover
Germany
Tel. 0511 73030

Three letter code	IATA No.	ICAO Callsign
HLF	617	Hapaglloyd

The well-known German shipping company Hapag-Lloyd set up the airline with the traditional name in July 1972. Flights started in March of the following year with three Boeing 727-100s acquired from All Nippon Airlines and its 727 fleet subsequently increased to eight aircraft by 1979. After lengthy negotiations Bavaria-Germanair was taken over in late 1978. This takeover provided Hapag-Lloyd with various BAC 1-11 and Airbus A300B4 aircraft. While the latter were integrated into the existing fleet, the BACs were sold and new Boeing 737-200 were ordered. A replacement of the fleet and its adaptation to future needs was decided in 1987. A total of six Airbus A300B4s were exchanged for Airbus A310s and Boeing 737-400s were ordered, the first of which arrived in Hanover in autumn 1990. When the Airbus A310 was introduced, Hapag-Lloyd was then in a position to provide flights to the USA as well. Around 3 million tourists were carried by Hapag-Lloyd in 1993 to a variety of destinations; this makes the airline one of the leading provider of charter flights in Germany.

Routes

Charter flights to the Mediterranean, to the Canary Islands, to Africa, Middle East, Far East, USA and the Caribbean.

Fleet

4 Airbus A310-200
3 Airbus A310-300
9 Boeing 737-400
5 Boeing 737-500

Photograph: McDonnell Douglas DC-8-62 (author's collection)

HAWAIIAN AIR

P.O. Box 30008 Int. Airport
Honolulu, 96820 Hawaii, USA
Tel. 808 525 5511

Three letter code	IATA No.	ICAO Callsign
HAL	173	Hawaiian

Founded on 30th January 1929 as Inter Island Airways in Honolulu by the Inter Island Steam Navigation Company. Flights started on 11th November 1929 between Honolulu and Hilo with Sikorsky S-36 amphibian flying boats, replaced later by larger S-43 versions. Air mail contracts were obtained in 1934 and during the following years the fleet included the larger again Sikorsky S-34 amphibians. A permanent route certificate was awarded on 16th June 1939. On 1st October 1941, the airline assumed its present name, Hawaiian Airlines, known now as Hawaiian Air and flight operations were changed over

to DC-3s. Increased expansion in the tourist business and route additions led to the acquisition of larger aircraft in 1952 such as Convair 340s, and from 1958 DC-6s. In 1966 the airline switched over to jet aircraft with the introduction of the DC-9-30. DC-8s were added to the fleet in 1983 and Lockheed TriStars in 1987, for charter flights to the American continent, the Pacific and Europe. A Honolulu-Los Angeles service was introduced on 12th June 1985 and was later extended to Las Vegas. In early 1991, Northwest Airlines paid $20 million for a 25% holding in the airline. Hawaiian Air sought Chapter

11 protection in 1993 as the result of financial difficulties.

Routes

There are 160 scheduled domestic services daily, and there are further flights to Pago Pago, Papeete, Tonga in the Pacific and to San Francisco, Las Vegas, Los Angeles and other destinations in the USA. Also, there are sightseeing flights with Dash 7s.

Fleet	Ordered
8 Lockheed L-1011 TriStar	8 DC-10-10
6 McDonnell Douglas DC-8-62/63	
14 McDonnell Douglas DC-9-51	
4 de Havilland DHC-7	

Photograph: Airbus A300B4 (author's collection)

IBERIA

130 Calle Velazquez, 28006 Madrid
Spain
Tel. 15858585

Three letter code	IATA No.	ICAO Callsign
IBE	75	Iberia

Iberia was originally established on 25th June 1927 and its first service was between Madrid and Barcelona using a German-built Rohrbach Roland trimotor. In 1928, Iberia merged with compania Espanola (founded in 1925) to form CLASSA with financial and technical help from Deutsche Lufthansa. On 31st December 1927 it entered into contract with the government to provide air services. During 1931, the airline was re-formed as LAPE (Lineas Aereas Postales Espanoles) and the name changed to Iberia in 1937, a year after DC-2s were ordered. The present-day Iberia was formed in 1940 as the result of the

merger of several airlines. After the Spanish Civil War, the German influence on the airline was still quite considerable, with Lufthansa holding 49% of the capital. In 1944 the Spanish government acquired all the shares and ordered DC-3s to add to the Ju-52 fleet. Iberia, as a pioneering European airline after the Second World War, opened up important routes to Buenos Aires (1946), Caracas and San Juan (1949), Havana, New York and Mexico (1954), Bogota (1958), Santiago and further destinations in early 1960. South America is thus traditionally one of the most important markets. DC-4s and

Lockheed Constellations were used, and the first jet aircraft was a DC-8 in 1961. The Caravelle was acquired in 1962 for short-distance and medium-distance flights; these were passed on to the subsidiary Aviaco in 1967 and DC-9s were bought. Iberia obtained its first large-capacity aircraft, the Boeing 747, in October 1970. In 1972 Boeing 727s were bought, and a year later DC-10-30s. A large-scale fleet replacement programme is underway in the 90s. MD-87s and A320s are replacing older DC-9s and Boeing 727s. Iberia has a stake in various companies such as VIASA, Aerolineas Argentinas and Ladeco.

Routes

Dense domestic network with the emphasis on Madrid and Barcelona. Scheduled services to the USA, the Caribbean, South and Central America, the Middle East, Africa and important destinations in Europe. Overseas hubs operate at Buenos Aires, Santo Domingo and Miami.

Fleet		Ordered
7 Boeing 747-200	8 Airbus A300B4	8 Airbus A340-200
30 Boeing 727-200ADV	22 Airbus A320	8 Airbus A321-100
14 McDonnell Douglas DC-9-32	8 Boeing 757-200	13 Boeing 757-200
24 McDonnell Douglas MD-87		
8 McDonnell Douglas DC-10-30		

Photograph: Boeing 757-200 (author's collection)

ICELANDAIR

Reykjavik Airport, 101 Reykjavik
Iceland
Tel. 1690100

Three letter code	IATA No.	ICAO Callsign
ICE	108	Iceair

Icelandair, or Flugfelag Islands HF, was formed on the north coast of Iceland as Flugfelag Akureyar on 3rd June 1937. In 1940, the headquarters of the airline was moved to the capital Reykjavik, and a Beech 18, two de Havilland Dragon Rapides and a further Waco YKS were bought. After the end of the Second World War, a scheduled service from Iceland via Prestwick to Copenhagen was set up for the first time in 1946. In April 1948. Flugfelag obtained its first Douglas DC-4, using it for a second route to London. The first flights to Germany took place as early as 1955; in 1965 its present title was adopted and

Fokker F-27s were put to use, and two years later Boeing 727s. Icelandair was set up in its present form on 20th July 1973 as the holding company for Flugfelag Islands and Loftfeidir (Icelandic Airlines formed on 10th March 1944). The company was a holding company after the merger but did not assume all operating responsibility until 1st October 1979. Since 1973 it had been Icelandic flying transatlantic services and Icelandair flying domestic and European services. In 1988 836,000 passengers flew with Icelandair. The DC-8s were replaced by modern Boeing 757s in 1989, the rest of the

fleet was continually replaced and Boeing 737s added. The F-27s were replaced by modern F-50s for regional routes, giving Icelandair a entirely new fleet. Icelandair is a public company, quoted on the stock market in Iceland, with 100% private shareholders. Associated companies include Eagle Air, Cargolux and domestic airlines North Air and East Air.

Routes

Icelandic regional services to around ten destinations. International routes to New York, Salzburg, Chicago, Luxembourg, Copenhagen, Frankfurt, London, Paris, Göteborg, Oslo, Stockholm.

Fleet

3 Boeing 757-200ER
4 Boeing 737-400
4 Fokker F-50

Photograph: Airbus A320 (Airbus Industrie)

INDIAN AIRLINES

113 Gurdwara Rakabganj Road
Parliament Street, New Delhi 110001, India
Tel. 11388951

Three letter code	IATA No.	ICAO Callsign
IAC	58	Indair

Indian Airlines Corporation was set up on 28th May, 1953 by the central government in Delhi and on 1st August 1953 formally acquired the routes and assets of eight independent airlines – Airways (India), Bharat Airways, Himalayan Aviation, Kalinaga Airlines, Indian National Airways, Deccan Airways, Air India and Air Services of India. They were all nationalised and combined to form Air India and Indian Airlines, with Indian Airlines being responsible for regional services. The airline's first flights were on 1st August 1953, and it used DC-4s, Vickers Vikings and DC-3s. Daily night airmail services were inaugurated on 5th November 1955 between the major Indian cities. In 1957 these aircraft were partly replaced by Vickers Viscounts, and by Fokker F-27 from May 1961 onwards. The airline's first jet aircraft was the Caravelle, acquired in February 1964. HS-748s manufactured under licence in India were also used, as were Airbus A300s, the first widebody aircraft. When the latest generation of aircraft, the Airbus 320, was introduced at the end of 1989/ beginning of 1990, some operational problems arose which had an effect on flights and on passenger numbers. Indian Airlines' flights are regionally divided up, from Delhi, Bombay, Calcutta and Madras. Indian Airlines has a stake of 50% in the regional airline Vayudoot. With over 20,000 employees and carrying more than 10 million passengers a year, Indian Airlines is one of the world's largest domestic carriers. It is an autonomous corporation under the control of the Ministry of Tourism and Civil Aviation.

Routes

Over fifty destinations in India are served, also international flights to Kabul, Dhaka, Chittagong, Male, Karachi, Katmandu, Lahore, Colombo, Bangkok and Singapore.

Fleet	Ordered
11 Airbus A300B4	5 Airbus A320
25 Airbus A320	
23 Boeing 737-200ADV	
3 Fokker F-27	

Photograph: de Havilland DHC-8-100 (author's collection)

INTEROT AIRWAYS

Georg-Haindl-Str. 4, 86153 Augsburg
Germany
Tel. 0821 705051

Three letter code	IATA No.	ICAO Callsign
IRT	614	Interot

Interot Air Service, a subsidiary of Interot Spedition, a forwarding company of Hamburg, has been operating regular charter services between Augsburg and Düsseldorf using Beechcraft 200 Super King Airs since 1979. Since 1986, this occasional service has been registered as a scheduled supplemental air service and the appropriate licence has been granted. Its first scheduled service operated in September 1986 between Augsburg and Düsseldorf. A second Beechcraft was acquired in order to be able to serve Hamburg from autumn 1987. The demand for these services is quite considerable, so that a Beechcraft 1900 was bought in September, followed by another one in December 1989. Interot obtained its licence as a scheduled airline in December 1989. In October 1990 a provisionally leased DHC-8-100 was used for the first time on the route to Düsseldorf. Three aircraft of this type were ordered. German reunification resulted in Interot acquiring new destinations from Augsburg and a change of name, to Interot Airways. The opening of Munich Airport gave Interot and Augsburg airport an unexpected boost, reflected in rising passenger numbers.

Routes

Düsseldorf, Hamburg, Dresden, Berlin, Augsburg, Leipzig.

Fleet	Ordered
1 Beechcraft 200 Super King Air	1 de Havilland DHC-8-300
2 Beechcraft 1900	
2 de Havilland DHC-8-100	
1 de Havilland DHC-8-300	

Photograph: Fokker 100 (author's collection)

IRAN AIR

P.O. Box 13187 Head Office, Mehrabad Airport, Teheran, Islamic Republic of Iran
Tel. 021 600 9111

Three letter code	IATA No.	ICAO Callsign
IRA	96	Iranair

Iran Air came into existence in February 1962 as the result of the fusion of Iranian Airways and Persian Air Service, by order of the government of the time. Iran Air had been established as a private company in 1944 and was known as Iranair. Persian, also in private hands, had initially begun freight services in 1955 with Avro Yorks. The routes and aircraft were taken over from Iran Air's predecessors. In 1965 Iran Air acquired Boeing 727s to open new routes to London and Frankfurt. In March 1976 a Boeing 747SP started scheduled flights to New York. The first Airbus A320s were used in 1978, mainly on much

travelled routes to neighbouring countries. Political developments in the early 80s following Ayatollah Khomeini's rise to power in 1979 and the departure of the Shah and war lasting several years with neighbouring Iraq resulted in considerable changes. Prior to 1979, Iranair had been one of the world's fastest growing airlines scheduling over 100 weekly international departures from Teheran to twenty-nine foreign cities from New York to Tokyo. It was the last airline to cancel its order for Concorde. In the mid-1980s, the number of weekly international flights had reduced to less than

thirty from Teheran. It was only from 1989 onwards that Iran Air was able to restructure itself. Fleet modernisation began in September 1990 with the delivery of the first Fokker 100s for regional flights. Further modernisation is failing at the moment because of the US economic embargo, which also applies to civil aircraft.

Routes

Iran Air flies to destinations in the Middle East and to Frankfurt, London and Paris. A domestic network connects the most important places with Teheran. There are intensive charter flights (pilgrimages) to Saudi Arabia.

Fleet

6 Fokker 100
3 Boeing 737-200
7 Boeing 727-200
4 Boeing 707
4 Boeing 747-200

1 Boeing 747-100
4 Boeing 747SP
5 Airbus A300B4

Ordered

2 Airbus A300-600
16 Boeing 737-400

Photograph: Boeing 727-200 (Uwe Gleisberg/Munich)

ISTANBUL AIRLINES

Incirli Cod. No: 50 Bakivöy
Istanbul, Turkey
Tel. 1 5703400

Three letter code	IATA No.	ICAO Callsign
IST	–	Istanbul

Istanbul Airlines (or Istanbul Hava Yollari) was set up in December 1985 by Turkish and West Geman interests in order to meet the increased demand for seats in aircraft to Turkey. Flights started on 14th March 1986 with SE 210 Caravelles. Two BAC 1-11 aircraft were also leased from Tarom. The first Boeing 737s came in November 1988. This aircraft was also used to set up a scheduled service providing better connections from Istanbul to other Turkish centres. The airline developed very quickly and further Boeing 737-400s were bought. In order to meet the demand for charter flights, Boeing 727s were also used, replacing the Caravelles.

Routes

Charter flights from Düsseldorf, Cologne, Hamburg, Hannover, Frankfurt, Munich, Saarbrücken and Stuttgart, as well as Vienna, Graz, Linz, Salzburg, Zürich and London to Istanbul. There are scheduled flights from Istanbul to Munich, Munich-Izmir, Amsterdam and further destinations in Turkey.

Fleet

7 Boeing 737-400
7 Boeing 727-200

Photograph: Boeing 747-400 (author's collection)

JAPAN AIRLINES

Dai 2 Tekko Bldg., Maronouchi 2-chome
Chiyoda-ku Tokyo 100, Japan
Tel. 03 2842610

Three letter code	IATA No.	ICAO Callsign
JAL	131	Japanair

JAL was set up on 1st August 1951 as Japanese Air Lines when civil aviation was activated again in the country after the Second World War. The first flight took place with a leased Martin 202 from Tokyo-Haneda to Osaka on 25th October 1951 flown by Northwest Airlines crew as it was forbidden at the time to use Japanese pilots. Exactly a year later the first flight with a DC-4 owned by the airline took place. In October 1953, a new JAL came into being as the national airline with a 50% government stake. In 1953 the DC-6 was introduced, and 2nd February 1954 saw the first international flight from Tokyo to San Francisco. In August 1960 the DC-8 was introduced for this route. The following year the Tokyo-London polar route and Paris/Copenhagen-Tokyo was opened with DC-8s. Convair 880s were introduced in 1962 and used for the first time to Frankfurt via South-East Asia. In 1967 a flight 'around the world' was set up. The first flights over Siberia to Europe were in March 1970, saving several hours compared to the polar route. In the same year, on 1st July the Boeing 747 was used, initially on Pacific routes. The DC-10-40 was specially designed for JAL and used from the mid-70s onwards. In 1979 Zürich became a new destination and in 1985 Düsseldorf. The airline also expanded to the USA in the eighties, with Atlanta as a new destination. The first Boeing 767 was integrated into the fleet in 1987. The Japanese Government sold its remaining 34.5% stake in JAL in November 1987 giving JAL a new corporate identity and resulting in the introduction of new colours for the aircraft. JAL carried 20 million passengers in 1993 and has been involved in a harsh cost-reduction plan to bring it back to profitability after several years of disappointing results. Japan Asia is a wholly-owned subsidiary (see page 173).

Routes

Domestic services connect Tokyo with Osaka, Komatsu, Kagoshima, Okinawa, Fukuoka, Hakodate and Sapporo. There are international services to sixty-three destinations in thirty-three countries, such as Australia, New Zealand, Brazil, USA, Canada, Korea, China, Singapore, Manila, Jakarta, Bangkok, the Middle East and Europe.

Fleet		Ordered
16 Boeing 767-200/300	10 Boeing 747F	10 Boeing 747-400
30 Boeing 747-400	15 DC-10-40	10 Boeing 777-200
14 Boeing 747-300		10 McDonnell Douglas MD-11
30 Boeing 747-100/200		

Photograph: McDonnell Douglas DC-10-30 (Josef Krauthäuser/Seoul)

JAPAN AIR SYSTEM JAS

Toranomon 18 Mori Bldg., 3-13 Toranomon
2-Chome, Minato-ku, Tokyo 105, Japan
Tel. 03 5078030

Three letter code	IATA No.	ICAO Callsign
JAS	234	Air System

Japan Air System (JAS) is the new name, in existence since 1st April 1988, for the former TOA-Domestic (TDA). Toa Domestic Airlines resulted from the merger of Japan Domestic and TOA Airways on 15th May 1971; the latter was founded on 30th November 1953. Japan Domestic had been formed in March 1964 through the amalgamation of North Japan Airlines, Nitto Aviation and Fuji Airlines. Toa Domestic operated flights with NAMC-YS-11s until the introduction of the first DC-9 jet aircraft in 1973. Airbus A300s have also been in use since 1980. The name was changed in 1988 and adapted to the new situation, as flights outside Japan had now also become possible. The first international flight was to Seoul in Korea. The first DC-10-30 was delivered to JAS on 30th March, 1988. For the first time JAS had an aircraft for intercontinental flights, and it is used for charter flights to Hawaii and Singapore. 7.9 million passengers were carried on all scheduled and charter flights up until the end of 1993, making JAS Japan's third largest airline. Commuter services in Japan's southern western Island are operated by Japan Air Commuter, which was set up in 1983 and in which JAS has a 60% stake and the government 40%. This uses principally Saab 340s.

Routes

To over forty domestic destinations such as Fukuoka, Akita, Hiroshima, Nagasaki, Osaka, Sapporo, Tokyo, Yakushima, Okinawa and others.

Fleet

		Ordered
2 McDonnell Douglas DC-10-30	9 Airbus A300B2	7 Airbus A300-600
9 McDonnell Douglas DC-9-41	8 Airbus A300B4	4 McDonnell Douglas MD-81
22 McDonnell Douglas MD-81	10 Airbus A300-600	10 McDonnell Douglas MD-90
8 McDonnell Douglas MD-87		7 Boeing 777-200
22 NAMC YS-11		

Photograph: McDonnell Douglas DC-10-40 (Josef Krauthäuser/Hong Kong)

JAPAN ASIA

Yurakucho Denki Bldg., 1-7-1 Chuyodaku
Tokyo 100, Japan
Tel. 3 3284 2972

Three letter code	IATA No.	ICAO Callsign
JAA	688	Asia

Japan Asia Airways is a wholly-owned subsidiary of Japan Airlines and was set up on 8th August 1975. The airline was set up for political reasons, as Japan Airlines wished to open up connections to the People's Republic of China, but only received permission when it gave up its Taiwan services. However, as the Taiwan flights are so lucrative, Japan Asia was formed as a face-saving operation and politicians in China and Japan were kept happy. Japan Air Lines had suspended Taiwan services in April, 1974 following the problems resulting from the Japanese Government's recognition of the People's Republic of China (Taiwan). Jet operations started on 15th September 1975 between the two countries. Expansion of services, to Manila and Hong Kong, took place in the mid-1980s. Japan Asia obtained the aircraft, first DC-8s, then later DC-10s, from its parent company. Around 1.5 million passengers flew with Japan Asia in 1993.

Routes

Tokyo, Osaka, Hong Kong, Taipei, Manila

Fleet

4 McDonnell Douglas DC-10-40
1 Boeing 747-100
3 Boeing 747-200/300

Photograph: Junkers 52,3m (Jörg Thiel/Frankfurt)

JU-AIR

Postfach, 8600 Dübendorf 1
Switzerland
Tel. 01-8232005

Three letter code	IATA No.	ICAO Callsign
JUA	–	–

Ju-Air, which was formed in 1982, may not be one of the oldest Swiss airlines, but it certainly flies the oldest aircraft in Switzerland, and in Europe. Ju-Air belongs to the 'Verein der Freunde des Museums der Schweizerischen Fliegertruppe' (Society of the Friends of the Museum of the Swiss Air Corps). Ju-Air acquired the three original Junkers aircraft in 1981 from this corps. Initially, so much money came in from a collection throughout Switzerland that it enabled one aircraft to be kept in an airworthy condition. Further donations over a period of time made it possible for all three aircraft to be preserved for civil aviation purposes. Flights with Ju-Air are offered at cost price, as the entire money is re-invested in the aircraft and their preservation.

Routes

Sightseeing flights and charter flights

Fleet

3 Junkers Ju 52,3mg4e
1 CASA 352-L

Photograph: Saab SF-340A (Uwe Gleisberg/Adelaide)

KENDELL AIRLINES

43 Tompson Street, Wagga Wagga NSW 2650
Australia
Tel. 69 215011

Three letter code	IATA No.	ICAO Callsign
KDA	678	Kendell

Set up in 1966 as a non-scheduled air carrier with the name PremiAir Aviation. The first aircraft was a Piper Apache for air-taxi work, followed by a Piper Cherokee Six. The name was changed to Kendell Airlines in 1971. Regular scheduled flights from Wagga Wagga to Melbourne started on 18th October 1971 using a Piper Navajo. de Havilland Herons arrived in 1975 and Swearingen Metros by 1979. Over the years Kendell developed in southern Australia into a regional airline now flying to four federal states. In 1985 the Saab SF-340 was introduced. TNT/News Corp, owners of Ansett, increased its shareholding in Kendell over the years and in 1986 when Ansett closed down Airlines of South Australia, Kendell took over a number of its routes. In October 1990, TNT/News Corp acquired 100% ownership after buying out Dan Kendell, the airline's founder. Kendell intends to be quoted on the Sydney stock market in 1994.

Routes

Wagga Wagga, Melbourne, Albury, Coona, King Island, Mildura, Portland, Mount Gambier, Tumut and other destinations in the south-east of Australia.

Fleet	Ordered
6 Saab SF-340 A	2 Saab 2000
8 Fairchild Sweringen Metro II	2 Swearingen Metro 23
2 Fairchild Sweringen Metro 23	

Photograph: Airbus A310-300 (author's collection)

KENYA AIRWAYS

Embakasi Airport, P.O. Box 19002
Nairobi, Kenya
Tel. 2822171

Three letter code	IATA No.	ICAO Callsign
KQA	706	Kenya

After the collapse of the multinational airline East African Airways, the flag carrier for Kenya, Tanzania and Uganda in 1976, the Kenyan government was compelled to set up its own national airline. With the aid of British Midland Airways and two leased Boeing 707s, flight operations started from Nairobi to London, Frankfurt, Athens and Rome in February 1977, one month after it was formed on 22nd January 1977. The leased aircraft were replaced by Boeing 707s of their own. The airline acquired modern aircraft from 1986 onwards, when it was possible to replace the Boeing 707s with Airbus A310s.

Today, the Boeing 707 is only used for cargo flights.

Routes

Many destinations in Africa plus in Europe and the Middle East including Athens, Frankfurt, Cairo, London, Mombasa, Nairobi, Paris, Rome, Zürich.

Fleet

3 Airbus A310-300
2 Boeing 737-200ADV
1 Boeing 757-200
3 Fokker 50

Photograph: Boeing 747-400 (author's collection)

KLM ROYAL DUTCH AIRLINES

P.O. Box 7700 1117 ZL Amsterdam
Airport Schiphol, The Netherlands
Tel. 020 6499123

Three letter code	IATA No.	ICAO Callsign
KLM	74	KLM

Formed on 7th October 1919, KLM is the oldest operating airline in the world. The first scheduled flights were from Amsterdam to London on 17th May 1920 with a DH 16. KLM has been flying to Germany since 1921. Mainly Fokker aircraft were used until the outbreak of the Second World War. In 1929 the route to Batavia (today called Djakarta) was opened, at that time the longest route. Its first transatlantic link came in 1934 with a route to Curacao using a Fokker F XVIII. Operations in the West Indies started in 1935. DC-2s were introduced in 1935, followed by DC-3s in 1936. KLM had one of the densest networks in Europe until 1940. Services around the West Indies continued during the Second World War and allows KLM to claim over 75 years of continuous operations. After 1945, reconstruction commenced with DC-3 aircraft. Convair 240s followed, replaced by the Convair 340 in 1953. The Vickers Viscount took over important routes in Europe from 1957 onwards, and was replaced by the Lockheed Electra in 1959. Overseas flights were initially operated using DC-4s, Lockheed Constellations and DC-6s and DC-7s as the last of the propeller aircraft. The first DC-8 was used to New York on 4th April 1960. Boeing 747s, introduced in 1971, and DC-10s took over the long-distance routes in the seventies. On the short-distance and medium-distance routes, KLM initially used DC-9s, which were later replaced by Boeing 737s and Airbus A310s added. The present flagship of KLM is the Boeing 747-400, which came into service in May 1989. KLM acquired a minority interest 20% in Northwest Airlines in 1993. Amongst other investments, KLM has a 14.9% stake in Air UK, 80% in Transavia and 100% of KLM Cityhopper. Over 6.5 million passengers flew with KLM in 1993.

Routes

KLM serves a dense European network from its home airport Amsterdam-Schiphol with passenger and cargo services to over 150 cities on all continents.

Fleet

16 Boeing 747-400
3 Boeing 747-300
12 Boeing 747-200 (some SUD)
4 DC-10-30
2 McDonnell Douglas MD-11

10 Boeing 737-400
16 Boeing 737-300
2 Boeing 737-200
6 Fokker 100
8 Airbus A310

Ordered

2 Boeing 737-400
3 Boeing 747-400
8 McDonnell Douglas MD-11

Photograph: Fokker 50 (Fokker BV)

KLM CITYHOPPER

Postbus 7700, 1117ZL Schiphol Oost,
The Netherlands
Tel. 020 6492227

Three letter code	IATA No.	ICAO Callsign
KLC	195	City

The present KLM Cityhopper is the successor in name to NLM Dutch Airlines, which was set up in 1966 and started scheduled flights between Amsterdam, Eindhoven and Maastricht on 29th August 1966. It used the proven Fokker F-27 Friendship. Regional international scheduled flights began in April 1974. In 1976 the name was changed to NLM Cityhopper and KLM acquired a majority interest. Netherlines was set up in 1984 and started flights between Amsterdam and Luxembourg on 8th January 1985. Further scheduled routes were opened up between 1985 and 1988 using Jetstream 31s. By 1987, NetherLines was owned by the Nedlloyd Group, who also owned Transavia. In 1988, KLM decided to buy NetherLines with the intention of asking NLM, which operated Fokker F-27s and F-28s, to merge the airlines together. The merger subsequently brought about the formation of KLM Cityhopper in early 1990 although the joint airline did not officially come into being until April 1991. Its base is Amsterdam-Schiphol, where the entire KLM infrastructure is used.

Routes

Extensive regional services including Amsterdam, Antwerp, Belfast, Berlin, Birmingham, Bremen, Bristol, Brussels, Cardiff, Düsseldorf, East Midlands, Eindhoven, Frankfurt, Guernsey, Hanover, Jersey, Luton, Luxembourg, Maastricht, Malmö, Paris, Rotterdam, Southampton, Strasbourg, Stuttgart.

Fleet

 3 Fokker F-28
10 Fokker 50
13 Saab SF 340

Photograph: Airbus A300-600 (Josef Krauthäuser/Hong Kong)

KOREAN AIR

C.P.O. Box 864, Seoul
Republic of Korea
Tel. 02 7517114

Three letter code	IATA No.	ICAO Callsign
KAL	180	Koreanair

Korean Air Lines had been formed in June 1962 by the South Korean Government to succeed Korean National Airlines which was established in 1947. The private company Hanjin Transport Group took over Korean Air Lines, which up to that time had been state-owned, with eight aircraft on 1st March, 1969. Its international routes were to Hong Kong and Osaka. In 1973, KAL obtained its first Boeing 747, used from May 1973 for the trans-Pacific services via Tokyo and Honolulu to Los Angeles. In the same year, a weekly service to Paris started, the first destination in Europe, with Boeing 707s. The Airbus A300B4 came into service in 1975, and was used for the East Asian market. DC-10 deliveries also started in 1975. In 1984 the name Korean Air was introduced and all their aircraft were given the present colour scheme. Frankfurt became the third destination in Europe that same year. In December 1986, KAL was a launch customer for the MD-11. Korean Air is developing into one of the largest airlines in the world with scheduled services to all five continents. New routes in 1993 included Brisbane, Cairo, Auckland, Beijing Taipei and Mexico.

Routes

Domestic connections to ten destinations, and international flights to Australia, to the USA with Los Angeles and New York, to several destinations in Japan, Singapore, Hong Kong, Bangkok, the Middle East and to Europe.

Fleet

2 Boeing 747SP
12 Boeing 747-400
3 Boeing 747-300
6 Boeing 747-200 F
6 Boeing 747-200
3 McDonnell Douglas DC-10-30
12 McDonnell Douglas MD-82

5 McDonnell Douglas MD-11
10 Airbus A300B4
20 Airbus A300-600
10 Boeing 727-200
2 Fokker F-28
5 Fokker 100

Ordered

22 Boeing 747-400
7 Boeing 777-200
6 Airbus A300-600
7 Airbus A330-300
4 Fokker 100

Photograph: Airbus A310 (Uwe Gleisberg/Munich FJS)

KUWAIT AIRWAYS

P.O. Box 394, 13004 Safat
Kuwait
Tel. 4740166

Three letter code	IATA No.	ICAO Callsign
KAC	229	Kuwaiti

Kuwait Airways Corporation came into existence in 1953 as a national airline set up by local businessmen as Kuwait National Airways. Its first route was from Kuwait City to Basra, flown for the first time in April 1954 with DC-3s. The present name was adopted in 1958 when in May 1958 the British airline BOAC took over the management of the airline and managed it until independence in 1962. A local charter airline, British International Airlines had been absorbed in April 1959. Vickers Viscounts replaced the DC-3s. Kuwait Airways operated a Comet 4C on the routes to London, Paris and Frankfurt. The airline became wholly-Government owned on 1st June 1963 and took over Trans Arabia. On 20th March, 1966 the first of a total of three HS-Tridents was introduced and Kuwait became one of the few operators outside the UK of the type. Three Boeing 707s followed two years later and took over all routes gradually. In 1978 Kuwait Airways acquired its first Boeing 747 Jumbo. Airbus aircraft had been ordered as successors for the Boeing 707s, with three Boeing 767s being added from 1986 onwards as part of continued fleet replacement. In 1989 1.7 million passengers were carried by Kuwait Airways. After the Iraqi occupation of Kuwait in summer 1991 flights were discontinued; some aircraft were destroyed, some were seized by Iraq and are slowly being returned and refurbished for service, whilst others were transferred abroad for lease. Restricted flights were provided by Kuwait Airways from Cairo. Since the end of the Gulf War KAC has resumed flights from Kuwait to Europe, such as to Geneva, Frankfurt, London and Munich. Kuwait Airways' colours were slightly altered in 1993.

Routes

Alexandria, Amsterdam, Athens, Abu Dhabi, Bahrain, Bangkok, Bombay, Colombo, Dakar, Damascus, New Delhi, Dubai, Istanbul, Jeddah, Cairo, Karachi, London, Madrid, Manila, Paris and Rome.

Fleet

Fleet		Ordered
4 Boeing 747-200	3 Airbus A320-200	4 Airbus A340-200
1 Boeing 767-200ER	3 Boeing 707-300	3 Airbus A300-600
3 Boeing 727-200ADV (leased out)		2 Airbus A321
5 Airbus A300-600		3 Boeing 747-400
8 Airbus A310-300		

Photograph: Boeing 727-200ADV (author's collection)

LAB-LLOYD AEREO BOLIVIANO
Casilla Correo 132
Cochabamba, Bolivia
Tel. 42 25918

Three letter code	IATA No.	ICAO Callsign
LLB	51	Lloyd Aereo

Set up by German immigrants on 15th September 1925, flights started on 25th July 1925 with a Junkers F-13 from Cochabamba to Santa Cruz. The Bolivian government had a stake in the airline, which got into financial difficulties in 1928, however. Company shares were sold to the Junkers company and the latter brought three further F-13s into the airline. The network of routes was steadily extended as far as the Brazilian and Argentinian border. Over the years further Junkers aircraft such as W 34s and Ju 52s were employed in the service of LAB. German influence disappeared in 1941 as the result of

American pressure and the company was nationalised on 14th May 1941 and Lodestars were introduced on flights after Panagna took an interest in operations. In 1948 Curtiss C-46s were added to the fleet. The first DC-4s were used on the new route to Asuncion or Porto Vila, followed in 1961 by DC-6s. In the late 60s LAB was reorganised and Fairchild FH-227s were acquired for regional routes, as well as a Lockheed Electra for international routes. In 1970 the change was made to Boeing 727s, and there were flights to Miami in the USA for the first time in 1975. Further routes to Santiago and

Caracas followed. A Boeing 707 is still used on cargo flights. LAB, one of the world's oldest airlines, is now 97.5% government owned.

Routes

As well as domestic Bolivian routes, there are regular flights to Miami, Panama, Caracas, Lima, Cuzco, Santiago, Buenos Aires, Sao Paulo and Rio de Janeiro.

Fleet

1 Boeing 707-320F
6 Boeing 727-100/200
2 Fokker F-27
1 Airbus A310-300

Photograph: Boeing 727-200ADV (author's collection)

LACSA

P.O. Box 1531 San Jose
Costa Rica
Tel. 506323555

Three letter code	IATA No.	ICAO Callsign
LRC	133	Lacsa

Pan American set up Lineas Aereas Costarricenses SA in December 1945 with the support of the government of Costa Rica and private interests. Flights started in 1950, to Miami. In June 1946 some domestic destinations were linked up for the first time to form a network of scheduled routes. They used Convair CV-440s, Curtiss C-46s and DC-6s. It became the national flag carrier in 1949. In 1952 TACA de Costa Rica, their only competitor in the country, was bought up. In 1967 LACSA acquired its first jet aircraft, a BAC-1-11-400. These were replaced by Boeing 727s in late 1970. The airline's domestic network was transferred in September 1979 to Servicios Aereos Nacionales (SANSA), a subsidiary. A fleet acquisition programme has earmarked the Airbus A320 as the aircraft of the 90s and the first one was delivered in late 1990.

Routes

Mexico City, Los Angeles, Miami, New York, Guatemala, Panama, San Juan, Caracas, Quito, Rio de Janeiro.

Fleet

3 Boeing 727-200ADV
5 Airbus A320
2 Boeing 737-200

Photograph: Boeing 727-100 (author's collection)

LADECO

Av. Bulnes 147 Santiago
Chile
Tel. 562723559

Three letter code	IATA No.	ICAO Callsign
LCO	145	Ladeco

Linea Aerea del Cobre Ltda., abbreviated LADECO, was set up as a private company on 3rd September 1958 to serve the copper mining region of northern Chile. Flight operations began on 1st November 1958, initially on the Santiago-El Salvador route. LADECO took over the rights to the routes from CINTA-ALA, as well as DC-3 aircraft. The DC-3s were equipped with more powerful Twin Wasp engines in order to be able to take off more easily from the high-altitude airport at Santiago. In 1965 larger DC-6s were added to the DC-3s and the network of routes expanded. In 1975 LADECO bought its first Boeing 727-100. When the DC-6s were taken out of service, more aircraft of this type were added. Two Boeing 707s were bought for long-distance routes in 1978 and 1979 and were used for flights to Miami and New York. The ageing fleet has been undergoing a process of replacement since 1992 with Boeing 737-300s and Boeing 757-200s.

Routes

Eighteen destinations in Chile, foreign flights to Asuncion, Sao Paulo, Rio de Janeiro, Guayquil, Bogota, Mendoza, Miami and New York.

Fleet

2 Boeing 707-320
2 Boeing 727-100
5 Boeing 737-200
2 Boeing 737-300
2 Boeing 757-200ER

2 Fokker F-27
4 BAe 1-11
1 McDonnell Douglas DC-8-71

Photograph: Boeing 767-200ER (Albert Kuhbandner/Paris)

LAM

P.O. Box 2060, Maputo
People's Republic of Mozambique
Tel. 1 734111

Three letter code	IATA No.	ICAO Callsign
LAM	68	Mozambique

DETA – Direccao de Exploracao dos Transportes Aereos – was set up in August 1936 as a department of the railways and harbours and airways administration in Laurenco Marques, the capital at that time of Mozambique, which was under Portuguese administration. An airfield was set up on the outskirts of the city for the first time and DETA's first flight, and also the first scheduled flight, was on 22nd December 1937 to Johannesburg with a Junkers Ju 52. De Havilland Moths and Dragonflies were also used. Further Ju 52s were used, but these were replaced after the end of the Second World War by Douglas DC-3s. July 1962 saw the first use of Fokker F-27s. The arrival of two Boeing 737s in December 1969 also heralded the start of the jet age for DETA. During the revolution in the seventies, flights practically came to a standstill. After independence in June 1975 and reorganisation, the national airline also received a new name: LAM-Lineas Aereas de Mocambique in May 1980. In 1993 Boeing 737-300s and Boeing 767s came into use. With the arrival of these aircraft, the colours of the airline were also changed.

Routes

Beira, Berlin-Schönefeld, Copenhagen, Dar-Es-Salaam, Durban, Harare, Johannesburg, Lichinga, Lisbon, Luanda, Lusaka, Madrid, Manzini, Nampula, Paris, Tete.

Fleet

1 IL-62M	2 CASA 212-200
2 Boeing 737-200ADV	2 Beech 200C
2 Boeing 737-300	1 Partenavia P.68C
1 Boeing 767-200ER	

Photograph: Boeing 767 (Wolfgang Grond/Frankfurt)

LAN CHILE

Huerfanos 757, Piso 8 Santiago
Chile
Tel. 2 6394411

Three letter code	IATA No.	ICAO Callsign
LAN	45	Lan

LAN Chile (Lineas Nacional de Chile) is one of the oldest airlines in South America. Set up on 5th March 1929 as Linea Aeropostal Santiago-Africa under the command of the Chilean Air Force, it initially provided mail flights. The airline was nationalised in 1932 when the present name was adopted. Lockheed Lodestars were used in 1948 to open a scheduled service to Buenos Aires, and also to Miami from 1958 with DC-6s. The SE 210 Caravelle was LAN's first jet aircraft, and was delivered in March 1964. In 1967 the Boeing 707 followed, and was used to open up a route to the Easter Islands and on to Tahiti. In 1974 the South Pole route was opened to Australia, the first airline to link South America with Australia. Three DC-10s were added to the fleet in 1980 and were used for flights to the USA and Europe. Boeing 767s were added in 1986 and later replaced the DC-10s. LAN Chile carried out the first ever Twinjet (Boeing 767-200ER) revenue service across the South Atlantic in September 1986. It was privatised in 1989. Regional and national flights have been further improved and extended with leased BAe 146s.

Routes

Miami, New York, Madrid, Paris and Frankfurt as well as in within South America, to the Easter Islands and to the South Seas.

Fleet

4 Boeing 767-200ER
1 Boeing 707-300
4 Boeing 737-200
2 BAe 146-200
2 McDonnell Douglas DC-8-71

Photograph: Antonov An-24 (Josef Krauthäuser/Bangkok)

LAO AVIATION

2, Rue Pan Kham, Vientiane
People's Democratic Republic of Laos
Tel. 21 8534

Three letter code	IATA No.	ICAO Callsign
LAO	627	Lao

As a result of the Vietnam War, which the Kingdom of Laos of that time was also involved in, three airlines were active in the early 70s: Royal Air Lao, Lao Air Lines and Civil Aviation Co. The last of these was operated by the Pathet Lao movement for a free Laos. This airline received help from North Vietnam. After the final takeover of power, the remaining aircraft belonging to the airlines were brought together to form Lao Aviation. It was established on 19th January 1976 by the People's Republic of Laos and took over from Royal Air Lao as the national flag carrier. The fleet consisted of Vickers Viscounts, Lockheed Hercules, Sikorsky S-58s, DC-3s and DC-4s. As there was no need for flights in Laos, these aircraft were sold or scrapped. Spare parts were not available to maintain these aircraft, so a new fleet was built up favouring Soviet aircraft. International flights between Vientiane and Bangkok and Hanoi were introduced and to Phnom-Penh, operated by Antonov An-24s. The present name of the airline was introduced in 1979. More recently the fleet policy has moved to the operation of Western and Chinese-built aircraft.

Routes

From Vientiane to Bangkok, Hanoi, Ho Chi Minh City, Luang Prabang, Pakse, Phnom Penh, Xieng Khouang.

Fleet

3 Antonov An-24
4 Harbin Y 12
2 ATR-42
2 Boeing 737-200
3 Xian Y 7

Photograph: Boeing 767-300ER (Uwe Gleisberg/Munich FJS)

LAUDA AIR

Office Building 1, 1300 Vienna-Schwechat
Airport, Austria
Tel. 0222 7970 2081

Three letter code	IATA No.	ICAO Callsign
LDA	231	Laudaair

Lauda Air was set up in April 1979, when Niki Lauda, the former Formula One motor racing world champion, took over a licence to operate non-scheduled flights from Alpair. Lauda had a 51% stake and Itas Austria 49%. Flight operations started on 24th May 1979 with two Fokker F-27s. After a phase of restructuring and conversion into a joint-stock company, the airline leased two Rombac 1-11s from Tarom in 1985. Boeing 737-200s and -300s were added and were later used to replace the Rombacs. At that time Lauda Air was primarily flying to Greece and Spain. In 1986 Lauda Air applied for a licence to operate scheduled flights to Australia, which it finally obtained in 1988. In that year Lauda Air obtained its first Boeing 767-300ER, followed by a second one in November 1989. Scheduled services to Sydney, Hong Kong and Singapore were further expanded. The airline has the rights to scheduled flights worldwide. The first European scheduled routes were started in late 1990, from Vienna to London-Gatwick and the same year obtained other licences for international services which had previously been reserved for Austrian Airlines. In autumn, Lufthansa acquired a 25% share in Lauda Air via Condor. Lauda Air flies in co-operation with the latter to Miami and Los Angeles. In another example of co-operation with Lufthansa Lauda now flies Canadair Regionaljets twice daily between Vienna and Brussels on behalf of the German airline. In 1993, it formed an Italian subsidiary, Lauda Air SPA.

Routes

Lauda Air has scheduled flights to Bangkok, Phuket, Hong Kong, Singapore and Sydney, Miami, Los Angeles. Charter flights especially to the Mediterranean; also from Salzburg, Graz and Linz in addition to Vienna.

Fleet	Ordered
3 Boeing 767-300ER	1 Boeing 737-400
2 Boeing 737-300	4 Boeing 777-200ER
2 Boeing 737-400	3 Canadair Regionaljet
3 Canadair Regionaljet	

Photograph: de Havilland DHC-8 (author's collection)

LIAT

P.O. Box 819 V.C. Bird Intl. Airport
St. Johns, Antigua
Tel. 809 462 0701

Three letter code	IATA No.	ICAO Callsign
LIA	140	Liat

Leeward Island Air Transport Services Ltd., LIAT for short, was set up in 1956 by two American businessmen. LIAT started flights from Antigua to Montserrat with a Piper Apache. A year later LIAT became part of British West Indian Airways who took a 75% stake. Beech Bonanzas and DH Herons were the ideal aircraft for small island hops to other islands in the Virgin Islands. The first HS-748 was acquired on 1st February 1965. In November 1971 the British company Court Line Aviation. took over the airline and introduced the BAC 1-11 and BN-Islanders. In 1974, after the collapse of Court Line in August, a rescue company was set up in November known as LIAT (1974) Ltd and it still has that company name. Its partners were the governments of six Caribbean island states, with further states acquiring a stake over the years. The first DHC-8s were bought in 1987, contributing to the expansion of the route network. In 1993 LIAT-The Caribbean Airline carried around half a million passengers. The small Caribbean Airlines, Inter-Island Air Services and Four Island Air are subsidiaries.

Routes

Anguilla, Antigua, Barbados, Caracas, Grenada, Guadeloupe, Guyana, Martinique, Montserrat, St. Croix, St. Kitts, St. Lucia, St. Maarten, St. Thomas, St. Vincent, San Juan, Trinidad, Tobago and Tortula.

Fleet

4 BAe HS-748
8 de Havilland DHC-8-100
6 de Havilland DHC-6
2 Pilatus BN-Islander

Photograph: Boeing 727-200 (Josef Krauthäuser/Frankfurt)

LIBYAN ARAB AIRLINES

Haiti Street, P.O. Box 2555
Tripoli, People's Republic of Libya
Tel. 602083

Three letter code	IATA No.	ICAO Callsign
LAA	148	Libair

The merger of Libiavia and United Libyan Airlines resulted in the formation of the the state-owned Kingdom of Libya Airlines in September 1964 in order to have a state airline. August 1965 saw the start of flights to Europe and North Africa as well as to the Middle East with two Caravelles. In 1969 some Fokker F-27s were added to the fleet for domestic services. 1969 also saw political changes in the country following the September revolution, as a result of which the airline changed its name to Libyan Arab Airlines on 1st September 1967. Boeing 707s, 727s and later Airbus A310s were added. Political and trade sanctions meant that the western built fleet could only be partly used. For this reason the fleet was expanded using Soviet Tupolev 154M aircraft from 1990 onwards. As a result of these political sanctions Libya no longer has any flight rights abroad. Jamahiriya Libyan Arab Airlines is now the official name of the national carrier of the Socialist People's Libyan Arab Jamahiriya. The charter services of the former Jamahiriya Air Transport (established in April 1982, it took over United African Airlines in 1983) are now integrated A sister cargo airline, Libyan Arab Air Cargo, has a fleet of Ilyushin 76 and Hercules.

Routes

Connections to neighbouring regions from Tripoli and Benghazi.

Fleet

15 Fokker F-27
 3 Fokker F-28
 9 Boeing 727-200
 3 Boeing 707-300

Photograph: McDonnell Douglas DC-8-63 (author's collection)

LINEAS AEREAS PARAGUAYAS

Oliva 455, Asuncion
Paraguay
Tel. 02191040

Three letter code	IATA No.	ICAO Callsign
LAP	705	Air Paraguay

Set up in 1962 as the national airline, it was established to provide international services to supplement the domestic network operated by Transporte Aereo Militar (TAM). The airline came under the control of the Air Force. LAP started flights in August 1963 with flights to Buenos Aires, Montevideo and Rio de Janeiro using three ex-Aerolineas Argentinas Convair 240s. They were replaced in 1969 by Lockheed L-188 Electras. The introduction of Boeing 707s in 1978 enabled the airline to provide overseas flights as well, to Europe, from 1979 onwards. A British Aerospace 146 was introduced at the end of 1992 for regional services, but it has been returned to the manufacturers.

Routes

From Asuncion to Asturias, Brussels, Buenos Aires, Frankfurt, Lima, Miami, Montevideo, Rio de Janeiro, Santiago, Sao Paulo.

Fleet

2 McDonnell Douglas DC-8-63/70
3 Boeing 707-300
3 Lockheed L-188 Electra
1 McDonnell Douglas DC-10-30

Photograph: Boeing 737-200ADV (Patrick Lutz/Berlin)

LITHUANIAN AIRLINES

8 Radunes, Vilnius Airport, Vilnius
Lithuania
Tel. 2637817

Three letter code	IATA No.	ICAO Callsign
LIL	874	Lithuanian Air

Lithuanian Airlines was the first airline of the Baltic republics which obtained independence from the former Soviet Union; it started its own flights in 1991. The aircraft were taken over from the former directorate of Aeroflot. Lithuanian immediately turned towards Western Europe and Scandinavia and started flights to those countries first. A leased Boeing 737 was first used to Copenhagen on 20th December 1991. Malev assisted in building up flights and trained the pilots on Boeing 737s. In late 1992 Lithuania was accepted into IATA. Lithuanian served London Gatwick and Heathrow with a weekly service to each starting on 3rd August 1992 but from 25th October the service became twice weekly to Heathrow from Vilnius.

Routes

Berlin, Frankfurt, Hamburg, Copenhagen, Kiev, Moscow, St. Petersburg, Tallin, Warsaw are served with scheduled flights. Charter flights to Athens and Istanbul.

Fleet

 6 Antonov An-24
 1 Boeing 737-200ADV
 9 Tupolev Tu-134 A/B
 6 Yakovlev Yak-40
12 Yakovlev Yak-42

Photograph: BAe 146-200 (Josef Gietl/Salzburg)

LOGANAIR

St. Andrews Drive, Glasgow Airport, Paisley
Renfrewshire PA3 2TG, United Kingdom
Tel. 041 8891311

Three letter code	IATA No.	ICAO Callsign
LOG	122	Logan

Duncan Logan Contractors set up Loganair in Glasgow on 1st February 1962. The Royal Bank of Scotland took over the airline in 1968. The partly unsurfaced runways of many airfields and airports it flies to meant that robust aircraft such as DHC-6 Twin Otters or Fokker F-27s had to be acquired as Scotland's airline, it had a comprehensive commuter network centred on Glasgow and Edinburgh, with flights radiating to northern Scotland, Orkneys and Shetlands and the Western Isles. Since 1973, Loganair has operated the Scottish Air Ambulance Service and has been involved in air freight operations throughout its existence. In December 1983 British Midland Airways acquired 75% of the shares from the Bank of Scotland. Flights were expanded and coordinated with Manx Airlines' and British Midland's network of scheduled routes. Loganair is a member of the Airlines of Britain Holdings group and obtains the necessary aircraft from the group, such as BAe 146s for scheduled and charter flights. It was also one of the first customers to receive the new BAe Jetstream 41. Over the years, services from Scotland to England, Ireland and into Europe have grown but from March 1994 all routes south of Scotland have been handed over to Manx Airlines, also a member of the Airlines of Britain Holdings group. Some of the Jetstream 31, 41 and 61 aircraft have also been disposed of to other airlines within the group. It is now expected that Loganair will operate Scottish regional routes, with most of their aircraft painted in British Airways colours under a franchise arrangement.

Routes

Belfast, Blackpool, Glasgow, Inverness, Kirkwall, Derry, as well as another twenty destinations in Scotland, Ireland, the Shetland Islands, the Orkneys and the Hebrides. Charter services to the Channel Islands.

Fleet

8 Shorts 360
5 Pilatus BN 2 Islander

Photograph: Boeing 767-200ER (author's collection)

LOT

Uliczka 17 Stycznia 39, 00906 Warsaw
Poland
Tel. 461251

Three letter code	IATA No.	ICAO Callsign
LOT	80	LOT

Aerolloyd Warsaw (subsequently Aerolot) and Aero were united to form the future state airline Polskie Linie Lotnicze-LOT on 1st January 1929 by order of the government. Aerolloyd had begun regular flights in September 1922 and started international services in 1925, Aero was formed in 1922. LOT Junkers F-13s flew to Vienna, Berlin, Moscow and Helsinki. As a result of the Second World War, a fresh start with Soviet aircraft could only be made in 1946. While the Ilyushin IL-14 was part of the fleet in the fifties, Western aircraft such as the Convair 240 or Vickers Viscount were also used. Tu-134 and Tu-154 jet aircraft were the mainstay of the short and medium-distance routes, while the IL-62M was used for long hauls. Western Boeing 767s have also been in use since 1989. The fleet is being brought up to Western standards as quickly as possible. LOT is also working on its services and is increasingly becoming a competitor for established airlines. In December 1992, LOT became a joint stock holder company, a transitional step towards privatisation, which the airline is aiming for in 1995. Its transatlantic services to the USA and Canada (where there are large expatriate populations) bring in a third of its revenue and LOT is looking for closer ties with an American airline.

Routes

Dense network of routes in Poland with An 24s and ATR-72s. European cities, Bangkok, Beijing, Singapore, Delhi, Montreal, Chicago, New York.

Fleet		Ordered
2 Boeing 767-200ER	3 Boeing 737-400	5 Boeing 767-300ER
14 Tupolev 154M	2 Antonov An-24	3 ATR-72
7 Tupolev Tu-134	5 ATR-72	1 Boeing 737-400
1 Boeing 767-300ER		
5 Boeing 737-500		

Photograph: Boeing 757-200 (Uwe Gleisberg/Frankfurt)

LTE INTERNATIONAL AIRWAYS

Gran Via Asima 4, 07009 Palma de Mallorca
Spain
Tel. 071 757051

Three letter code	IATA No.	ICAO Callsign
LTE	–	Fun Jet

LTE-Lineas Transportadores Espanola was set up on 29th April 1987. 25% of the shares were held by LTU; more was not legally possible, and the rest were held by Spanish shareholders. Flights started on 1st November 1987 with two Boeing 757s. The aircraft came from the LTU-subsidiary LTS and their colours were a slightly altered blue and white. Today, LTU is the sole owner of LTE.
LTE operates domestic flights to Barcelona and Madrid. It has also been providing long-distance charters from these airports since 1990. In 1991 the colour scheme was changed, and since then it has been expanded to a total of five Boeing 757s. LTE has been particularly active in the new federal states in Germany after reunification and operates from airfields with low passenger volume.
Within the LTU group, aircraft are exchanged and subleased as needed.

Routes

Charter flights from Germany, Austria, Switzerland, also Finland, Norway, Italy to the Spanish mainland, to the Balearic and Canary Islands. Also flights to the Dominican Republic and Kenya.

Fleet

5 Boeing 757-200

Photograph: McDonnell Douglas MD-11 (author's collection)

LTU

Parsevalstr. 7a, 40468 Düsseldorf
Germany
Tel. 0211 9418 0

Three letter code	IATA No.	ICAO Callsign
LTU	266	LTU

LTU was formed as Lufttransport Union on 20th October 1955 by an Englishman, Mr Dromgoole, but the chief partner, and soon to become sole owner, was the Duisburg building contractor Conle. The present name was adopted in 1956 to avoid confusion with another company of the same name. Frankfurt was the first base but transferred to Düsseldorf in 1960. The first aircraft, Vickers Vikings, were in use until 1963. Further aircraft used were Bristol 170s, Fokker F-27s and DC-4s, until flights with jet aircraft started, in the form of the first Caravelles in 1965. From 1969 onwards LTU was one of the first charter airlines to only use jet aircraft. In addition to the Caravelles, Fokker F-28 Fellowships were also used from 1968. 1973 saw the start of the age of large-capacity aircraft, with the acquisition of the first Lockheed L-1011 TriStars. This was also the aircraft which enabled LTU to make the breakthrough to become Germany's largest charter airline. Up to eleven TriStars were used by LTU, allowing it to include faraway tourist destinations. LTU took a financial stake in LTS when it was formed in 1983. In 1989 it also applied for a licence to operate as a scheduled air carrier; the licence was granted on some routes from autumn 1990 onwards. The purchase of the first MD-11s in late 1991 began a renewal of the fleet, replacing the TriStars. LTU took over control in 1992 of Spanish charter operators LTE International Airways, in which LTU had a 25% stake since 1987.

Routes

Long-distance destinations are Miami, New York, Los Angeles, Bangkok, Mombasa, Recife, Male, Havana, Puerto Plata. LTU also provides flights from Cologne, Düsseldorf, Berlin, Hamburg and Munich to classic tourist destinations in the Mediterranean, to the Canary Islands, Turkey, Greece, North Africa.

Fleet	Ordered
6 Lockheed L-1011-100 TriStar	5 Airbus A330-300
3 Lockheed L-1011-500 TriStar	
4 McDonnell Douglas MD-11	

Photograph: Boeing 757-200ER (author's collection)

LTU-SÜD

Postfach 231844, 85327 Munich
Germany
Tel. 089 97810

Three letter code	IATA No.	ICAO Callsign
LTS	–	LTS

LTS was set up in 1983 as a subsidiary of LTU. In June 1984, after delivery of the first Boeing 757s, charter flights started from its home base in Munich, the first service being between Munich and Ibiza. From then on the blue jet aircraft of Lufttransport Süd took off for destinations in the Mediterranean and the Canary Islands and Kenya. The airline was renamed and its colours changed to those of the parent company LTU in January 1988 and the first Boeing 767s were delivered in 1989. LTU Süd carries around 2 million passengers annually.

Routes

LTU serves destinations in the Mediterranean, Bangkok, Kenya, the Maldives, Brazil and the Caribbean from Munich, Düsseldorf, Hamburg and Berlin, in association with LTU.

Fleet

7 Boeing 757-200
4 Boeing 767-300ER

Photograph: Airbus A320-200 (Airbus Industrie)

LUFTHANSA

von Gablenz-Str. 2-6, 50679 Cologne
Germany
Tel. 0221 8261

Three letter code	IATA No.	ICAO Callsign
DLH	220	Lufthansa

The 'old' Lufthansa, founded in 1926, was put into liquidation by the victorious powers in the Second World War. In early 1950 the German government made efforts to acquire air sovereignty and set up an independent national airline. For this purpose 'Luftag' was set up in 1953, which was renamed after the old Lufthansa in 1954. The first flight with a Convair 340 was on 1st April 1955, and the first flight abroad was to New York on 8th June 1955 with a Lockheed Constellation. An expansion of the network to South America, the Middle and Far East took place in the next few years. In 1960 Lufthansa made use of Boeing 707s on transatlantic flights for the first time; Boeing 720s were acquired for routes to Africa and the Middle East. Lufthansa was the first customer outside the USA to obtain the Boeing 727 for medium-distance routes in April 1964. Lufthansa was the first to order the Boeing 737, delivered from 1967; it has been the 'workhorse' of the airline on short-distance routes for many years and is being replaced with the latest model. The age of widebody aircraft started in March 1970 with the introduction of Boeing 747s. With orders for DC-10s and later for Airbus aircraft, Lufthansa not only awards contracts to its main supplier Boeing but also supports the European Airbus consortium. Lufthansa is well-known for its fleet replacement policy; the entire 747-100 fleet was exchanged for 747-200 models. The A310 replaced the A300B4, which had been introduced in 1980, as early as April 1983; the last Boeing 707s were taken out of service on 31st December 1984. In 1989 two new aircraft were introduced, the Boeing 747-400 and the Airbus A320. Lufthansa will also be the launch customer for the new A321. It has had a co-operation agreement since 1993 with United Airlines. In 1993 28 million passengers flew with Lufthansa.

Routes

Lufthansa flies to over 190 destinations worldwide; in Germany it goes under the name of 'Lufthansa Express'.

Fleet

		Ordered
9 DC-10-30	10 Boeing 747-200SCD	20 Airbus A321-100
36 Boeing 737-200ADV	16 Boeing 747-400	4 Airbus A340
42 Boeing 737-300	10 Airbus A340	4 Boeing 747-400
6 Boeing 737-400	33 Airbus A320	
33 Boeing 737-500	12 Airbus A310-300	
4 Boeing 747-200	13 Airbus A310-200	
5 Boeing 747-200F	11 Airbus A300-600	

Photograph: Canadair Regionaljet (author's collection)

LUFTHANSA CITYLINE

Postfach 1111, Am Holzweg 26
65830 Kriftel, Germany
Tel. 016192 4070

Three letter code	IATA No.	ICAO Callsign
DLT	683	DLT

DLT-Deutsche Luftverkehrsgesellschaft mbH is the successor of OLT (Ostfriesische Luftransport GmbH) and was set up in 1974. OLT was founded on 1st November 1958 as Ostfriesische Luftaxi but changed its name of 13th September 1974. However DLT was formed on 1st October 1974 through the re-organisation of OLT, with Lufthansa having a 26% shareholding. With Shorts 330s, some Twin Otters and HS-748s supplemental flights were operated on behalf of Lufthansa. In 1987 Embraer EMB-120s were introduced, but these aircraft were soon too small for further expansion and were replaced by Fokker 50s.

Today, Lufthansa has a 50% share in DLT, which is responsible for regional flights, which cannot be served economically with jet aircraft (Boeing 737s). In 1990 DLT carried almost a million passengers. In order to provide passengers with a better means of identification with the parent company, the airline was renamed Lufthansa Cityline. This was also reflected in the external appearance of the airline. When the Canadair Regionaljets were introduced, the 'crane on the tail' was also added. Lufthansa Cityline has been a wholly-owned subsidiary of Lufthansa since 1st January 1993 and is now responsible for

Lufthansa's European non-stop services using aircraft with up to 100 seats.

Routes

LH Cityline flies from all the German commercial airports and connects a total of forty-seven destinations, such as Copenhagen, Paris, Geneva, Nice, Venice, Vienna, Prague, Brussels, Milan, Turin, Rome, Budapest, Oslo, Göteborg, Amsterdam, Basle, Toulouse, Bologna, Florence, Verona, Trieste, Linz, Glasgow, Sofia, Barcelona.

Fleet	Ordered
20 Fokker 50 3 Canadair Regionaljet	10 Canadair Regionaljet

Photograph: Fokker 50 (author's collection)

LUXAIR

BP 2203, 2987 Luxembourg Airport
Grand Duchy of Luxembourg
Tel. 4798311

Three letter code	IATA No.	ICAO Callsign
LGL	149	Luxair

The Société Luxembourgeoise de Navigation Aérienne, or Luxair for short, was set up in 1961 as Luxembourg Airlines with the support of the government, of banks and Radio Luxembourg and technical assistance provided by KLM. Regular flights started on 2nd April 1962 with a Fokker F-27 to Amsterdam, Frankfurt and Paris. Luxair started using Vickers Viscounts in 1966 and SE 210 Caravelles in March 1970. These were replaced in 1977 by Boeing 737s. Leased Boeing 707s were added to the fleet in 1980 for long-distance flights. One Airbus A300B4 was used at Luxair, but only for a short time, as it was too large for the airline's needs. The Airbus was then exchanged for a Boeing 747SP, which was used from then on for long-distance flights. A fleet replacement programme started in 1989 with the delivery of the first Fokker 50s. Lufthansa took a 13% share in Luxair in December 1992. The Luxembourg government has no more than a 20% stake. Subsidiaries include Cargolux (24.5%), Lionair, Luxair Executive and Luxair Commuter.

Routes

Luxembourg, Paris, Nice, Hamburg, Frankfurt, Munich, Saarbrücken, Amsterdam, London, Copenhagen, Geneva, Rome, Palma de Mallorca, Malaga and Nairobi. In addition to scheduled services, Luxair also offers charter flights.

Fleet	Ordered
1 Boeing 747SP	3 Fokker 50
3 Boeing 737-200	
2 Boeing 737-400	
2 Boeing 737-500	
4 Fokker 50	

Photograph: Boeing 737-300 (author's collection)

MAERSK AIR

Dragoer Airport, 2791 Copenhagen
Denmark
Tel. 534444

Three letter code	IATA No.	ICAO Callsign
DMA	349	Maerskair

The A.P. Moeller shipping company set up Maersk Air as a subsidiary in February 1969. It was originally intended purely as a charter business. Flight operations started in December 1969 with a HS-125 and a Fokker F-27. The young airline's urge to expand resulted in its taking over Falckair, a domestic airline, plus its routes to Odense and other destinations in 1970. In November 1971, Maersk joined with SAS and Cumber Air to create Danair, based at Copehagen. Maersk now has a 38% stake in Danair. Air Business, another regional airline, was acquired in May 1983. it had been operating

between Esbjerg and Stavanger. The route from Billund to Sonthad was opened with de Havilland DHC-7s. Further scheduled services connect Copenhagen with Billund and Ronne. In addition to scheduled and charter flights, Maersk Air has also earned considerable turnover from the aircraft leasing business including the lease of four Boeing 737-300s to British Airways. The Maersk Air Group includes Maersk Air (Denmark) and Maersk Air (UK), each wholly-owned by AP Moller Group (Maersk Line). Maersk Air UK was established in July 1993 and operates BAe One Elevens and Jetstream 31s out of Birmingham

under a franchise agreement with British Airways following the de-merging of the TPL Group (The Plimsoll Line) comprising Brymon Aviation and Birmingham European Airways (previously Birmingham Executive Airways until 1989). In August 1993, Brimingham European became wholly-owned by Maersk Air (Denmark) and was renamed Maersk Air (UK), and Brymon because a wholly-owned subsidiary of British Airways.

Routes

Scheduled and charter flights, of which seven are to scheduled destinations, also to the neighbouring European countries and to the Faroe Islands.

Fleet

8 Fokker 50
2 Boeing 737-200
11 Boeing 737-300
1 Boeing 737-400
5 Boeing 737-500

1 Shorts 360
1 BAe 125

Ordered

3 Boeing 737-600

Photograph: Boeing 747-400 (Albert Kuhbandner/Munich FJS)

MALAYSIA AIRLINES

Jalon Sultan Ismail Bangumon MAS
50250 Kuala Lumpur, Malaysia
Tel. 03 2610555

Three letter code	IATA No.	ICAO Callsign
MAS	232	Malaysian

Malaysian Airline System came into existence on 3rd April 1971 after the former MAS (Malaysia-Singapore Airlines) was split up with the suspension of the joint Malaysia-Singapore Airlines agreement and the new MAS was set up by government decree as the national carrier. Its history dates to the formation of Malayan Airways in 1937 but operations only started in May 1947 with two Airspeed Consuls. Following the formation of the Federation of Malaysia November 1963, Malayan became Malaysian Airways, with BOAC and Qantas the majority shareholders. Malaysian absorbed Borneo Airways in 1965. When Singapore separated from Malaysia in 1967 the airline changed its name to Malaysian-Singapore Airlines. Subsequently, Singapore's Government pushed for extension of the airline's international routes while Malaysia wanted greater emphasis on Malaysian domestic route expansion. The rift brought about the new MAS which started operations on 1st October 1972. Destinations in Malaysia were served with nine F-27s and three Britten-Norman Islanders. Weekly flights to London started in 1974 with Boeing 707s. Further destinations in Europe such as Amsterdam, Zürich and Frankfurt were soon to follow. In 1976 the first DC-10-30 was delivered, and in 1982 two Boeing 747-200s were added, which were also used for flights to the US from 1985 onwards. At the end of 1985 the Malaysian Government reduced its stake to 70% and further to 55% by 31st March 1987 including 5% stakes by the Sarawak and Sabah State Governments. On 15th October 1987 MAS introduced new colours and the name was shortened (Airline System was omitted). Malaysian will take delivery of its first Airbus A330 as a replacement for DC-10s in December 1994.

Routes

Around thirty-five domestic destinations, plus connections to Australia, Japan, Korea, Hong Kong, Indonesia, the Philippines, Thailand, Taiwan in East Asia, the Middle East and Europe.

Fleet

9 Boeing 747-400
1 Boeing 747-300
2 Boeing 747-200
3 Boeing 737-500
38 Boeing 737-400

1 Boeing 737-300
11 Fokker 50
6 de Havilland DHC-6
6 McDonnell Douglas DC-10-30
4 Airbus A300B4

Ordered

1 Boeing 747-400
19 Boeing 737-400
10 Airbus A330-300

Photograph: Boeing 737-300 (author's collection)

MALEV-HUNGARIAN AIRLINES

V. Roosevelt ter 2, 1051 Budapest
Hungary
Tel. 118 9033

Three letter code	IATA No.	ICAO Callsign
MAH	182	Malev

Malev was originally established on 26th April 1946 as a joint Hungarian/ Soviet undertaking with the title Maszovlet, with a fleet of eleven Lisuvior Li-2s and six Polikarpov Po-2s. Flight operations began on 15th October 1946 on domestic routes and international flights started the next year. On 25th November 1954 the Hungarian government gained complete control and the airline adopted the name Magyar Legiközlekedesi Vollat (MALEV). When Ilyushin IL-18s were delivered, in May 1960, flights started to European destinations such as Amsterdam, Vienna and Moscow. With the development of Hungary's road system, domestic services were gradually trimmed through the late 1950s and 1960s, with the last flights operated in 1969. The Tupolev 134 was the first jet aircraft in 1968, followed by the Tu-154 in 1973. Replacement of Soviet-built aircraft with Boeing 737s started in 1989 and Malev was one of the first eastern bloc countries to acquire western airliners. Boeing aircraft are also used for long-distance routes. The first Boeing 767 was acquired by Malev in 1992. The airline became a public limited company from 30th June 1992.

Routes

Regular flights from Budapest to Zürich, Vienna, Cologne, Frankfurt, Munich, Stuttgart, Tel Aviv, Algiers, Abu Dhabi und further destinations in Europe. In addition to scheduled flights, charter flights are also operated.

Fleet

12 Tupolev Tu-154	2 Boeing 767-200ER
6 Tupolev Tu-134	
3 Yakovlev Yak-40	
3 Boeing 737-200	
3 Boeing 737-300	

Photograph: BAe ATP/Jetstream 61 (BAe photograph)

MANX AIRLINES

Ronaldsway Airport, Ballasalla, Isle of Man
IM9 2JE, United Kingdom
Tel. 0624 824111

Three letter code	IATA No.	ICAO Callsign
MNX	916	Manx

Manx Air Charter was founded immediately after the Second World War, in 1947. It went bankrupt in 1948 and was integrated into Silver City. It was only in 1982 that the fine-sounding name of this airline was revived. Manx Airlines was founded on 1st November of that year by British Midland Airways with a 75% stake and the rest held by British and Commonwealth Shipping Line – the latter has a stake in Air UK. Flights started from Ronaldsway to London-Heathrow using Fokker Friendships and Vickers Viscounts. The airline also acquired a Saab SF 340 and BAC 1-11s, plus a BAe 146 as its first jet aircraft which replaced the Saab 340 in 1988. The Viscount 800 was replaced by BAe ATPs in 1989. British Midland assumed full control of the airline in 1988 and Manx Airlines is a member of the Airlines of Britain group. In 1993 Manx acquired the new Jetstream 41. In addition to scheduled flights, charter flights are also operated. On 28th March 1994, Manx became the largest regional airline in Europe based on the size of its network of routes following the takeover of a number of routes and aircraft from sister airline Loganair. With its base still at Ronaldsway, Isle of Man, it has hubs at Cardiff, Southampton, Manchester, Glasgow and Belfast City.

Routes

Scheduled services to Aberdeen, Belfast, Birmingham, Blackpool, Brussels, Cardiff, Cork, Dublin, Glasgow, Jersey, Liverpool, London, Luton, Manchester and Paris.

Fleet

8 BAe Jetstream 41
15 BAe ATP/Jetstream 61
2 BAe 146-200
2 Shorts 360-100

Photograph: Boeing 737-400 (Dirk Herforth/Hanover)

MARKAIR

P.O. Box 6769 Anchorage, Alaska 99502
USA
Tel. 907 243414

Three letter code	IATA No.	ICAO Callsign
MRK	478	Markair

Air Interior was founded in 1946 as an all-freight airline. It changed its name in 1972 to Alaska International Air. Finally, in 1984 its name was changed to the well-known name 'Markair'. A regular passenger service in addition to cargo flights was also started on 1st March 1984, using Boeing 737s. Markair expanded considerably, buying Wien Air Alaska and expanding its activities. Several smaller airlines act as feeder airlines for Markair under the name of 'Markair Express'. Over 400,000 passengers flew with Markair in 1989. After a destructive price battle with Alaska Airlines, the airline had to place itself under the protection of creditors on 11th June 1992. After reorganisation, the airline was able to notch up positive results again in late 1993. Wholly-owned subsidiary, MarkAir Express serves over 100 Alaskan communities.

Routes

Passenger flights in Alaska from Anchorage, Fairbanks, Juneau, Borrow, Bethel, Kotzebue, Nome, Prudhoe Bay and to cities in the 'lower 48' including Portland, Seattle, New York, Chicago and Las Vegas.

Fleet

6 Boeing 737-200
2 Boeing 737-300
3 Boeing 737-400

Photograph: Boeing 747-200 (Josef Krauthäuser/Hong Kong)

MARTINAIR

Postbus 7507, 1118 ZG Schiphol
The Netherlands
Tel. 020 6011222

Three letter code	IATA No.	ICAO Callsign
MPH	129	Martinair

Martin Air Holland, or to be precise Martin's Luchtvervoer Maatschaappij N.V, was founded on 24th May 1958 by Martin Schröder using a single Douglas DC-3. The airline was originally called Martins Air Charter, until the present name was introduced in April 1968. Sightseeing and air taxi flights were provided. A smaller airline, Faiways Rotterdam, was taken over in January 1964. KLM acquired a 25% stake in the airline, and further shares were sold to a shipping company. Martinair obtained DC-7s, Lockheed Electras and DC-8s from KLM. Using these aircraft, Martinair went into the charter business in a big way. In 1973 Martinair acquired DC-10s, in 1984 it obtained Airbus A310s and introduced the first Boeing 747 in 1988. Martinair maintains and operates under contract the Dutch government's VIP Fokker F-28 and is the launch customer for the new convertible freighter version of the MD-11. Main shareholder is Royal Nedlloyd Group with 49.2% and KLM holds nearly 30%.

Routes

Passenger and cargo charter flights all over the world.

Fleet

3 Boeing 747-200
5 Boeing 767-300ER
2 McDonnell Douglas DC-10-30
1 Dornier 228

Ordered

4 McDonnell Douglas MD-11CF

Photograph: Airbus A310-200 (Frank Schorr/Frankfurt)

MEA – MIDDLE EAST AIRLINE
P.O. Box 206, Beirut
Lebanon
Tel. 1316316

Three letter code	IATA No.	ICAO Callsign
MEA	76	CedarJet

MEA, whose full title is Middle East Airline SA, was founded in May 1945 as a private company, by a group of Lebanese businessmen and started a de Havilland Rapide service between Beirut and Nicosia on 20th November and to Baghdad on 15th February 1946. In 1949 Pan American acquired a stake in the airline, and the first thing it did was to replace the three DH.89As with DC-3s in order to obain more capacity for the transportation of cargo. Pan American withdrew from the airline in 1955, its stake being acquired by BOAC. Scheduled services started on 2nd October 1955 to London using Vickers

Viscounts. Karachi and Bombay followed. Its first jet aircraft was the de Havilland Comet 4B, used for the route to London from 6th January, 1961 onwards. Further expansion came in March 1963 when an agreement was reached for joint development with Air Liban. The two companies formally merged in November 1965 and Air Liban's DC-6s and SE210 Caravelles joined the fleet. Boeing 707s came into service in 1968, and in 1969 Lebanese International Airways (LIA) together with its fleet, route and staff was taken over. This merger was desired by the government, as several of LIA's and MEA's aircraft

had been completely destroyed during an Israeli attack on Beirut airport in 1968. MEA acquired its first Boeing 747 in May 1975. Flight operations have been repeatedly disrupted by the fighting – verging on civil war – which has been going on for more than ten years, but MEA is the only airline maintaining the link with the outside world in the face of all adversity. In addition, subcharters are operated for other airlines. New aircraft are also being acquired, such as two Airbus A310s, which were leased in order to be able to take Boeing 707s out of service.

Routes

The official schedule gave over thirty destinations in the Middle East, Europe, Asia and Africa in autumn 1993.

Fleet

8 Boeing 707-300
4 Boeing 720B
3 Boeing 747-200
2 Airbus A310-200

Photograph: BAe 146-200 (Frank Schorr/Frankfurt)

MERIDIANA

193 Corso Umberto, 07026 Olbia,
Zona Industrielle, Italy
Tel. 789 52600

Three letter code	IATA No.	ICAO Callsign
ISS	191	Merair

Meridiana resulted from the strategic merger of the Italian airline Alisarda and the Spanish airline Universair in 1991. Up until the Spanish airline Meridiana went bankrupt in late 1992, the two partners had coordinated their operations while remaining relatively independent. Alisarda was founded on 24th March, 1963 in Olbia as an air taxi and general charter company using two Beech-C45s and began operations that same year. Scheduled passenger services were added on 1st June 1966 initially with Nord 262s, later replaced by Fokker Friendships. Later services took place to destinations in France, Switzerland and within Italy using DC-9s from 1975. Other destinations followed seasonally such as Frankfurt or Munich, initially with charter and later with scheduled flights. Two MD-82s were acquired in 1984. A third-level company, Avianova was established in 1986. Avianova's equity is now shared 50% each by Meridiana and ATI. On 1st September 1991 Alisarda changed its name to Meridiana and by 1992 it had become the largest privately owned airline in Italy. In 1992 Gatwick was served for the first time.

Routes

Barcelona, Bologna, Cagliari, Catania, Florence, Frankfurt, Genoa, London, Milan, Munich, Naples, Nice, Olbia, Palermo, Paris, Pisa, Turin, Zürich.

Fleet	Ordered
3 BAe 146-200	4 BAe/Avro RJ 85
6 McDonnell Douglas DC-9-51	
8 McDonnell Douglas MD-82	

Photograph: McDonnell Douglas DC-9-32 (Björn Kannengiesser/Medan)

MERPATI

Jolan Angkasa 2, Kotak pos 323
Jakarta 10002, Indonesia
Tel. 21413608

Three letter code	IATA No.	ICAO Callsign
MNA	621	Merpati

The Indonesian government founded Merpati Nusantara Airlines on 6th September 1962 to take over the network of internal services developed by the Indonesian Air Force. Since 1958. Initial flight operations started on 11th September 1962 connecting Jakarta with domestic points. In 1964, Merpati took over the routes previously operated by the KLM subsidiary de Kroonduif, which had been flown by Garuda since 1962. This predecessor had been particularly active in West Guinea. Scheduled services had started in January 1964. Merpati used the following aircraft: DC-3s, HS-748s, Vickers Viscounts, Vickers Vanguards, NAMC-YS 11s, Dornier 28s, Pilatus Porters. Numerous CASA aircraft manufactured in Indonesia under licence are also used, such as the IPTN 235s, replacing older aircraft. On 28th October 1978 the airline was taken over by Garuda, although Merpati continues to operate under its own name. When the first DC-9s arrived in autumn 1990, new, modern colours were introduced for the aircraft. Merpati has been integrated into the Garuda Indonesia Group since September 1989.

Routes

Balikpapan, Bandar Lampg, Bandung, Banjarmasin, Denpasar, Dumai, Ketapang, Kupang, Maumere, Medan, Padang, Palankarya, Paembang, Pekanbaru, Pontianak, Rengat, Semarang, Surabaya, Tanjung Pinan, Waingapur.

Fleet

		Ordered
14 IPTN-CN-235-10	2 Lockheed L-382 Hercules	68 ITPN-250
11 IPTN-212 AB4/CC4 Aviocar	9 DC-9-32	9 Fokker 100
14 Fokker F-27	11 de Havilland DHC-6 Twin Otter	16 IPTN-CN235
27 Fokker F-28	3 Fokker 100	
5 BAe ATP		

Photograph: Airbus A320-200 (author's collection)

MEXICANA

Xola 535, Colonia de Valle 03100 Mexico City
Mexico
Tel. 660 4433

Three letter code	IATA No.	ICAO Callsign
MXA	132	Mexicana

The Compania Mexicana de Aviacion is one of the oldest airlines in the world. It was founded on 12th July 1921 initially in order to fly wage payments to the oilfields near Tampico, as transporting this money overland was no longer safe. The airline adopted its present name on 20th August 1924. In March 1929, Charles Lindbergh piloted the carrier's first international flight between Mexico City and Brownsville, USA via Tampico, its base. From 1929 to 1968 Pan American had a majority interest in Mexicana. Aerovias Centrales was bought in 1935, and Transportes Aereos de Jalinco in 1955. In

addition to DC-3s and DC-6s, Comet 4Cs were used on routes to Havana, Los Angeles and New York starting in 1960. The Boeing 727 was introduced in 1966 and the DC-10 in 1981. The Mexican Government became the major shareholder on 15th July 1982 when it increased its stake to 58%. However on 22nd August 1989 it became a private company. A necessary reorganisation involved changes to flight operations and to the network of routes. Airbus A320s were added to the relatively old Mexicana fleet from mid-1991. Aeromexico joined as a partner, so that schedules could be

co-ordinated in order to save costs. The Fokker 100, the 100-seat jet aircraft, was introduced in 1993 for routes with low passenger volume.

Routes

Mexicana operates scheduled and charter services in the Caribbean, Central America, South America and the USA. A dense network of routes connects around thirty destinations in Mexico.

Fleet	Ordered
37 Boeing 727-200ADV	6 Airbus A320
5 McDonnell Douglas DC-10-15	8 Fokker 100
10 Fokker 100	
22 Airbus A320	
1 McDonnell Douglas DC-8-71	

Photograph: Tupolev 154B (author's collection)

MIAT-MONGOLIAN AIRLINES

Ulan-Bator Airport
People's Republic of Mongolia
Tel. 1072240

Three letter code	IATA No.	ICAO Callsign
AMO	289	Mongolian

The airline, founded in 1956, is known under a variety of names such as 'Mongolian Airlines', 'Mongoflot' or 'Air Mongol'. MIAT was built up with the aid of the USSR and Aeroflot. The first flight was on 7th July 1956 from Ulan Bator to Irkutsk using an Antonov 24. Equipment in the shape of Lisunov Li-2s (Soviet built Douglas DC-3s) and crews were initially supplied by the Soviet airline and international routes were opened to Peking and Inkutsk to connect with Aeroflot's service to Moscow. A service to Peking was soon discontinued due to lack of demand. MIAT obtained a Boeing 727 from Korean Airlines as part of 'development aid' and co-operation. Other activities of the airline include agricultural flying and air ambulance work.

Routes

Services from Ulan Bator to destinations in Mongolia, such as Darchan and Eerdenet. There are further connections to Moscow and Irkutsk. Charter flights to Korea and Japan.

Fleet	Ordered
1 Tupolev Tu-154B	2 Boeing 757-200
18 Antonov An-24/26	
1 Boeing 727-100	
7 Harbin Y 12	

Photograph: Douglas DC-9-32 (Björn Kannengiesser/Fort Lauderdale)

MIDWEST EXPRESS

4915 South Howell Ave.
Milwaukee, Wisconsin 53207, USA
Tel. 414 747 4000

Three letter code	IATA No.	ICAO Callsign
MEP	453	Midwest

Midwest was established after deregulation in November 1983 to provide passenger service in the Midwest and Southeast of the USA. The airline is a subsidiary of KC Aviation, which is itself the established avaition division of Kimberley-Clark, the major paper products company. The initial fleet was a DC-9 and a Convair 580 but more DC-9s soon followed. Flight operations started on 29th April 1984 with a DC-9, on the route Milwaukee-Boston. Over the years the routes were extended as far as Dallas and to Los Angeles. Altogether around twenty destinations in the USA are served.

In 1992 around 808,000 passengers booked flights with Midwest Express.

Routes

Milwaukee, Dallas, Minneapolis, Appleton, Atlanta, Boston, Detroit, Fort Lauderdale, Grand Rapids, Indianapolis, Lansing, Los Angeles, Madison, New York, Philadephia, San Francisco, Washington.

Fleet

8 McDonnell Douglas DC-9-14/15
6 McDonnell Douglas DC-9-32
2 McDonnell MD-88

Photograph: Boeing 737-300 (author's collection)

MONARCH

Luton Airport, Luton, Bedfordshire
LU2 9NU, United Kingdom
Tel. 0582 40 00 00

Three letter code	IATA No.	ICAO Callsign
MON	974	Monarch

Monarch Airlines is a well-known British charter airline founded on 5th June 1967 by Cosmos Tours. Flight operations started on 5th April 1968 with a Bristol Britannia flying between Luton and Madrid. Its initial fleet was two Britannia aircraft. Its destinations were holiday regions in the Mediterranean. In 1971 the first jet aircraft was acquired, a Boeing 720. BAC 1-11s followed in 1975, Boeing 707s in 1978 and the first Boeing 737 in 1980. Its first Boeing 757 arrived in 1983. Licences to operate scheduled services from Luton to Mahon, Palma and Malaga were awarded in the mid 1980s and its first service to Mahon, started on 5th July 1986. Long-haul charter services to the USA were introduced in 1988. Apart from the charter business, Monarch is also very active in aircraft leasing. For example, the entire Euroberlin fleet has been leased from Monarch for years and two Airbus A300s were leased to Compass Airlines in Australia, although were returned when Compass got into financial difficulties. Monarch carried around 3.2 million passengers on its own flights in 1993. A scheduled service between Luton and Palma was being launched in 1994.

Routes

Charter flights, particularly to the Mediterranean, East Africa, the Caribbean and the USA; ski charters to Austria, Switzerland and Munich in winter.

Fleet

8 Boeing 737-300
8 Boeing 757-200/200ER
4 Airbus A300-600
4 Airbus A320-200

Photograph: Boeing 737-300 (Francois Stock via HARD/Los Angeles)

MORRIS AIR

260 East Morris Ave., Salt Lake City, UT 84115
USA
Tel. 801-4836464

Three letter code	IATA No.	ICAO Callsign
MOA	–	Morris Air

June Morris set up a travel agency in Salt Lake City, specialising early in her own operator tours. As the agency did not have its own air carrier permit, flights to Los Angeles, Las Vegas, Hawaii, Mexico and other destinations were provided by various airlines. Thus Ryan International, American Trans Air and Sierra Pacific flew these routes regularly on behalf of Morris. It was only in 1992 that Morris Air obtained permission to operate the previously regular charter flights as scheduled flights. Up to that point Morris had been operating more than 300 weekly flights. With eleven Boeing 737-300s in its own colours, Morris was able to expand its network of routes at a phenomenally high speed and quickly became a rival to the established airlines, as passengers were being carried at low priced tariffs.

This situation resulted in Morris Air being bought by Southwest Airlines in December 1993. Morris Air will be integrated into Southwest at a cost of $130 million in the period up to 1995; up to this point Morris will operate independently and build up further routes.

Routes

Twenty-eight destinations in the west of the US, from Anchorage to San Diego.

Fleet

21 Boeing 737-300

Photograph: Fokker F-28 (Josef Krauthäuser/Bangkok)

MYANMA AIRWAYS

104 Strand Road, Yangon
Myanmar (Burma) Socialist Republic
Tel. 1 80710

Three letter code	IATA No.	ICAO Callsign
UBA	209	Unionair

Originally established in 1948 by the Burmese government as the 'Union of Burma Airways', the airline changed its name in December 1972 to Burma Airways Corporation, and finally on 1st April 1989 to Myanma Airways. In between lie more than forty years of flight operations, which started in 1948 with de Havilland Doves. These were followed by DC-3s and Vickers Viscounts, and the introduction of national and international services. The first F-27 was delivered in October 1963. In 1969 a Boeing 727 replaced the Vickers Viscount on international flights. After the F-28 was delivered in 1977, Myanma only used Fokker aircraft. A co-operation was agreed with Royal Brunei in 1993 which provides for international flights to be operated by a joint airline.

Routes

Yangon, Akyab, Bangkok, Bhamo, Kalemyo, Kawthaung, Kengtung, Khamti, Mandalay, Penang, Singapore and around ten further domestic destinations.

Fleet

5 Fokker F-27-600
3 Fokker F-28

Photograph: McDonnell Douglas DC-10-30

NIGERIA AIRWAYS

PMB 1024, Ikeja
Nigeria
Tel. 01 900810

Three letter code	IATA No.	ICAO Callsign
NGA	87	Nigeria

West African Airways Corporation started operations in the former British colony of West Africa in 1946. Nigeria Airways was established in 1958 to take over the Nigerian operations of WAAC with the name WAAC (Nigeria) Ltd. The Nigerian Government assumed full ownership of the airline on 1st May 1959. Flight operations in the new independent state of Nigeria were started with the aid of BOAC using aircraft leased from the latter in on 1st October 1958. Boeing 377 Stratocruisers were used to open a route from Lagos to London, and from 1st April 1962 the de Havilland Comet 4B was used on this route. In 1961 the state took control of the airline, and a Boeing 707 was the first aircraft owned by the recently established airline. The present title was formally adopted on 22nd January 1971 although it had been used for commercial purposes since 1958. A Boeing 707 took over operating the Lagos-London service in 1971 from ex-BOAC Vickers VC-10 aircraft which had been introduced in 1969. When the first Douglas DC-10s arrived in October 1976, Nigeria Airways had its first widebody aircraft. Two Airbus A310s were delivered in 1983 and another two in 1984. They are primarily used on African routes. Over the last few years financial difficulties have been encountered and costs have been reduced and unprofitable services suspended to improve results.

Routes

Abidjan, Abuja, Accra, Banjul, Benin, Calabar, Conakry, Contonou, Dakar, Douala, Enugu, Freetown, Ilorin, Jedda, Johannesburg, Jos, Kaduna, Kano, Libreville, Lome, London, Makurdi, Malabbo, Monrovia, New York, Port Harcourt, Rome, Sokoto and Yola are the destinations.

Fleet

2 McDonnell Douglas DC-10-30
4 Airbus A310-200
2 Boeing 707-320F
8 Boeing 737-200ADV

Photograph: Airbus A320 (author's collection)

NORTHWEST

Minneapolis/St. Paul Intl. Airport
St. Paul, MN 55111, USA
Tel. 612 726 1234

Three letter code	IATA No.	ICAO Callsign
NWA	12	Northwest

This airline was founded on 1st August 1926 in Minneapolis/St.Paul as Northwest Airways. In the early years it operated flights with a Stinson Post from Chicago to St.Paul. Regular passenger services began in 1933 using Douglas DC-3s from Seattle to Winnipeg. In 1934 a competitor, Northern Air Transport, was taken over. The name was also changed to Northwest Airlines in 1934. On 15th July 1947 the first polar route was opened using DC-4s. This route was from Seattle via Anchorage to Tokyo and on to Manila. From that time onwards the airline was called Northwest Orient Airlines. Northwest was able to fly to various destinations in China until Mao Tse Tung took power. Taiwan, Seoul and Okinawa followed in 1950. Boeing Stratocruisers were used on the routes to East Asia. Lockheed Constellations, DC-6s, DC-7s and Lockheed L-188 Electras were the most important aircraft during the propeller age until the first DC-8s arrived. They were used for the route from Seattle to Chicago, and were then used to replace the propeller aircraft on the Asia routes. On 30th April, NW acquired its first widebody aircraft, a Boeing 747, followed by DC-10-40s in late 1972. In 1979 Northwest crossed the Atlantic to Copenhagen and London. Unlike many other airlines, Northwest's growth was solely internal until 1986, when Republic was bought. Since then there have been many financial difficulties with regard to adapting and integrating the fleets. In 1988 the old name, Northwest Airlines, was adopted again. When the first Airbus A320s were delivered in late 1989, Northwest also introduced the new colour scheme. Northwest works in close co-operation with KLM, which holds 20% of the voting shares and has feeder arrangements with four airlines, Mesaba, Big Sky, Precision, and Express Airlines I, who fly as 'Northwest Airlink' and with NW flight numbers.

Routes

Glasgow, Paris, Amsterdam, Frankfurt, Tokyo, Osaka, Seoul, Okinawa, Shanghai, Taipei, Hong Kong, Saipan, Guam, Manila, Bangkok, Singapore, Montego Bay, Grand Cayman, Montreal, Winnepeg, Toronto and Edmonton ; in addition there are over 150 destinations in the USA which are served by Northwest Airlines.

Fleet

		Ordered
149 McDonnell Douglas DC-9 series 14/15/31/32/51	68 Boeing 727-200	4 Boeing 747-400
8 McDonnell Douglas MD-82	33 Boeing 757-200	40 Boeing 757-200
21 McDonnell Douglas DC-10-40	41 Boeing 747-100/200	16 Airbus A320
8 McDonnell Douglas DC-10-30	12 Boeing 747-400	
	49 Airbus A320	

Photograph: McDonnell Douglas MD-83 (André Dietzel/Munich FJS)

OASIS

Calle Gobelas 17, 28023 Madrid
Spain
Tel. 13729102

Three letter code	IATA No.	ICAO Callsign
AAN	–	Oasis

Founded in 1986 in Malaga as Andalusair, it started flights on 27th May 1988 flying a Malaga to Manchester charter service with a 165-seat MD-83 but only for a short time. After a few months the Oasis hotel group acquired a stake in the airline, taking over a controlling interest and the management as well. The name was then changed and the MD-83s appeared in a wide variety of colours. The colours that have finally gained acceptance were a blue tail with a white fuselage. In 1992 Oasis acquired its first Airbus A310. That year Oasis had a fleet of six MD-83s, three of them on lease from the Guinness Peat Aviation Group. The airline cooperates with the Mexican airline Aerocancun and they lease aircraft to each other whenever the need arises, usually in Europe in the summer and Mexico in the winter Oasis is based at Palma. It also has an interest in the US operator Private Jet (see page 228), again with some seasonal fleet exchanges.

Routes

Charter flights from Western Europe, the United Kingdom, Scandinavia to Spain. Also flights to Cuba, Mexico and the Dominican Republic.

Fleet

2 Airbus A310-200
1 Airbus A320-200
3 McDonnell Douglas MD-83

Photograph: BAe BAC 1-11-400 (author's collection)

OKADA AIR

Airport Road, Benin City
Nigeria
Tel. 019 63881

Three letter code	IATA No.	ICAO Callsign
OKJ	–	Okadaair

A consortium of companies founded Okada Air in 1983, led by Chief Igbenidian, in order to operate regional and international charter flights. Flight services were started using BAC 1-11s followed by DC-8s and Boeing 707s. Its first foreign destination was London. There are also occasional charters to Frankfurt or Zürich. Okada also flies subcharter for other airlines as well as cargo. A network of domestic scheduled services is in being, joining such cities as Lagos, Kano, Kaduna and Port Harcourt. It is one of the largest operators of BAe 1-11s.

Routes

Charter flights to Europe, to the Middle East and to ad hoc destinations.

Fleet

```
 1 Boeing 707-300C
19 BAe 1-11-400
 5 Boeing 727-200ADV
```

Photograph: Airbus A320-320 (André Dietzel/Munich FJS)

ONUR AIR

Sipahioglu Caddeshi 5, Yesilyurt, Istanbul
Turkey
Tel. 1573 2382

Three letter code	IATA No.	ICAO Callsign
OHY	–	Onur Air

The airline, which was only founded in 1992, is a subsidiary of the Turkish tour operator 'TK Air Travel'. Flight operations started in May 1993 with new Airbus A320s. The airline intends to start scheduled services in addition to charter and inclusive tour flights. During the high season, further Airbus A320s are leased in addition to the airline's own aircraft. The intention is also to build up a domestic network of routes from Istanbul by the late nineties.

Routes

Charter flights from every major German airport and many European airports to destinations in Turkey.

Fleet	Ordered
3 Airbus A320-200	1 Airbus A320

Photograph: Airbus A300-600 (Airbus Industrie)

OLYMPIC AIRWAYS

96 Syngrou Ave., Athens 11741
Greece
Tel. 19292111

Three letter code	IATA No.	ICAO Callsign
OAL	50	Olympic

Olympic Airways was founded on 6th April 1957 by no less a person than Aristotle Onassis. The well-known shipowner took over an airline called TAE Greek National Airlines which had been in existence since July 1951 (through a merger of three airlines TAE, Hellas and AME), and belonged to the Greek state. By the time of the first oil crisis Onassis had turned Olympic into a modern airline, but the oil situation caused Olympic difficulties and it suspended flight operations for several months in 1974. In order to avert complete bankruptcy, the Greek state intervened and took over Olympic from 1st January 1976

when operations resumed. After the airline was completely restructured and unprofitable routes abandoned, things slowly took a turn for the better again. Olympic operates not only scheduled services but also charters. Right at the start of flight operations, in April 1957. Olympic had a fleet of 13 DC-3s and one DC-4 and a year later DC-6Bs started flying from Athens to London via Rome and Paris. Comet 4Bs went into service in 1960. Boeing 707s inaugurated a non-stop Athens-New Tork service on 1st June 1966 and later long-distance routes to New York, Johannesburg and Australia. Boeing 727s were

introduced in 1969 and NAMC YS-11As in 1970 to replace DC-3s on local networks. Boeing 720s supplanted the DC-6Bs on long-haul routes from 1972. The first Boeing 747 came to Olympic while it was still under Onassis' control. As part of a fleet replacement policy, the airline's Boeing 707s and Boeing 727s were replaced by new Boeing 737-400s and Airbuses by 1992, and all of these aircraft were painted in attractive colours. In 1993 around 7 million passengers flew with Olympic, although 4 million of these were domestic passengers flying with the subsidiary Olympic Aviation. (see page 221)

Routes

From Athens to New York, Chicago, Toronto, to all the important cities in Western Europe, the Middle East, to Singapore and Sydney.

Fleet		Ordered
4 Boeing 747-200	2 Airbus A300-600	2 Airbus A300-600
3 Boeing 727-200	8 Airbus A300B4	6 Boeing 737-400
11 Boeing 737-200		
6 Boeing 737-400		

Photograph: Dornier 228 (DASA)

OLYMPIC AVIATION

96 Syngrou Ave., Athens 11741
Greece
Tel. 19292111

Three letter code	IATA No.	ICAO Callsign
OAV	–	Olympic

Greece with its numerous islands, its fragmented and mountainous mainland is dependent not only on a dense network of ferry connections but also on properly functioning regional flight services. In order to open up smaller islands for tourists and to save tourists long transfer times, Olympic Aviaton was founded on 1st August 1971 with the objective of building up regional flight services. First of all runways had to be laid, extended or repaired on many islands. As many runways do not have a hard surface, robust aircraft such as Short Skyvans and Dornier 228s were used. Initially it was privately-owned but became

Government-owned in 1974. Flights are operated to those places where the parent company, Olympic Airways, cannot operate its aircraft, plus the airline operates as a feeder service to international flights to Athens. It is also responsible for charter and air-taxi operations. Since 1st January 1992, the airline has been operationally independent of Olympic Airways, of which it is a wholly-owned subsidiary.

Routes

From Athens domestic airport to over thirty destinations in the Aegean, the Peloponnese and the Greek mainland.

Fleet

7 Dornier 228-200	4 ATR-42
5 Shorts 330	1 Agusta A 109
4 ATR-72	1 Aerospatiale AS.350 Ecureuil

Photograph: Boeing 747-200 (Josef Gietl/Frankfurt)

PAKISTAN INTERNATIONAL

PIA Building, Quaid-e-Azam Internationa Airport
Karachi 75200, Pakistan
Tel. 21 457 2011

Three letter code	IATA No.	ICAO Callsign
PIA	214	Pakistan

Pakistan Airlines was founded by the government in 1951 and began Super Constellation services on 7th June 1954 providing a valuable connection between East and West Pakistan. International routes to Cairo and London followed on 1st February 1955 and on 10th March the same year the airline was reorganised after formal amalgamation with Orient Airways, which had been founded on 23rd 1946 prior to the partitioning of India. On domestic flights Convair CV-240s and DC-3s were used. They were replaced by Vickers Viscounts and later by HS-Tridents.

In 1960 long-distance flights changed over to Boeing 707s and in 1961 these aircraft were used for flights to New York for the first time. The airline's first large-capacity aircraft was a DC-10-30 in 1974. Two Boeing 747s were leased from TAP-Air Portugal in 1976, and then later bought. In 1971 many flights and connections were suspended due to the war situation and the secession of East Pakistan which became Bangladesh. After the airline was reorganised, flight operations picked up again in late 1972 and routes which had been abandoned, eg New York, were

resumed. The government is still the majority shareholder but private investors hold a 44% stake.

Routes

From Karachi and Islamabad to Lahore, Dubai, Teheran, Baghdad, Amman, Damascus, Cairo, Tripoli, Moscow, Istanbul, Athens, Rome, Frankfurt, Copenhagen, Amsterdam, Paris, London, New York, Toronto, Tokyo, Beijing, Zürich, Manila, Singapore, Kuala Lumpur, Bangkok, Katmandu, Nairobi, Jeddah, Bahrain and to over twenty domestic destinations.

Fleet

Fleet		Ordered
8 Boeing 747-200	7 Airbus A300B4	1 Airbus A310-300
5 Boeing 707	14 Fokker F-27	
7 Boeing 737-300	2 de Havilland DHC-6	
4 Airbus A310-300		

Photograph: Fokker F-28 (Uwe Gleisberg/Munich FJS)

PALAIR MACEDONIAN

Nef 1, 91001 Skopje
Macedonia
Tel. 91 411083

Three letter code	IATA No.	ICAO Callsign
PMK	–	Palair

Palair Macedonian was founded in 1991, after the Yugoslavian airline JAT was forced to discontinue flight operations. The connections to Western Europe were maintained using leased Tu-154s; this was particularly important for the numerous immigrant workers from former Yugoslavia and Turkey. In spite of the lack of infrastructure in Skopje, the rates of increase in the number of flights at this airport are enormous, and Palair leased two more Fokker 100s in October 1993. Palair Macedonian is only operating charter flights at the moment, but it intends to start operating regular scheduled flights in 1994/95.

Routes

Amsterdam, Berlin, Brussels, Düsseldorf, Frankfurt, Munich, Paris, Salzburg, Vienna, Zürich.

Fleet

2 Fokker F-28
2 Fokker 100
1 Tupolev Tu-154B

Photograph: Boeing 737-300 (Josef Krauthäuser/Manila)

PHILIPPINES

1, Legaspi P.O. Box 954, Manila
The Philippines
Tel. 02-8180111

Three letter code	IATA No.	ICAO Callsign
PAL	79	Philippine

Philippine Air Lines was founded on 25th February 1941 from the remains of an earlier company, Philippine Air Transport Company (PATCO) formed by a leading industralist. A few services were started on 15th March 1941 with twin-engined Beech aircraft but these were soon suspended in late 1941 due to the Japanese invasion. After the liberation of the Philippines, PAL resumed services on 14th February, 1946 with five DC-3s. Far East Air Transport, a competitor, was taken over in 1947 together with its routes to Hong Kong, Shanghai, Bangkok and Calcutta, as well as five DC-4s. In that same year PAL opened a scheduled route to San Francisco. All international flights, excepting the Hong Kong services, were suspended in March 1954 following the crash of a DC-6. However, this did allow PAL to expand its domestic routes all the more. It was only in 1962 that the first foreign route, to San Francisco, was opened again in co-operation with KLM. The first BAC 1-11s arrived in May 1966; starting in 1969 flights were operated to Europe again using DC-8s. Amsterdam, Frankfurt and Rome were served. In 1974 two domestic airlines, Air Manila and Filipinas, were bought. Its first leased DC-10-30s arrived in that same year, replacing the DC-8s. Boeing 747s took over from the DC-10s in 1986 and Airbus A300B4s, the latter being referred to as the 'lovebus', were introduced in 1979. Fokker 50s were acquired in 1988, replacing the older HS-748s. In 1990 the airline started taking BAC 1-11s out of service, and they have been replaced by Boeing 737-300s. A 67% controlling share in the airline was sold to PR Holdings, a consortium of local banking investors, in 1992. The Government presently holds the remainder. Having been formed over fifty years ago, Philippine Airlines claimed to be the longest-serving airline in Asia.

Routes

Amsterdam, Frankfurt, London, Paris, Rome, Los Angeles, New York, San Francisco, Dharan, Dubai, Bangkok, Brisbane, Ho Chi Minh City, Hong Kong, Seoul, Taipei, Tokyo, Sydney, Singapore, Kuala Lumpur, Karachi, and in addition a dense network of domestic routes.

Fleet		Ordered
10 Boeing 747-200	10 Fokker 50	4 Boeing 737-300
2 DC-10-30	7 Shorts 360-300	2 Boeing 747-400
8 Airbus A300B4	11 Boeing 737-300	6 Airbus A340-300

Photograph: Boeing 737-200ADV

PLUNA

Colonia 1021, P.O. Box 1360 Montevideo
Uruguay
Tel. 2 916591

Three letter code	IATA No.	ICAO Callsign
PUA	286	Pluna

Primeras Lineas Uruguayas de Navegazion Aera was founded in September 1935 by the Marquez Vaeza brothers. Flight operations started on 20th November 1936 with two de Havilland DH.90 Dragonflies. The airline expanded and ordered another DH.86B, until operations had to be discontinued on 15th March 1943. After the end of the Second World War, the government of Uruguay acquired 83% of the shares in the airline, and on 12th November 1951 the remaining capital shares were also transferred to the state. Services were operated to neighbouring states using DC-3s, and a domestic network was built up. In addition to DC-3s, de Havilland Herons and Vickers Viscounts were employed. In late 1967 PLUNA took over the route network and the aircraft belonging to CAUSA. PLUNA acquired its first jet aircraft, a Boeing 737-200, in late 1969. PLUNA's sole overseas route was a weekly connection to Madrid. Boeing 707s have been used on this route since 1982. An air-bridge between Montevideo and Buenos Aires has been operated in conjuction with Aerolineas Argentinas using Boeing 737s of both airlines. Domestic flights are flown by arrangement with TAMU, the transport wing of the Uruguayan Air Force. PLUNA entered into a co-operation with Spanair in 1993 for the flights from Montevideo to Madrid; the latter airline operates the flights with Boeing 767s, as PLUNA does not have any aircraft of its own available.

Routes

Artigas, Asuncion, Buenos Aires, Madrid, Melo, Paysandu, Porto Alegre, Rio de Janeiro, Santiago de Chile, Sao Paulo.

Fleet

1 Boeing 707-300
3 Boeing 737-200ADV

Photograph: Boeing 737-300 (Uwe Gleisberg/Sydney)

POLYNESIAN

Beach Road, Apia
Western Samoa
Tel. 21261

Three letter code	IATA No.	ICAO Callsign
PAO	162	Polynesian

After the collapse of its predecessor, Samoan Airlines, Polynesian Airlines Ltd. was founded on 7th May 1959. Its first flight was from Apia to Pago Pago, using a Percival Prince in 1960. After state independence in 1962, further routes to the Cook Islands were opened on 5th July 1963 and a DC-3 was acquired. In 1968 Polynesian obtained a DC-4, and from January 1972 onwards modern turboprop aircraft were acquired in the form of two HS-748s. Modernisation became possible after the state acquired a stake in the airline with a 70% stake. in 1977 the internal operations of Air Samoa were taken over. Polynesian entered the jet age in 1981 with the delivery of a Boeing 737, followed by new routes to Australia. Various GAF-Nomads, BN Islanders and DHC Twin Otters were also acquired for regional routes. In the early 90s Polynesian acquired the latest Boeing 737-300. A Boeing 767 leased from Air New Zealand followed in 1993; it was used on routes to the US.

Routes

Apia, Auckland, Nine, Noumea, Pago Pago, Papeete, Nadi, Vila, Sydney, Vara'u, Tongatapu and Los Angeles.

Fleet

2 Boeing 737-300
1 Boeing 767
1 de Havilland DHC-6 Twin Otter
1 Pilatus BN 2 Islander

Photograph: Fokker 100 (Stefan Schlick/Frankfurt)

PORTUGALIA

Avenida Almirante Gago Coutinho 88,
1700 Lisbon, Portugal
Tel. 18486693

Three letter code	IATA No.	ICAO Callsign
PGA	–	Portugalia

Portugalia was founded as a regional scheduled airline on 25th July 1989 and started flights a year later, on 7th July 1990 with Fokker 100s leased from Guinness Peat Aviation. In the first two years the airline made a loss of US$12 million. It made its first small profit in 1993. Portugalia is based in Lisbon and is also active in the charter business.

Routes

Amsterdam, Brussels, Faro, Frankfurt, Cologne/Bonn, London, Lisbon, Madrid, Paris, Porto, Strasbourg, Turin.

Fleet

5 Fokker 100

Photograph: McDonnell Douglas MD-83 (Björn Kannengiesser/Miami)

PRIVATE JET

P.O. Box 228 Atlanta GA 30085
USA
Tel. 404 939 5001

Three letter code	IATA No.	ICAO Callsign
PJE	333	Pee Jay

Private Jet Expeditions was founded as a 'travel club' in 1989 and started club flights using a Boeing 727. The Spanish airline Oasis acquired a stake in 1991, as did other private investors, and the airline's activities were expanded into a charter and scheduled airline. The first MD-83s were delivered in late 1991 and will be the airline's standard aircraft in the future. Private Jet is one of the 'discount' airlines in the US and primarily provides flights several times daily on routes which are in heavy demand, in competition with the established airlines.

Routes

Atlanta, Chicago, Miami, Newark, also charter flights to the Caribbean and to holiday resorts in the USA.

Fleet

12 McDonnell Douglas MD-83
 1 McDonnell Douglas MD-87
 1 McDonnell Douglas MD-82
 1 Boeing 727-100

Photograph: Boeing 767-200ER (Josef Krauthäuser/Bangkok)

QANTAS

P.O. Box 489, International Square,
Sydney NSW 2000, Australia
Tel. 2 236 3636

Three letter code	IATA No.	ICAO Callsign
QFA	81	Qantas

Queensland and Northern Territory Aerial Service Ltd having been formed on 16th November 1920, QANTAS for short, celebrated its seventieth anniversary in 1990. Two Avro 504s were stationed in Longreach; initially the airline operated taxi and sightseeing flights, and the first routes from Charleville to Cloncurry were flown in November 1922. Qantas aircraft were also used to set up the famous Flying Doctor Service in 1928 and in the same year began the first scheduled air service in Australia between Brisbane and Toowoomba, a distance of 80 miles. In co-operation with Imperial Airways, Qantas served the London-Brisbane route, with Qantas flying the last leg from Singapore to Brisbane from 1934. The airline called itself Qantas Empire Airways from 1934 to 1967. QEA employed Short Empire flying boats, because of their greater capacity, on this route, which went as far as Sydney from 1938, until the outbreak of the Second World War. During the war, Qantas operated flights for the armed forces, while flights in Australia itself virtually came to a standstill. After the war the entire fleet was modernised and Lockheed Constellations, DC-3s and DC-4s were acquired. In 1947 the Australian government acquired a controlling interest in Qantas. When seven Boeing 707s were delivered from 1959 Qantas entered the jet age, at the same time introducing new colours for the aircraft. Boeing 747s were introduced in 1973 and have formed the backbone of the fleet for over twenty years. Boeing 767s, the second generation of large-capacity aircraft, were acquired starting in 1985 bringing another new colour scheme that is familiar to us today. In 1992 domestic operator Australian Airlines was taken over. and incorporated into its network in 1993. In 1992, British Airways took a 25% stake in the Australian national airline.

Routes

Flights to Japan, Europe, the US, to Harare, Argentina, Canada and the Far East, as well as to the Pacific area. A dense domestic network after the takeover of Australian.

Fleet

Fleet		Ordered
18 Boeing 747-400	33 Boeing 737-300/400	2 Boeing 767-300ER
2 Boeing 747SP	4 Airbus A300B4	9 Airbus A320
7 Boeing 747-200		
6 Boeing 747-300		
20 Boeing 767-200/300ER		

Photograph: NAMC YS-11A (author's collection)

REEVE ALEUTIAN

4700 West Intl. Airport Road
Anchorage, Alaska 99502, USA
Tel. 907-2431112

Three letter code	IATA No.	ICAO Callsign
RVV	338	Reeve

The airline was founded by Bob Reeve an Alaskan pilot and airline pioneer in Valdez, Alaska on 25th August 1932. It flew initially under the name of Reeve Airways and operated charter flights for various firms initially using a single-engined Eaglerock aircraft. In 1948 the US government invited tenders for flights to the Aleutian Islands in the northwestern part of the US. Reeve obtained the licence in January 1948, initially for a period of five years, on account of its experience on the 1,800 mile long route. The present title was adopted in April 1951. The DC-3 was the appropriate aircraft for use on flights to reach these inhospitable and sparsely populated places and the type was introduced in 1946 between Fairbanks, Anchorage and Seattle. DC-4s enabled the airline to open up the group of Pribilof Islands. DC-6s were added to the fleet in 1962;. Lockheed Electras were introduced in 1968 and Boeing 727s in 1983. The only scheduled service outside Alaska is the link with Seattle. As Reeve Aleutian flies combined cargo/passenger aircraft to supply the islands, the proportion of passengers is lower than with other airlines.

Routes

Scheduled and charter flights from Anchorage to Seattle and to destinations in the Aleutian Islands.

Fleet

2 Boeing 727C
3 Lockheed L-188 Electra
3 NAMC-YS-11A

Photograph: McDonnell Douglas MD-82 (Martin Bach/Reno)

RENO AIR

690 East Plumb Lane, Reno NV 89500
USA
Tel 702 829 5750

Three letter code	IATA No.	ICAO Callsign
ROA	384	Reno Air

Reno Air was founded in 1990 and obtained permission to operate flights between Reno and Los Angeles in April 1992. It started flight operations to these destinations in June 1992. Reno Air promoted its flights with low fares and good service and expanded its network of routes. There were seven MD-82s in use in late 1992, and by means of purchases and leasing the airline was able to more than double the fleet by late 1993. Unprofitable routes were consistently cancelled and abandoned in favour of new connections. The airline's base and hub is Reno-Cannon International Airport. The airline is publicly owned.

Routes

Burbank, Las Vegas, Los Angeles, Ontario, Orange County, Phoenix, Portland, Reno, San Diego, San Jose, Seattle, Tucson.

Fleet

17 McDonnell Douglas MD-82/83

Photograph: de Havilland DHC-8-100

RHEINTALFLUG

Flugplatz, 6845 Hohenems
Austria
Tel. 05576 3222

Three letter code	IATA No.	ICAO Callsign
RTL	915	Rheintal

Founded in 1977 as a non-scheduled airline, regular flights began in 1984 from Hohenems (Vorarlberg) to Vienna. Then in 1988 the airline was able to set up a new route, from the neighbouring airport of Altenrhein (Switzerland) to Vienna using a Grumman Jetprop Commander 900. Rheintal also connected Friedrichshafen with Vienna from autumn 1989 with a daily off-peak return flight using a de Havilland DHC-8-100. Since then only DHC-8s have been used. 30,000 passengers used the flights of this regional airline in 1993. Cities such as Graz, Linz and Zürich are served on behalf of Austrian Airlines.

Routes

Hohenems/Bregenz, Altenrhein, Zürich, Friedrichshafen to Vienna. Also charter and non-scheduled flights.

Fleet

3 de Havilland DHC-8-100
1 Cessna 414

Photograph: Boeing 757-200 (author's collection)

ROYAL AIR MAROC

Aeroport Arifa, Casablanca
Morocco
Tel. 364184

Three letter code	IATA No.	ICAO Callsign
RAM	147	Marocair

The name Royal Air Maroc was introduced on 28th June 1957, after Morocco had obtained its independence from Spain and France. The state-owned airline Royal Air Maroc emerged from the Société Air Atlas and Avia Maroc Aérienne, which together formed the Compagnie Chérifienne de Transport Aériens (CCTA) on 25th June 1953. Initially there were only domestic services and some routes to France initially using Junkers Ju 52s but they were soon replaced by DC-3s. In 1957 a Lockheed Constellation came into use and was employed on the newly introduced international routes. In July 1958 Air Maroc acquired its first Caravelle. Boeing 707s were bought in 1975 for long-distance routes. Boeing 727s came into service on regional and long-distance routes in 1970. When the first Boeing 757 was delivered in July 1986 a fleet replacement programme was carried out. The first ATR-42 was received on 24th March 1989 and is used on domestic routes. In 1993 RAM acquired another large-capacity aircraft, a Boeing 747-400. RAM is controlled by the Moroccan Government which holds 92.7% of the shares.

Routes

To Europe, North Africa, Middle East, USA, South America as well as numerous charter services.

Fleet

1 Boeing 747SP	5 Boeing 737-500
1 Boeing 747-200	4 Boeing 737-400
1 Boeing 747-400	6 Boeing 737-200
2 Boeing 707-300	10 Boeing 727-200
2 Boeing 757-200	3 ATR-42

Photograph: Boeing 767 (Josef Krauthäuser/Bangkok)

ROYAL BRUNEI

P.O. Box 737, Bandar Seri Begawan
Brunei
Tel. 40500

Three letter code	IATA No.	ICAO Callsign
RBA	672	Brunei

Royal Brunei Airlines was founded on 18th November 1974 as the national airline of Brunei Negara Darussalam and began flight operations over Bandar Seri Begawan-Singapore route on 14th May 1975. A few Boeing 737-200s were the mainstay of the airline until three Boeing 757s were acquired, the first arriving on 6th May 1986. When this aircraft was delivered, Royal Brunei also painted all of its aircraft in new colours. With the introduction of Boeing 757s long-haul routes were launched and a London Gatwick service commenced. A leased Boeing 767 arrived in June 1990, and with two more delivered in 1991 and 1992, they have taken over some 757 routes while the 737s have been disposed of. The Airbus A340 delivered in 1993 is used by the Sultan of Brunei as his personal aircraft when needed. New routes for 1993 were Bahrain, Beijing, Cairo and Zürich.

Routes

Bangkok, Darwin, Dubai, Jakarta, Kota Kinabalu, Kuala Lumpur, Kuching, Manila, Perth, Singapore, Taipei, London, Zürich, Frankfurt and Hong Kong are in the network of scheduled routes.

Fleet	Ordered
3 Boeing 757-200	2 Fokker 50
5 Boeing 767-300ER	
1 Boeing 727-200ADV	
1 Airbus A340	

Photograph: Airbus A310-300 (author's collection)

ROYAL JORDANIAN

P.O. Box 302, Amman
Jordan
Tel. 06 672872

Three letter code	IATA No.	ICAO Callsign
RJA	512	Jordanian

King Hussein declared the establishment of the Jordanian national airline Alia on 8th December 1963 by virtue of law and succeeded Jordan Airways, also known as Jordanian Airways, which itself has succeeded Air Jordan of the Holy Land two years previously. Alia (meaning high flying) was named after King Hussein's daughter. Flight operations were started from 15th December 1963 Amman to Beirut, Cairo and Kuwait with two Handley Page Heralds and a DC-7. In 1964 a second DC-7 was added to the fleet. With the introduction of the SE210 Caravelle, a European route to Rome was

opened for the first time in 1965. Paris and London followed in 1966. The DC-7s were destroyed during the Israeli-Arab Six Day War and later replaced by F-27s. The Jordanian Government assumed full control of Alia in 1968. In 1969 the network of routes was expanded to include Munich, Istanbul and Teheran, followed by Frankfurt in 1970. In 1971 Alia acquired its first Boeing 707; the Caravelle was replaced in 1973 by Boeing 727s and finally, in 1977, two Boeing 747 'Jumbos' were bought. Flighs to the USA started in 1984, to New York and Los Angeles. Alia was the first of the Arab national carriers to

commence scheduled services to the USA using the 747s. TriStars joined the fleet in 1981. When the Airbus A310 was introduced in 1986, a new colour scheme was introduced. The airline then adopted the name Royal Jordanian. During the Gulf War the airline suffered severe losses, so that some aircraft had to be leased. In 1992 Berlin, Jakarta and Aden were included for the first time in the network of scheduled routes; flights to Athens were also resumed. The airline is to become a public limited company. Arab Wings, founded in 1975 is a subsidiary, operating a small executive aircraft fleet.

Routes

Middle East, Europe with Vienna, Athens, Berlin, Frankfurt and Zürich, USA, Bangkok, Jakarta and Singapore are served regularly. Charter flights primarily as pilgrimage flights.

Fleet	Ordered
3 Boeing 707-320 CF	4 Airbus A320
2 Boeing 727-200	5 Airbus A340
5 Lockheed L-1011-300	
6 Airbus A310-300	
2 Airbus A320	

Photograph: Boeing 757-200 (author's collection)

ROYAL NEPAL AIRLINES

RNAC Building, P.O. Box 401, Kantipath,
Kathmandu, 711000, Nepal
Tel. 1 220757

Three letter code	IATA No.	ICAO Callsign
RNA	285	Royal Nepal

Royal Nepal Airlines Corporation Ltd. was founded by the government on 1st July 1958, replacing Indian Airlines, which had operated domestic services for some eight years on Nepal's behalf. External services to such points as Delhi and Calcutta continued to be operated by Indian Airlines until 1960 when Royal Nepal took over DC-3s and later, Fokker F-27 Friendships, were the ideal aircraft for the harsh climate of Nepal because they are undemanding. Three HS-748s came into use in 1970, and the first Boeing 727 in June 1972. However, the airfield at mountainous Kathmandu had to be extended by that time, which was a difficult business; even today, it is not possible for jumbo jets to take off and land there. The Boeing 727 was used to open a route to Delhi. The delivery of the first Boeing 757s in 1987 and 1988 marked at the same time a fleet replacement programme and the expansion of services to European destinations.

Routes

Bangkok, Calcutta, Delhi, Dacca, Dubai, Frankfurt, Hong Kong, Karachi, London, Singapore and to over thirty regional destinations in Nepal.

Fleet

2 Boeing 757-200
2 Boeing 727-100
3 BAe HS-748
9 de Havilland DHC-6
1 Pilatus PC-6 Turbo Porter

Photograph: BAe BAC 1-11-500 (Martin Bach/Frankfurt)

RYANAIR

College Park House, Nassau Street, Dublin 2
Republic of Ireland
Tel. 01 794444

Three letter code	IATA No.	ICAO Callsign
RYR	224	Ryanair

Founded in May 1985, Ryanair can be seen as a rival to Aer Lingus, as far as regional services and flights to Britain are concerned. London European Airways were acquired in 1986. No airline has served more towns in Ireland, nine airports in all at one time, than Ryanair. It uses ATR-42s and BAC/Rombac 1-11s but in 1994 has introduced Boeing 737-200s on services from the UK mainland to Dublin. The route Dublin-Munich was taken over from Aer Lingus, a service which Ryanair has been serving since 1988 and the Liverpool-Dublin route was also taken over. Luton-Dublin services were a main route for Ryanair when it moved onto UK routes but since the expanion of Stansted, it has increased its presence there to the detriment of Luton. Prestwick is being served from May, 1994 and Ryanair is the only operator flying scheduled services from the famous Scottish airport. 120,000 passengers were carried in the financial year '92/'93. The One Elevens are being replaced by Boeing 737-200s, acquired from Britannia Airways, and Air Malta with a new colour scheme.

Routes

Regional services in Ireland and Britain. From nine Irish airports to Luton, Birmingham, Cardiff, Leeds, Liverpool, Manchester, Prestwick and Stanstead. Charter flights to Germany.

Fleet

3 ATR-42
4 BAe/Rombac-BAC 1-11
6 Boeing 737-200s

Photograph: Boeing 727-100 (author's collection)

RYAN INTERNATIONAL AIRLINES

1600 Airport Road, Wichita, KS 67209
USA
Tel. 316 9420141

Three letter code	IATA No.	ICAO Callsign
RYN	–	Ryan International

Ryan Aviation has been in existence since 1972 as an airline operating charter flights as a subcontractor for Emery Express and began operations on 3rd March 1973 as DeBoer Aviation. Ryan International was a division of these operations until it was sold in 1985 to the PHH group. In February 1989 Ronald Ryan bought the company back and started an airfreight service from Indianapolis for the US Mail using eight DC-9s and nine Boeing 727s. The airline operates on behalf of Emery Worldwide using further Boeing 727s. Ryan sought further activities in the Pacific. A Boeing 727 flies freshly caught fish from Saipan to Japan. A further aircraft for passenger flights is standing by in Cleveland for a tour operator. Ryan International is not at present operating any aircraft in its own colours; all the aircraft have the colours of the particular client, and only some small lettering indicates the name of the operator.

Routes

Extensive freight routes on behalf of the US Mail, for Emery Worldwide and others.

Fleet

  7 McDonnell Douglas DC-9-15F
20 Boeing 727F
  1 Boeing 727C

Photograph: Boeing 737-200ADV (Thomas Ziegler/Munich FJS)

SABENA WORLD AIRLINES

35 rue Cordinal Mercier 1000 Brussels
Belgium
Tel. 02 7233111

Three letter code	IATA No.	ICAO Callsign
SAB	82	Sabena

The Société Anonyme Belge d'Exploitation de la Navigation Aérienne (SABENA) was founded on 23rd May 1923 to succeed the Syndicat National pour l'Etude des Transports Aériens (SNETA), formed in 1919. Sabena began revenue flights on 1st April 1924 over the Rotterdam-Strasbourg route via Brussels. The carrier was a pioneer in establishing many African services, and flights to the Congo began in 1925. In 1938 SABENA flew a network of 5,970 km in Europe. Between May 1940 and October 1945 European services were suspended, but African operations continued through the Second World War. After the war SABENA extended its network very rapidly. DC-3 aircraft were used in Europe, and they were replaced in 1950 by Convair 240s. A route to New York was opened in 1947 using DC-4s and later DC-6s, and also from Brussels to the Congo. The famous DC-7 'Seven Seas' followed in 1957. There were drastic changes for SABENA in 1960, when the state of Zaire was founded and previous routes to the Congo had to be abandoned. The first Boeing 707s were also added to the fleet in 1960 and were used for flights to the US. SE 210 Caravelles were used for the European routes, then from 1967 Boeing 727s and from 1973 Boeing 737s. The Boeing 737-200 was supplemented by the more modern Boeing 737-300 from 1987 onwards. SABENA acquired its first wide body aircraft in 1971 and 1974. Long-distance routes are today served by DC-10s and Boeing 747s. The Airbus A310-300s are used on heavily frequented routes. Sabena entered into a close partnership with Air France in 1993, resulting in Air France acquiring a 49% stake in Sabena and taking over Sabena's ordered Airbus A340s. There is a charter subsidiary, Sobelair (see page 247).

Routes

Routes from Brussels to Africa are particularly well represented, with twenty-seven destinations on offer. The network of routes extends to the Far East, to the US and to every major city in Europe.

Fleet

1 Boeing 747-100	3 Boeing 737-400
1 Boeing 747-200	6 Boeing 737-500
2 Boeing 747-300	2 DC-10-30
13 Boeing 737-200	3 Airbus A310-200/300
6 Boeing 737-300	4 de Havilland DHC-8

Photograph: Boeing 727-200ADV (Björn Kannengiesser/Miami)

SAETA

Avenida C.J. Arosemeria KM 2.5 Guayaquil
Ecuador
Tel. 203559

Three letter code	IATA No.	ICAO Callsign
SET	156	Saeta

SAETA SA-Ecuatoriana de Transportes Aereos started as a non-scheduled air carrier using DC-3s. The airline, which was founded in January 1967, entered the scheduled services business in 1969 with routes from Quito to Guayaquil, Esmeraldas and Tulcan. Two Vickers Viscounts were used, later replaced by SE 210 Caravelles in June 1975. A DHC-6 Twin Otter was used at times for short-distance routes. SAETA also started flights to neighbouring countries with a Boeing 727 delivered in 1981. Its latest aircraft is an Airbus A310-300, which came into use in 1992. In 1993 SAETA took over the routes to New York and Miami from Ecuatoriana and has applied to serve Los Angeles from Quito, its base. It also operates cargo charters to Panama, Curacao and Colombia.

Routes

Bogota, Curacao, Guayaquil, Esmeraldas, Los Angeles, Miami, New York, Panama, Quito

Fleet

2 Airbus A310-300
1 Boeing 707-300
1 Boeing 727-200ADV
2 Boeing 727-100

Photograph: Boeing 737-200 (author's collection)

SAHSA

Ave. Colon y 4a Calle, Teguciagalpa
Honduras
Tel. 2201 31234

Three letter code	IATA No.	ICAO Callsign
SHA	274	Sahsa

Honduran business people established this airline on 8th March 1945 with the support of Pan American World Airways, which held 40% of the shares. Flight operations started on 22nd October 1945 with a DC-3 on domestic routes, followed by regional air services to Guatemala. A controlling interest in TACA de Honduras was acquired in 1953 and in ANSAH in 1957. Pan American sold its SAHSA shares in 1970 to TAN. Apart from DC-3s, Convair 440s, Convair 580s, Curtiss C-46s and Lockheed L-188 Electra were used. In January 1974 SAHSA acquired its first jet aircraft, a Boeing 737. Further Boeing 737s have replaced the older propeller aircraft. It merged with TAN (Transportes Aereos Nacionales) in 1991, adopting the SAHSA name. The Honduran airline ANHSA is a subsidiary, with which it coordinates certain domestic services. Shareholders are Ingesa with 62% and TAN Airlines with 38%.

Routes

Belize, Guatemala City, Houston, La Ceila, Managua, New Orleans, Panama, San Andres, San Jose.

Fleet

4 Boeing 737-200
2 DC-3
1 Lockheed L-188 Electra

Photograph: Boeing 747-100 (author's collection)

SAUDIA

P.O. Box 620, Jeddah 21231
Saudi Arabia
Tel. 26860000

Three letter code	IATA No.	ICAO Callsign
SDI	65	Saudia

Saudia, the national carrier of the Kingdom of Saudi Arabia, was founded in late 1945 as the Saudi Arabian Airlines Corporation. Flights began on 14th March 1947 with a fleet of three DC-3s. In the early fifties, five Bristol Freighter 21s, DC-4s and Convair 340s were used. The jet age began for Saudia in April 1962 with the introduction of the Boeing 720B, and with this aircraft the airline started operating long-distance flights. This opened up routes to Cairo, Karachi and Bombay, and in 1968 to destinations in Europe with London, Rome, Geneva and Frankfurt. In 1975 Saudia acquired its first widebody aircraft, the Lockheed L-1011, and in June 1977 it also obtained Boeing 747s. Its expansion policy has always been very cautious, making Saudia the largest airline in the Arab world for years, and with about 11 million passengers Saudia is one of the world's largest international airlines. Also operated in Saudia colours and as part of their fleet are various royal household and government executive aircraft. Saudia intends to replace its entire fleet in the mid-90s; the bulk of the aircraft order intentions so far announced are to come from Beoing following strong political pressure from the United States.

Routes

Around thirty domestic destinations and another fifty abroad such as Cairo, Casablanca, Nairobi, Amsterdam, Athens, Frankfurt, Geneva, Istanbul, London, Madrid, Paris, Rome, Bangkok, Bombay, Delhi, Jakarta, Manila, Tokyo, Seoul, New York and Washington.

Fleet

2 Boeing 747SP	19 Boeing 737-200ADV
8 Boeing 747-100	11 Airbus A300-600
10 Boeing 747-300	17 Lockheed L-1011 TriStar
2 Boeing 747-200	1 McDonnell Douglas DC-8-63

Photograph: Boeing 767-300ER (Josef Krauthäuser/Bangkok)

SCANDINAVIAN-SAS

16187 Stockholm-Bromma
Sweden
Tel. 08 7970000

Three letter code	IATA No.	ICAO Callsign
SAS	117	Scandinavian

SAS-Scandinavian Airlines came into existence on 1st August 1946 after the merger of DDL (Denmark), DNL (Norway) and ABA/SLA (Sweden), all of which were formed in the early 1920s, except for DDL, formed in 1918. The realisation that these three countries could not operate flights independently meant that old plans from 1940 were revived after the war. SAS started scheduled flights on 9th September 1946, with a DC-4 from Stockholm to New York via Copenhagen. A route to Buenos Aires was opened in late 1946 and to Bangkok as early as 1949. SAS started flights to Johannesburg in 1953 for the first

time with the more powerful DC-6s. SAS's pioneering effort was to explore the polar routes to Los Angeles and Tokyo, which were opened on 15th November 1954 and 24th February 1957 respectively. In Europe, Saab Scandias and Convair 440s were used in addition to DC-3s. SAS's first jet aircraft was the SE 210 Caravelle, and the first of these was used in 1959 on the route Copenhagen-Beirut. The DC-8 followed in 1960 for intercontinental routes, replacing DC-6s and DC-7s. In early 1971 SAS acquired its first widebody aircraft, a Boeing 747. DC-10-30s and A300B4s were added to the SAS fleet in the late

seventies. Structural changes to the airline and adjustment of capacity led to the sale of the Boeing 747s and Airbus A300s in the mid-'80s. MD-80s and Boeing 767 aircraft were ordered. In 1993 the domestic airline Linjeflyg was completely taken over, and co-operation with other airlines increased. Scandinavian SAS Commuter, formed on 24th September 1989 is another subsidiary operating inter Scandinavian routes with a large fleet of Fokker 50s. SAS has interests in several other airlines, including Greenlandair, Spanair (49%) and Airlines of Britain Holdings – British Midland's parent (40%).

Routes

Dense network of routes in the countries which have a stake in the airline: Sweden, Norway and Denmark. Tokyo, Los Angeles, New York, Bangkok, Singapore, South America, Africa and destinations in Europe's most important cities.

Fleet		Ordered
36 McDonnell Douglas DC-9-21/41	11 Boeing 737-500	3 Boeing 737-500
16 McDonnell Douglas MD-87	19 Fokker F-28	2 Boeing 767-200
48 McDonnell Douglas MD-81/82/83		6 McDonnell Douglas MD-90
14 Boeing 767-300ER		
3 Boeing 737-300		

Photograph: Airbus A320-200 (Frank Schorr/Munich FJS)

SHOROUK AIR

1191 Corniche El Nil, Cairo
Egypt
Tel. 2771400

Three letter code	IATA No.	ICAO Callsign
SHK	273	Shorouk

Shorouk Air is a joint venture set up by Egypt Air and Kuwait Airways in 1992, to operate charter flights from Western Europe to Egypt, as well as scheduled flights to the Middle East. It intends to operate cargo flights for Kuwait Air using the ordered Boeing 757-200PFs. Shorouk also flies subcharter for Air Sinai and Egyptair.

Routes

Cairo, Berlin, Beirut, Düsseldorf, Frankfurt, Hamburg, Munich

Fleet

2 Airbus A320-200

Ordered

3 Airbus A320-200
2 Boeing 757-200PF
2 Boeing 757-200

Photograph: Boeing 737-300 (Björn Kannengiesser/Singapore)

SILKAIR

77, Robinson Road 01-06 SIA Buildg.
Singapore 0106, Singapore
Tel. 2212277

Three letter code	IATA No.	ICAO Callsign
SLK	629	Silkair

Tradewinds Charters was founded in October 1976 as a subsidiary of Singapore Airlines to carry out non-scheduled passenger flights. Its operations consisted of inclusive tour charters, oil-crew changes and ad-hoc charters. Some flights were operated in the region from Seletar Airport until 1988. As a charter airline it leased its aircraft from SIA when needed. Using MD-87s on scheduled flights to five destinations in Malaysia and Brunei, Tradewinds became the second scheduled airline in Singapore. In 1991 the airline was renamed Silkair. New routes were opened to Cebu, Medan, Phnom Penh and Ho Chi Minh City. Apart from scheduled flights, the airline continues to offer charter services from its base at Singapore Changi airport. It launched a scheduled service to Kunming in China on 3rd February 1993 and further new services to China and Thailand were due to start in 1994. It is planned to double the fleet by the end of the decade.

Routes

From Singapore to Kota Kinabalu, Kuala Lumpur, Cebu, Medan, Phnom Penh among others.

Fleet

4 Boeing 737-300
2 Airbus A310-200

Photograph: Boeing 747-300 (author's collection)

SINGAPORE AIRLINES

P.O. Box 501, Singapore 9181
Singapore
Tel. 5423333

Three letter code	IATA No.	ICAO Callsign
SIA	618	Singapore

Singapore Airlines was formed on 28th January 1972 as the wholly Government-owned national airline of Singapore to succeed the jointly operated Malaysia-Singapore Airlines. Operations began on 1st October 1972, when the latter, which had up to that time been operated jointly by Singapore and Malaysia, was dissolved. Boeing 707s and 737s were taken over from MSA, but soon the changeover was made to Boeing 747-200s, in 1973. Since then Singapore Airlines has been one of those airlines undergoing a particularly lively phase of expansion. An agreement with British Airways in 1977 saw the inauguration of a joint service using Concorde on the London-Bahrain-Singapore route. However, soon afterwards a ban on supersonic travel through its airspace by the Malaysian Government brought suspension of the service. It did resume again but was not a success and was finally ended in 1980. With the acquisition of further Boeing 747s, routes to Australia, New Zealand, the US and Europe were be expanded. There were daily flights to San Francisco via Honolulu as early as 1979. In 1978, DC-10s arrived and between 1978 and 1983 up to six Boeing 727s were used. 1981 saw Airbus A300s being introduced on regional services and Boeing 757s were also acquired but SIA decided to rationalise its fleet on Airbus A310s and Boeing 747s. Its first two Boeing 747-400s were delivered in December 1988 and began non-stop services between Singapore and London Heathrow in early 1989. SIAs first pure freighter entered service the same year. In November 1990 Singapore Airlines, Delta Airlines and Swissair announced a trilateral purchase of equity, each to a maximum of 5% of each others stock, with attendant commercial co-operation. Singapore regularly receives the top awards for service and quality.

Routes

Singapore Airlines serves around sixty cities in a total of thirty-seven countries from New Zealand, Australia, the USA, Japan, Korea, Philippines, China, Hong Kong, Mauritius, India, Pakistan and the Gulf region to Europe, where Frankfurt, Zürich and Vienna are served.

Fleet	Ordered
21 Boeing 747-400	2 Airbus A310-300
14 Boeing 747-300	20 Boeing 747-400
4 Boeing 747-200	7 Airbus A340-300
3 Boeing 747F	
21 Airbus A310-300	

Photograph: Boeing 737-400 (Uwe Gleisberg/Munich FJS)

SOBELAIR

131, Ave. Frans Courten, 1030 Brussels
Belgium
Tel. 022162175

Three letter code	IATA No.	ICAO Callsign
SLR	–	Sobelair

Société Belge de Transports par Air SA was established on 30th July 1946 and operations began the following year with a DC-3. The intention was to operate charter flights, mainly to the Belgian Congo, with DC-4s. In 1948 Sabena acquired a controlling interest in Sobelair. From 1957 to 1962 a domestic network of routes was set up using Cessna 310s on behalf of Sabena within the Congo to supplement the main services operated by Sabena. Apart from a DC-6, Sobelair also obtained ex-Sabena SE 210 Caravelles as its first jet aircraft. Up to 1960, the major activity had involed scheduled passenger services between Belgium and Zaire but since the early sixties, the airline has been primarily operating charter flights to popular holiday areas in the Mediterranean. After the last Boeing 707 was sold in 1988, Sobelair has used only Boeing 737s. Following Sabena's introduction of new colours, Sobelair also introduced a complementary new scheme in spring 1993.

Routes

Destinations in the Mediterranean, the Canary Islands and North Africa and other subcharters or charter flights.

Fleet

4 Boeing 737-200ADV
1 Boeing 737-300
2 Boeing 737-400

Photograph: Boeing 737-400 (Uwe Gleisberg/Cairns)

SOLOMONS

P.O. Box 23, Honiara
Solomon Islands
Tel. 30704

Three letter code	IATA No.	ICAO Callsign
SOL	193	Solomon

Solair, a subsidiary of Macair (Melanesian Airline Charter Company) was founded on 1st May 1968. This had been preceded by the takeover of Megopade Airways' routes; the latter was an airline serving the Solomon Island capital Honiara from Papua New Guinea since 1963. Solair's first flight was on 1st June 1968. In September 1975 Solair was bought by Talair, also an airline from Papua New Guinea following Talair's acquisition of Macair. It was only after some time that Solair became the property of the island administration, which acquired 49% of the shares in April 1979 and finally in 1982 and 1985 all of the Solair shares. In the mid 1980s a Brisbane service from the Solomon Islands was introduced in association with Air Pacific. The present name, Solomon Airlines, was introduced in early 1990. With a Boeing 737 now in the fleet, direct services to Nadi and Cairns started in 1993.

Routes

Auckland, Brisbane, Cairns, Honiara, Nadi, Port Moresby, as well as around twenty destinations in the Solomon Islands.

Fleet

2 Pilatus BN2-Islander
1 de Havilland DHC-6-300
1 Piper Aztec
1 Boeing 737-400

Photograph: Boeing 747-200 (Uwe Gleisberg/Munich FJS)

SOUTH AFRICAN AIRWAYS

39, Wolmarans Street, Johannesburg
2000, Transvaal, Republic of South Africa
Tel. 11713 2600

Three letter code	IATA No.	ICAO Callsign
SAA	83	Springbrook

South African Airways was founded on 1st February 1934, when Union Airways passed into government ownership and became a subsidiary of South African Railways. Operations started the same day with a fleet of single-engined Junkers F-13s, later supplemented by a large number of Ju 52s and Ju 86s. Numerous routes were operated, including to Nairobi, until the outbreak of the Second World War. South West African Airways had been acquired in February 1935 and gave SAA an extensive network of regional services. November 1945 saw the start of the 'Springbok' service to London,

using DC-4s, DC-7s and Lockheed Constellations. The latter were used by SAA to open a route to Perth in Australia in November 1957. When the Boeing 707 was introduced in October, 1960, this route was extended to Sydney, and a further long-distance route to Rio de Janeiro was opened in 1969. SAA has had to restrict its routes to a few European routes for political reasons: many African states withdrew its flyover rights. In order to be able to operate direct flights, Boeing 747SPs and later Boeing 747-300s with extreme ranges were ordered. Airbus A300s and Boeing 737s were ordered to expand the

regional and domestic service, replacing the Vickers Viscounts and older aircraft. After the independence of Namibia and South Africa's adopting a conciliatory political course, SAA is now obtaining more scheduled flights rights again in Africa. In 1992 SAL/SAA flew weekly to Munich, and this was raised to two flights in 1993. There are also new flights to Hamburg. Russian aircraft are being acquired for the first time, IL-76s, for cargo flights. SAA has also acquired a 20% stake in the new feeder airline South African Express.

Routes

Abidjan, Amsterdam, Hong Kong, Hamburg, Lisbon, London, Manchester, Munich, Paris, Port Louis, Rio de Janeiro, Rome, Taipei, Tel Aviv, Vienna, Zürich. Regional flights to around fifteen destinations in southern Africa.

Fleet

17 Boeing 737-200	6 Boeing 747-200
8 Airbus A300B4	2 Boeing 747-300
3 Boeing 747SP	4 Boeing 747-400
4 Ilyushin IL-76	7 Airbus A320-200

Photograph: Boeing 737-300 (author's collection)

SOUTHWEST AIRLINES

P.O. Box 37611 Love Field, Dallas
Texas 75235, USA
Tel. 214 902 1100

Three letter code	IATA No.	ICAO Callsign
SWA	526	Southwest

The airline first appeared on 15th March 1967 under the name of Air Southwest, but it took some time until flight operations could start. The established airlines tried their utmost to prevent the troublesome newcomer from flying, as the airline intended to set up a 'one-class service' with particularly low fares. A major legal controversy for many years involved Southwest's use of Love Field airport in Dallas. Other airlines and some municipal officials made attempts to force the carrier to shift operations to more distant Dallas-Fort Worth Regional Airport, which was then a small airport. In March 1971 the airline's name was changed to Southwest Airlines and in June 1971 Southwest flew for the first time from Dallas to Houston and San Antonio. After deregulation in the US, Southwest's fortunes soared. The airline bought Muse Air on 25th June 1985 and it was renamed TranStar airlines on 17th February 1986 but operations of this subsidiary stopped on 1st July 1987 due to mounting losses. The cost-conscious airline is considered to be one of the winners of this deregulation having expanded from its initial services within the state of Texas only, to cover a wide part of the continental USA. Using a homogeneous fleet of Boeing 737s, more and more passengers have been flown to an increasing number of destinations in the US every year. Its base is Love Field airport in Dallas, Texas. Utah-based Morris Air was acquired in December 1993, and is planned to be integrated into Southwest in 1995. The aircraft illustrated is in a non-standard 'whale' colour scheme, promoting Sea World. The normal colour scheme is that still showing on the tail fin.

Routes

To over thirty destinations, mainly in the southwest of the US such as Austin, Dallas, Houston, Las Vegas, San Francisco, Los Angeles, San Antonio, San Diego, Tulsa.

Fleet	Ordered
43 Boeing 737-200	47 Boeing 737-300
80 Boeing 737-300	
25 Boeing 737-500	

Photograph: McDonnell Douglas MD-83 (Björn Kannengiesser/Salzburg)

SPANAIR

Airport P.O. Box 50086 Palma de Mallorca
07000, Spain
Tel. 71 492012

Three letter code	IATA No.	ICAO Callsign
SPP	–	Sunwing

The tour operators Vingresor AB and Scandinavia & Viajes Marsono SA founded their own charter airline by the name of Spanair in 1987. The airline is based on the holiday island of Majorca. Operations commenced during March 1988 and a fleet of new MD-83s were leased from Irish Aerospace and Guinness Peat Aviation and are used mainly to fly Scandinavian holidaymakers to the sunny beaches of Spain. Spanair also flies from German airports, and from Zürich and Salzburg. The first revenue flight took place on 1st June, 1988 from Palma to Bilbao. When Boeing 767-300ERs were acquired in 1992 flights were also operated to destinations in the USA, Mexico and the Caribbean. In 1993 Spanair carried 2 million passengers for the first time. SAS, through its subsidiary, SAS Leisure has a 49% holding in Spanair but its stake could be sold in 1994 if a buyer for loss-making SAS Leisure is found.

Routes

Charter flights from North and Central Europe to Spain, the Balearic Islands and the Canary Islands. From Spain to New York, Orlando, Cancun, Puerto Plata, Punta Cona, Montevideo.

Fleet

9 McDonnell Douglas MD-83
2 Boeing 767-300ER

Photograph: Fokker 50 (author's collection)

SUDAN AIRWAYS

P.O. Box 253, Khartoum
Sudan
Tel. 74133

Three letter code	IATA No.	ICAO Callsign
SUD	200	Sudanair

Sudan Airways was founded in February 1946 by the Sudanese government as a subsidiary of Sudan Railways System and a contract was signed for technical and flying assistance from the British company Airwork. Domestic service began in July 1947 with a fleet of four de Havilland Doves. In November 1954, the first foreign connection was the route to Cairo, which was served using DC-3s. On 8th June 1959 a scheduled service was opened via Cairo-Athens-Rome to London using Vickers Viscounts, and Comet 4Cs from 1962 onwards. The first Fokker F-27 was delivered in January 1962 and the first de Havilland Comet on 13th November 1962. The second jet generation was introduced in 1972 in the form of the Boeing 707, which was used for regular flights to Europe. For domestic services mainly F-27s were used, replaced in spring 1990 by the modern Fokker 50s. New aircraft in Sudan's fleet introduced in 1992/93 are the Airbus A310 and A320.

Routes

Abu Dhabi, Athens, Baghdad, Bahrain, Bangkok, Belgrade, Bombay, Brussels, Damascus, Dharan, Dubai, Istanbul, Cairo, Jakarta, Jeddah, London, Ndjamena, Nyala, Port Sudan, Tripoli.

Fleet

6 Boeing 707-300
2 Boeing 737-200
2 Fokker 50
3 de Havilland DHC-6

1 Airbus A310-300
1 Airbus A320-200

Photograph: Boeing 737-300 (Uwe Gleisberg/Munich FJS)

SUN EXPRESS

Falez Hotel, Konyaalti Merkii, 07050 Antalya
Turkey
Tel. 473858

Three letter code	IATA No.	ICAO Callsign
SXS	–	Sunexpress

On 11th September 1989 Lutfhansa (40% of the shares), Turkish Airlines (40% of the shares) and Turkish investors (20%) established the airline Sun Express with headquarters in Antalya. Flight operations started with a leased Boeing 737-300 on 4th April 1990. Its first flight was from Nuremberg to Antalya. Two further Boeing 737-300s were acquired in 1991; also, additional aircraft are leased from Lufthansa when needed. For the first time after two years of getting the airline started and of making losses, a profit was made in 1992/93.

Routes

Brisk charter services from airports in Germany, Austria, Switzerland, England and other Western European countries to Izmir, Antalya and other Turkish destinations.

Fleet

3 Boeing 737-300
1 Boeing 737-400

Photograph: McDonnell Douglas MD-11 (B.I. Hengi/Zürich)

SWISSAIR

Postfach CH-8058 Zürich Airport
Switzerland
Tel. 1 812 1212

Three letter code	IATA No.	ICAO Callsign
SWR	85	Swissair

On 26th March 1931 Basler Luftverkehr (Balair) and Ad Astra Aero AG merged to form Schweizerischer Luftverkehrs AG. Balair had begun operations in 1926 with a Zürich-Berlin service but Ad Astra had been founded in September 1919 and began Savoia flying boat operations between the Swiss lakes. The company called itself Swissair and continued the routes of its predecessors. It used Fokker F VIIbs and the famous Lockheed Orion on the route Zürich-Munich from 1932 and Curtiss Condors were acquired in 1934. In 1935 Swissair acquired Douglas DC-2s and DC-3s in 1937, which were used on the route to London. Post-war services resumed on 30th July 1945 with DC-3s as the mainstay of the fleet, but DC-4s arrived in 1947 and transatlantic services started in 1949. Convair 240s were added to the fleet in 1949, with Convair 440s later. Alpair Bern was taken over in 1947 and from then on Swissair was the official carrier of Switzerland. DC-6Bs and DC-7s were the last propeller aircraft before Caravelles and DC-8s were introduced in 1960. Convair 990 Coronados were used for flights to the Far East from September 1961. The first DC-9 was delivered on 20th July 1966 and eventually replaced the Caravelles. Swissair's first jumbo jet was a Boeing 747 in January 1971, followed by the DC-10 a year later. Airbus A310s were also added to the fleet – Swissair was a launch customer in 1978 – and the fleet is now in the process of being replaced. The first MD-11s were acquired in early 1991. Swissair regularly carries more passengers worldwide than Swizerland has inhabitants. In 1993 around 8 million passengers flew with Swissair. Swissair has controlling interests in Crossair and Balair CTA, and further shares in Austrian and Delta Airlines.

Routes

Swissair flies from Zürich, Geneva and Basle to the USA, Canada, South America, Africa, the Middle East and Far East. All the important cities in Europe are served daily, in some cases several times daily.

Fleet

		Ordered
10 Fokker 100	5 Boeing 747-300	1 McDonnell Douglas MD-11
25 McDonnell Douglas MD-81/82		5 Airbus A319
10 Airbus A310-200/300		16 Airbus A320
12 McDonnell Douglas MD-11		8 Airbus A321

Photograph: Boeing 747SP (Josef Krauthäuser/Munich-Riem)

SYRIANAIR

P.O. Box 417, Damascus
Syria
Tel. 220700

Three letter code	IATA No.	ICAO Callsign
SYR	70	Syrianair

The airline was founded in October 1961 by the Syrian government, after its predecessor Syrian Airways (founded on 21st December 1946) had formed United Arab Airlines with Misrair. However, this union only held for less than two years. Egyptian carrier Misrair had been renamed UAA in February 1958 and Syrian Airways merged with it on 23rd December 1958. After the break with Egypt, Syrian Arab Airlines, to give the airline its full name, took back its fleet and routes from UAA. Syrian Airways had operated domestic and regional routes from Damascus; Syrian Arab inherited these and started operating into Europe with DC-6Bs, serving Paris and London from 1964 and also flying east to Karachi and Delhi. Depending on the political orientation of the particular government, both Western aircraft and Soviet-built aircraft are used. SE 210 Caravelles were introduced in 1965, and Boeing 747SPs in 1976. The first Boeing 727 was delivered in March 1976 to supplement Caravelle services. In the early 1980s Tu-134s were acquired followed by Tu-154s and they have provided good service for some ten years.

Routes

From Damascus there are services in Syria to Aleppo, Latika, Kameschii. Internationally, the airline's network extends from Delhi through various destinations in the Middle East and North Africa to Europe with services to Munich, Frankfurt, Berlin-Schönefeld, Moscow, Rome, Prague, Copenhagen and Paris.

Fleet

6 Yakovlev Yak-40
1 Antonov An-24
5 Antonov An-26
6 Tupolev Tu-134B
3 Tupolev Tu-154M

4 Ilyushin IL-76M
2 SE 210 Caravelle 10B
2 Boeing 747SP
3 Boeing 727-200ADV

Photograph: Lockheed L-1011-500 TriStar

TAAG ANGOLA AIRLINES

R. da Missao, C P 3010 Luanda
People's Republic of Angola
Tel. 2332990

Three letter code	IATA No.	ICAO Callsign
DTA	118	DTA

Direccao de Exploracao dos Transportes Aereos (DTA – Angola Airlines) was established by order of the Portuguese government in September 1938. Flight operations could only begin in 1940, as the infrastructure was completely lacking. With an initial fleet of three de Havilland Dragon Rapides, scheduled services were started on 17th July 1940 on domestic routes and also on an international route between Luanda and Pointe Noire in the Congo Republic (then French Equatorial Africa), where connections were available to various European destinations. In that year the airline's name was changed to DTA-Linhas Aereas de Angola and remained unchanged until 1973. For political reasons flight operations were suspended between 1973 and the country's independence from Portugal in November 1975, with a few exceptions. When the airline was renamed TAAG – Linhas Aereas de Angola, it became the flag carrier of the new people's republic. Boeing 707s and 737s were acquired in the late 1970s/early 1980s and were the types used on its longer routes with Fokker F-27s used on domestic services. Around a million passengers a year are carried.

Routes

From Luanda to Berlin-Schönefeld, Bissau, Brazzaville, Sal, Kinshasa, Lisbon, Lusaka, Maputo, Paris, Moscow, Rio de Janeiro, Rome, Havana. TAAG also operates regional flights in Angola.

Fleet

1 Lockheed L-1011 TriStar
2 Ilyushin IL-62M
3 Boeing 707
5 Boeing 737-200ADV

6 Fokker F-27
2 Yakovlev 40
1 Pilatus Britten-Norman 2A Islander

Photograph: Boeing 737-300 (author's collection)

TACA

Edifico Garibe 2 Piso San Salvador
El Salvador
Tel. 232244

Three letter code	IATA No.	ICAO Callsign
TAI	202	Taca

TACA International Airlines was founded in November 1939 in El Salvador as TACA El Salvador, at that time as a division of TACA-Airways SA, a multinational organisation comparable to the present-day Air Europe, operations began on the Salvador-Tegucigalpa-Managua-San Jose trunk route. In 1942 flights started for the first time with DC-3s to Bilbao in the Panama Canal zone, and a year later to Havana. TACA International succeeded TACA El Salvador in 1950, and acquired all remaining assets of the origianl TACA Corporation in 1960. The airline also made use of DC-4s, Vickers Viscounts and DC-6s until the first jet aircraft, a BAC 1-11 was taken into service in 1966. Twenty years later TACA acquired its first widebody aircraft, a Boeing 767. In 1992 around half a million passengers were carried with TACA. TACA International is privately owned and the only surviving member of the once all-powerful TACA air transport system in Central America. The well-known airline pioneer, Lowell Yerex had formed TACA originally in Honduras in 1931.

Routes

From San Salvador to Belize, Guatemala, Houston, Los Angeles, Mexico City, Miami, Montego Bay, New Orleans, Panama, San Francisco, San Jose and Tegucigalpa.

Fleet	Ordered
4 Boeing 737-300	1 Boeing 767-200ER
4 Boeing 737-200	1 Boeing 767-300ER
1 Boeing 767-200	

Photograph: Fokker F-27 (author's collection)

TAM

Rue Monsenhor Antonio Pepe 94
CEP 04357 Sao Paulo, Brazil
Tel. 11 5777711

Three letter code	IATA No.	ICAO Callsign
TAM	877	TAM

TAM is Brazil's principal third-level airline, set up by VASP Brasilian Airlines and Taxi Aereo Marilia on 12th May 1976 to operate scheduled services in the interior of Sao Paulo State. Operations began on 12th July 1976 and 'domestic' routes have been added within the state and to other states of Brazil using Fokker F-27s from the start. For less frequented routes, aircraft built in Brazil are used, Embraer 110 Bandeirantes. In October 1990 the first jet aircraft, Fokker 100s, were put into service. The airline intends to continue to expand with a mixed fleet composed of Fokker 100s and F-27s. TAM is based at Congonhas airport in Sao Paulo from where it operates a shuttle service to Rio de Janeiro, in competition with the Air Bridge Shuttle operated in pool with Varig, Cruzeiro do Sul, VASP and Transbrasil. TAM is owned by VASP (23%) and Taxi Aereo Marilia (77%).

Routes

Dense domestic network from Sao Paolo to Brasilia, Merilla, Porta Pora, Rio de Janeiro, Belo Horizonte and Asuncion.

Fleet

4 Embraer 110C Bandeirante
8 Fokker F-27
12 Fokker 100

Photograph: Lockheed L-1011 TriStar (Björn Kannengiesser/Rio de Janeiro)

TAP AIR PORTUGAL

Edifico 225, Aeroporto Lisboa 1704 Lisboa
Portugal
Tel. 01 8470250

Three letter code	IATA No.	ICAO Callsign
TAP	47	Air Portugal

Transportes Aereos Portugueses-TAP was established on 14th March 1945 by the Portuguese government. Flight operations began on 19th September 1946 with a converted C-47 (DC-3) from Lisbon to Madrid and Casablanca was served by a Lockheed L-18 Lodestar. Routes were also opened to Luanda and Laurenco Marques in Mozambique on 31st December 1946, followed in 1947 by London and Paris. All these flights were operated using DC-4s. TAP became a joint-stock company, partly with private shareholders, on 1st June 1953. From then until the Portugeuse Government

nationalised it on 15th April 1975, TAP was privately controlled (80% private and 20% government holdings). A 1953 merger combined TAP and Aero Portuguesa (a carrier established in 1934). Lockheed L-1049 Constellations were used for long-distance routes. A South American service to New York started in 1966. When Caravelles were commissioned in 1962, followed by Boeing 707s in 1966 as well as Boeing 727s a year later, this provided TAP with a completely jet fleet. In 1972 TAP obtained its first widebody aircraft, a Boeing 747. The confusion of the revolution in Portugal brought flights partly to a

standstill in 1975, and it was only in 1977, after reorganisation, that it was possible to operate flights to their full extent. In 1975 the airline's aircraft were given their present colours, the TAP logo also being altered. Its present name was adopted in 1979. Two new aircraft were integrated in 1984, the Lockheed L-1011 for long-distance routes and the Boeing 737 for short and medium-distance routes. The first Airbus A320-200s arrived in 1992 and the TriStars will be taken out of service in 1994/95. TAP has a 30% stake in the Portuguese regional airline LAR (Linhas Aereas Regionais).

Routes

TAP serves around ten domestic destinations as well as destinations in Africa, South America and the US; plus extensive services to major destinations in Europe.

Fleet	Ordered
7 Lockheed L-1011-500 TriStar	4 Airbus A340-200
13 Boeing 737-300	
10 Boeing 737-200	
5 Airbus A310-300	
6 Airbus A320-200	

Photograph: Boeing 737-300 (Boeing via Kauders/Seattle)

TAROM

Otopeni Airport Bucharest
Romania
Tel. 333127

Three letter code	IATA No.	ICAO Callsign
ROT	281	Tarom

Transporturi Aeriene Romana Sovietica (TARS) was established as a Romanian-Soviet airline in 1946 to succeed the pre-war state airline LARES. Operations began with a fleet of Lisunov Li-2s provided by its Russian partner.The Romanian state acquired the shares in 1954 and it was renamed TAROM (Transporturile Aeriene Romane). TAROM flew IL-14s from 1958 to destinations in Eastern and Western Europe and the first IL-18s were placed in service in 1963. In 1968 TAROM acquired its first BAC 1-11 (they were later built in Romania under licence). IL-62s and Boeing 707s were commissioned in 1973 and 1974, and the Boeing 707s were used to open a route to New York. The IL-62s allowed extension of services to Africa and the Far East. TAROM flies both charter and scheduled flights and carried 1.2 million passengers in 1993. Boeing delivered the first 737-300 in late 1993. The intention is to bring the entire fleet up to 'Western' standard by the mid-90s. LAR-Liniile Aeriene Romane was formed in 1975 as the charter subsidiary of TAROM using BAC 1-11s. It was re-formed n 1991 as a joint-stock company, one third owned by the Romanian Government. Its fleet is leased from TAROM as required.

Routes

Beijing, New York, Abu Dhabi, Karachi, Athens, Cairo, Tel Aviv, Rome, Vienna, Zürich, Frankfurt, Düsseldorf, Berlin, Amsterdam, Copenhagen, Paris, London, Madrid, Lisbon, Casablanca, Prague, Warsaw, Moscow, Tirana.

Fleet

3 Ilyushin IL-62M
3 Boeing 707
8 Tupolev 154 B
14 Rombac/BAe BAC 1-11
2 Boeing 737-300

4 Ilyushin IL-18
18 Antonov An-24
2 Airbus A310-300

Ordered

3 Boeing 737-300
1 Airbus A310-300

Photograph: ATR-42 (author's collection)

TAT

BP 0237, 37002 Tours Cedex
France
Tel. 47423000

Three letter code	IATA No.	ICAO Callsign
TAT	–	TAT

Founded in 1968 as Touraine Air Transport, the company grew from a local taxi service into an important French regional airline maintaining regular scheduled services throughout mainland France and to Corsica. It began scheduled operations in March 1969 with a Tours-Lyon service. Over the years various companies such as Air Alpes, Air Alsace, Taxi Avia France, Air Paris and Air Languedoc were taken over. Over the years, the airline has entered into contract with Air France to provide feeder services for the national airline. A subsidiary, TAT Export, created in 1984 to undertake international charters and a scheduled service was operated between West Berlin and Saarbrucken. Transport Aérien Transregional, as the airline was subsequently called, has a mixed fleet for the various tasks, but the intention is to standardise the fleet in the long term. In 1990 over 2.5 million passengers were carried, and a new colour scheme introduced. However, another important change in its colour scheme came with British Airways taking a 49.9% stake in the carrier in January, 1993 and the aircraft now have a BA/TAT livery. British Airways has an option to buy the remaining shares before 1997. From March 1993 new scheduled service expansion started and in June 1994 it was to launch services between London Heathrow and Paris Orly, following the resolution of an international dispute regarding access by 'foreign' airlines to Paris' second airport.

Routes

Charter flights to forty national and ten international destinations, some of them on behalf of other airlines. Charter flights.

Fleet

		Ordered
12 ATR-42	2 Embraer Brasilia	6 ATR-72
8 ATR-72	14 Fokker 100	4 Fokker 100
5 Boeing 737-200	5 Beech KingAir 200	
7 Fairchild FH-227	1 Beech 1900	
22 Fokker F 28		

Photograph: Boeing 737-300 (author's collection)

TEA-BASEL

Postfach 238, 4030 Basle
Switzerland
Tel. 061 3253348

Three letter code	IATA No.	ICAO Callsign
TSW	–	Topswiss

The main and original Trans European Airways – TEA was formed on 6th December 1970 as a Belgian charter airline and flights started on 2nd June 1971. Within the combine of the trans-European TEA airline, a Swiss operation was established in May 1988 with its headquarters in Basle. New Boeing 737-300s were delivered in March 1989 and were used for the first flight on 23rd March 1989. One aircraft was leased to Australia from November 1989 to mid-March, so that the first operating year ended without loss as 20,000 passengers flew with the new airline. TEA (UK) was another company formed by the TEA but TEA failed and so did TEA UK. TEA (France) is another company, with no connection with TEA-Basel; this began operations in October 1989. In 1993 the airline made a profit for the first time. TEA-Basel established a subsidiary on Cyprus, and also established TEA-Hellas. During the winter some aircraft are leased out.

Routes

To twenty-five destinations in the Mediterranean and to Mombasa.

Fleet	Ordered
5 Boeing 737-300	1 Boeing 737-300

Photograph: Boeing 747-400 (Josef Krauthäuser/Bangkok)

THAI AIRWAYS INTERNATIONAL

89 Vibhavachi Rangit Road
Bangkok 10900, Thailand
Tel. 02 5130121

Three letter code	IATA No.	ICAO Callsign
THA	217	Thainter

Thai Airways was able to look back in May 1990 on thirty years of flight operations. The airline was established on 24th August 1959 as a joint venture between SAS and the Thai Airways Company, which operated regionally to take over Thai Airways international routes. Thai had a 70% stake and SAS 30%. Flight operations started to neighbouring countries, to Hong Kong and Tokyo, using DC-6Bs. As early as 1963 the airline changed over to jet aircraft, to Caravelles, and in 1969 it changed to DC-9-41s. When four-engined DC-8-33s arrived, Thai expanded its network

to Australia in April 1971, and then to Copenhagen starting in June 1972. A route to Frankfurt was opened in 1973. In May 1975, when a DC-10-30 was delivered, Thai also introduced a new colour scheme. Thai has been in state ownership since April 1977 after SAS gave up their 15% shareholding to the Thai Government on 31st March, the fleet is being continually expanded, with Airbus A300s and Boeing 747s being brought in to the fleet in 1975 and 1979 respectively. The United States was served from April 1980. New destinations in the US have been added. On 1st April 1988 Thai

International and Thai Airways merged in preparation for the privatisation of the airline. Thai Airways had originally been formed on 1st November 1951 by the merger of Siamese Airways and Pacific Overseas Airlines (Siam). By taking over Thai Airways, Thai International somewhat surprisingly had taken over the airline of which it was once a subsidiary. Thai is one of the world's largest operators of the Airbus A300/310 which are used on regional routes. More are due in the mid 1990s.

Routes

Today, Thai serves destinations on four continents with destinations such as Seattle, Dallas, Sydney, Melbourne, Perth, Brisbane, Vienna, Zürich, Düsseldorf, Frankfurt, Seoul, Tokyo, Hong Kong, Amsterdam, Paris, Rome, Copenhagen, Stockholm and others. There is an extensive domestic network.

Fleet

		Ordered
3 Boeing 737-200ADV	16 Airbus A300-600	8 Airbus A330-300
7 Boeing 737-400	6 Boeing 747-200	5 Airbus A300-600
2 Airbus A310-200	2 Boeing 747-300	8 Boeing 777-200
1 Airbus A310-300	7 Boeing 747-400	6 Boeing 747-400
4 McDonnell Douglas MD-11	2 ATR 42	
12 Airbus A300B4	2 ATR 72	

Photograph: Ilyushin IL-18 (Gottfried Auer/Salzburg)

THE BERLINE

Postfach 145, 10251 Berlin
Germany
Tel. 030 67872113

Three letter code	IATA No.	ICAO Callsign
TBL	–	Beroliner

The Berline, Berlin-Branden-burgisches Luftfahrtunternehmen GmbH, was founded on 1st November 1991. Five Ilyushin IL-18 turboprop aircraft were acquired from the stocks of the former East German state airline Interflug, which had been wound up after German reunification. Two of these aircraft were converted into freighters and provided with a cargo door at the side. Since February 1993 the airline also used Fokker 100s. It offered ad hoc charter and passenger flights from its base airport, Berlin-Schönefeld, and carried over 60,000 passengers in the first year of operation, but lack of capital backing for further expansion resulted in the airline ceasing operations at the end of march 1994.

Routes

Athens, Berlin, Dresden, Erfurt, Düsseldorf, Nuremberg, Palma de Mallorca, Saloniki, Ibiza and further destinations in the Mediterranean, as well as to England and France.

Fleet

4 Ilyushin IL-18
3 Fokker 100

Photograph: Airbus A340-300 (André Dietzel/Munich FJS)

THY-TURKISH AIRLINES

Attatürk Hava Limani, Yesilköy
Istanbul, Turkey
Tel. 1 5747300

Three letter code	IATA No.	ICAO Callsign
THY	235	Turkair

THY resulted from Turkiye Devlet Hava Yollari (DHY – Turkish State Airlines), founded on 20th May 1933, when the state took over the latter in February 1956. The airline then adopted its present name and became a joint state and privately owned operation with a fleet of DC-3s and de Havilland Herons. THY acquired its first Vickers Viscount on 21st January 1958 and together with Fokker F-27s operated local services and international flights to Nicosia and Rome. In 1960 flights started to the first destinations in Western Europe, including Frankfurt. In August 1967 DC-9s were commissioned, and on

1st December 1972 the airline's first large-capacity aircraft, a DC-10. F-27s and F-28s were used for regional services. Boeing 727-200s were acquired in 1974, as was the first Airbus A310. THY set up Kibris Turk Hava Yollari (Cyprus Turkish Airlines) as a subsidiary on 4th December 1974 and scheduled services began in February 1975. It has a fleet of three Boeing 727s and uses THY's aircraft as well for flights from Ercan in Cyprus to Turkey. For a long time THY concentrated more on expanding its domestic routes than on international routes. It was only in the late 70s that the international routes were expanded

with the inclusion of connections to the most important European centres. This was due to the large number of immigrant workers who had settled all over Europe. The first destination overseas was New York, in 1990, using Airbus A310s. In that same year THY took a new colour scheme for its aircraft. The capacity of the fleet was increased, with the first Airbus A340s and further Boeings being added in 1993. Domestic subsidiary airline THT was fully merged into THY in 1993. The Turkish Government now owns 99% of THY's shares.

Routes

More than thirty domestic routes. New York, Tokyo, Bangkok, Kuala Lumpur, Singapore, Bombay, Delhi, Algiers, Tunisia, Tripoli, Cairo, almost all German airports, Vienna, Zürich and further destinations in Europe and the Middle East.

Fleet		Ordered
9 McDonnell Douglas DC-9-32	14 Airbus A310-200/300	6 Boeing 737-400
10 Boeing 727-200ADV	2 Airbus -A340-300	1 Boeing 737-500
2 Boeing 737-500	2 BAe RJ100	3 Airbus A340-300
15 Boeing 737-400		

Photograph: Boeing 707-320C (Josef Krauthäuser/Frankfurt)

TMA OF LEBANON

P.O. Box 11-3018 Beirut International Airport,
Beirut, Lebanon
Tel. 1 831433

Three letter code	IATA No.	ICAO Callsign
TMA	270	Tango Lima

Trans-Mediterranean Airways SAL was founded in 1953 in order to operate cargo flights, mainly for oil companies. Two Avro York aircraft were employed. When TMA acquired its first Douglas DC-4 in 1959, it opened a scheduled route to Teheran and Frankfurt. TMA was certified by the Lebanese Government on 12th February 1959 for the carriage of freight on scheduled services. Large aircraft, DC-6s, were acquired from 1963 on. Capacity was further expanded with the acquisition in 1966 of a Boeing 707 leased from Trans World Airlines. On 14th April 1971 TMA inuagurated the first round-the-

world cargo service from Beirut eastwards and back to Beirut. Scheduled services were extended to Tokyo. Two Boeing 747s were bought and converted to cargo aircraft. These jumbo aircraft were first used in 1974. The continuing political tensions in the Middle East also led to losses over the years: two DC-6s were blown up by Israeli commando units and a Boeing 707 was destroyed in 1982 by a bomb. Apart from cargo, TMA also flies subcharters for other airlines and uses its aircraft for pilgrimage flights to Mecca.

Routes

Charter flights to Europe, the US, Middle East and Far East.

Fleet

7 Boeing 707-320C

Photograph: BAe 146 QT (Martin Bach/Munich FJS)

TNT EXPRESS

Archway House 114-116 St. Leonards, Windsor, Berkshire, SL4 3DG, United Kingdom
Tel. 0753 842168

Three letter code	IATA No.	ICAO Callsign
TNT	–	Nitro

TNT, which originated in Australia, is one of the largest cargo organisations in the world. TNT Express Worldwide is part of the TNT Group which began operations in 1968 TNT came to Europe in 1984 and in 1987 the European airfreight system was established and a special version of the BAe 146, the QT (or 'quiet trader'), was ordered. This particularly quiet aircraft is not subject to night-flight restrictions and can therefore be used on overnight flights. TNT does not operate its own aircraft but charters them to partners such as Air Foyle, Euralair, Malev, City Air, Mistral Air, Eurowings, Pan Air and Pacific East Asian Cargo. The cargoes are flown in a star-shaped pattern from around forty European cities to the central hub at Cologne/Bonn. There the freight is distributed, transferred, and sorted, when the aircraft then leave the hub again. All this takes place at night-time. A DC-8 is operated on weekdays between Cologne and New York. A further hub was established in Manila in 1993 covering the Far East region, in conjuction with Pacific East Asia Cargo Airlines (formerly Air Philippines).

Routes

Around forty destinations in Europe, Singapore, Taipei, Manila, Brunei, New York.

Fleet

2 Cessna Citation II
21 BAe 146-200/300 QT
1 McDonnell Douglas DC-8-73F

Photograph: Boeing 747-100 (Uwe Gleisberg/Munich FJS)

TOWER AIR

Hangar B, JFK International Airport, Jamaica,
New York 11430, USA
Tel. 718 5534300

Three letter code	IATA No.	ICAO Callsign
TOW	305	Tee Air

Tower Air was founded as a pure charter airline in August 1982. Flights were marketed to Europe and Israel without the airline possessing its own aircraft; the flights were carried out by Metro International Airways on Tower Air's behalf. By Spring 1983, Tower became the general sales agent for Metro International's scheduled services and on 1st November 1983 Tower Air took over from Metro on the New York-Brussels-Tel Aviv route with its only Boeing 747. One year later, the airline entered the domestic American scheduled business as a 'low fare operator'. It entered competition with PeoplExpress with flights between New York and Los Angeles, but with little success, and so these loss-making schedules were discontinued in 1984. Two more Boeing 747s were delivered in 1985 and a fourth in 1988. In the rest of the 1980s charters were flown between the USA and a number of European destinations and scheduled flights were added from New York to Oslo and Stockholm. Special contract charters for the US Military Airlift Command have also been flown on a regular basis. In 1992 scheduled flights to Berlin were offered for the first time.

Routes

Athens, Berlin, Buenos Aires, Hong Kong, Los Angeles, Miami, New York, Paris, Rome, Sao Paulo, San Juan, Taipei are served regularly.

Fleet

10 Boeing 747-100

Photograph: Boeing 737-200 (author's collection)

TRANSAERO

2 Smolensky Pereulok 3/4, 121099 Moscow
Russia
Tel. 095 2411190

Three letter code	IATA No.	ICAO Callsign
TSO	670	Transaero

Transaero was founded in late 1991 as one of the first private joint-stock companies in Russia and the first non-Aeroflot company approved for scheduled passenger services in Russia. The shareholders are Aeroflot and aircraft manufacturers Ilyushin and Yakovlev. Flight operations commenced in early 1992 with Tu-154s. Thousands of emigrants were flown from Russia to Israel in a spectacular action which caught the media's attention and gave the airline publicity. Two Boeing 737-200s were leased in late 1992 and two IL-86 acquired, as well as IL-76s for cargo flights. Additional aircraft are leased from Aeroflot when needed. In November 1993, Transaero launched its first international route between Moscow and Tel Aviv. It has been approved to begin non-stop services from Moscow to six US cities in 1994 and fleet expansion is to take place using several Boeing types.

Routes

Moscow, Kiev, Sochi, Surgut, Norilsk, and also charter flights to Antalya, Dubai, Istanbul, Sharjah, Varna.

Fleet	Ordered
2 Boeing 737-200	1 Boeing 757
1 Boeing 757	3 Boeing 737-200
1 Ilyushin IL-76 M	4 Boeing 767-300ER
2 Ilyushin IL-86	

Photograph: ATR-72 (Patrick Lutz/Hamburg)

TRANS ASIA AIRWAYS

139 Cheng Chou Road, Taipei
Republic of China
Tel. 2 715 2766

Three letter code	IATA No.	ICAO Callsign
TNA	170	Foshing

Founded in 1951 as Foshing Airlines, this airline experienced more downs than ups and returned its licence in 1965. It was then reactivated in 1990 and since then it has made rapid progress. It was renamed Trans Asia Airways in 1992 in order to better reflect the airline's ambitions with regard to an international network of routes. Its first jet aircraft was an A320, which was delivered in August 1992. The airline also opened international routes to Cambodia and the Philippines in 1992. It is the first Asian customer airline for the Airbus A321, the first to be delivered in July 1995.

Routes

In Taiwan and to Phnom Penh as well as Manila.

Fleet

5 ATR-42
13 ATR-72
2 Airbus A320-200

Ordered

3 ATR-72
4 Airbus A300-600
2 Airbus A321

Photograph: Boeing 737-200ADV (Uwe Gleisberg/Munich FJS)

TRANSAVIA

Postbus 7777, 1118 ZM Schiphol
The Netherlands
Tel. 020-6046518

Three letter code	IATA No.	ICAO Callsign
TRA	979	Transavia

Transavia Airline, was formed as Transavia Limburg in 1965 and changed its name to Transavia Holland in 1967 and to Transavia Airlines in 1986, has been operating flights since 16th November 1966 when it operated a charter service to Naples. Initially, flights to the Mediterranean were offered with DC-6s. The airline acquired its first jet aircraft, a Boeing 707, followed by an SE-210 Caravelle, as early as 1969; this aircraft was replaced by the Boeing 737 in 1974 as the airline operated a large share of the Dutch market in holiday flights. Transavia introduced a scheduled service from Amsterdam to London on 26th October 1986; otherwise, the airline operates charters and provides aircraft leasing. In 1993 around 1.4 million passengers flew with Transavia. Transavia is a subsidiary of KLM which, since 1991 has an 80% shareholding and its base is Amsterdam-Schiphol.

Routes

Scheduled flights Amsterdam-London Gatwick and to Mediterrenean destinations. Charter flights to the Mediterranean, North Africa, the Canary Islands, also to the Alpine regions in winter.

Fleet	Ordered
6 Boeing 737-200ADV	4 Boeing 757-200
8 Boeing 737-300	
2 Boeing 757-200	

Photograph: Boeing 737-300 (author's collection)

TRANSBRASIL

Rua General Panteleao Telles 40
CEP-04355 Sao Paulo, Brazil
Tel. 011 533 7111

Three letter code	IATA No.	ICAO Callsign
TBA	653	Transbrasil

The Brazilian meat wholesaler Sadia started flight operations as Sadia SA Transportes Aereos on 5th January 1955 with a DC-3, primarily to transport freight from Concordia to Sao Paulo. The airline entered the passenger business on 16th March 1956 and then proceeded to develop routes in Brazil's south east. Close co-operation with REAL and Transportes Aeros Salvador began in 1957; the latter was taken over by Sadia in 1962 and thereby expanded services into northeastern Brazil after the collapse of REAL. The aircraft they used were Handley Page Heralds and, from 1970, BAC 1-11s: Boeing 727s were used from

1974 onwards. Sadia changed its name to Trans Brasil in June 1972 and transferred its headquarters to Brasilia. In June 1976, Transbrasil joined with the government of the state of Bahia to form the regional Nordeste airline which took over many local routes, allowing Transbrasil to concentrate on mainline route development. A cargo service to Miami was introduced in March 1978. Fleet replacement began in July 1983 with the purchase of Boeing 767s; the Boeing 727s were replaced by modern Boeing 737-300s and 400s starting in 1987. The airline divides up its scheduled and charter routes with Varig. The

airline has announced plans to establish a new regional subsidiary, Interbrasil Star which will operate EMB-120 Brasilias.

Routes

Scheduled services to over thirty destinations in Brazil and charter flights in the region, to the Caribbean and to the US.

Fleet	Ordered
4 Boeing 767-200	5 Boeing 767ER
15 Boeing 737-300/400	
1 Boeing 767-300ER	

Photograph: de Havilland DHC-6 Twin Otter (author's collection)

TRANSPORTES AEREOS DE CABO VERDE

Caixa Postal 1, Praia
Republic of Cape Verde
Tel. 613215

Three letter code	IATA No.	ICAO Callsign
TCV	696	Transverde

Transportes Aereos de Cabo Verde (TACV) was founded on 27th December 1958 to succeed a local flying club which had served internal points from May 1955 using de Havilland Doves until its bankruptcy in 1958. TACV began flights in January 1959. In 1971 the first of three Britten-Norman Islanders was commissioned. Operations were suspended for a time in 1967, while re-organisation took place with the help of the Portuguese national carrier TAP. After the country gained its independence from Portugal on 5th July 1975, TACV became the flag carrier of the recently established republic. After the acquisition of a BAe HS-748 in 1973, a weekly flight to Dakar in Senegal was set up; this remained TACV's sole foreign destination for many years. TACV-Cape Verde Airlines became a public company in 1983. Together with TAP-Air Portugal it also provides a direct flight to Lisbon with a TCV flight number, but using a TAP Airbus.

Routes

From the capital, Praia, to Dakar and to the islands of the Republic of Cape Verde such as Sal, Sao Vincente, Sao Nicolau, Boa Vista.

Fleet

2 BAe HS-748
2 de Havilland DHC-6 Twin Otter
1 Embraer 120 Brasilia
2 CASA 212

Photograph: McDonnell Douglas MD-83 (Josef Krauthäuser/Agadir)

TRANSWEDE

P.O. Box 530, 19045 Stockholm-Arlanda
Sweden
Tel. 076060070

Three letter code	IATA No.	ICAO Callsign
TWE	–	Transwede

The present-day Transwede was founded on 1st April 1985 under the name of Aerocenter Trafikflyg AB. Initially it operated charter flights throughout Europe using F-27s. The next aircraft in the fleet were three SE 210 Caravelles and used to operate inclusive tour charters from Sweden and Norway to the Mediterranean area. At the same time as these aircraft were acquired, the airline's name was changed and the aircraft were painted blue, yellow and white. In 1986 two further MD-83s were added to the fleet, which was continually expanded in the following years. As well as Boeing 737s, new MD-83s and

MD-87s were added to the fleet, while the Caravelles were sold to the airline's Turkish subsidiary, Sultan Air. In 1991, Norway Airlines of Oslo, Transwede of Stockhom and Sterling Airways of Copenhagen formed an alliance called the Transnordic Group aimed at reducing Scandinavian air fares and the airlines' costs by co-operation between the members. All three launched services to London but Norway and Sterling have since had these problems while Transwede continues to grow. In the long term the intention is to have a fleet with only one type of aircraft. The decision was taken to acquire

more MD-83s, and Fokker 100s were bought for short-distance routes and domestic services in 1993, as changes in the market situation had made this necessary. More Fokker 100s are due for delivery in 1994 and 1995. In Summer 1994, Transwede had twenty scheduled flights weekly to London Gatwick from Stockholm.

Routes

Charter flights to destinations in the Mediterranean, to the Alps (winter charters), to the Canary Islands and North Africa. Scheduled flights outside Scandinavia.

Fleet

4 McDonnell Douglas MD-83
2 McDonnell Douglas MD-87
1 Fokker 100

Ordered

4 Fokker 100

Photograph: McDonnell Douglas MD-82 (author's collection)

TRANS WORLD AIRLINES

100 South Bedford Road Mt. Visco
New York 10549, USA
Tel. 914 2423000

Three letter code	IATA No.	ICAO Callsign
TWA	15	TWA

Founded on 1st October 1930 as Transcontinental and Western Air as the result of a merger between Transcontinental Air Transport (a part of Western Air Express formed in 1925) and Pittsburg Aviation Industries Corporation. TWA was the first airline to operate scheduled service from coast to coast in the USA, it opened up California for flights and was the joint initiator of such famous aircraft as the DC-1/2 and the DC-3. DC-2s started to arrive in 1934 and the larger DC-3 in 1936, followed by the first of five Boeing 307 Stratoliners in 1940. Howard Hughes, who had a controlling interest in TWA, placed an order with Lockheed in 1939 for an aircraft which would fly coast to coast in less than nine hours; the Constellation went into service in 1944. TWA's first overseas service operated on 5th December 1945 between Washington and Paris. On 21st May 1950 the airline changed its name to Trans World Airlines. London and Frankfurt became part of the network of routes as early as September 1950. On international flights the Constellation was used, and in the US DC-3s and Martin 404s. The first jet, a Boeing 707, came into service in March 1960. In August 1969 a round-the-world service was set up. TWA acquired its first Boeing 747 in December 1969. A second widebody type, the L-1011 TriStar, was added in 1972. The latest aircraft in TWA's fleet is the Boeing 767. Ozark Airlines was acquired in 1986. In recent years TWA has hit hard economic times, but emerged from Chapter 11 bankruptcy protection on 3rd November 1993, now 45% owned by its employees. It had been drastically slimmed down, notably with the sale in 1991 of routes to London to American Airlines, but is now rebuilding. Feeder services are operated by Trans World Express, formerly Pan Am Express, bought from the Pan Am liquidator in 1991.

Routes

TWA flies in Europe to Frankfurt, Amsterdam, Brussels, London-Gatwick, Munich, Geneva, Vienna and Zürich. Its most important American hub is St. Louis. Together with TWA Express more than 100 destinations are served.

Fleet		Ordered
46 DC-9/15/31/32/41	11 Boeing 747-100/200	20 Airbus A330-300
33 McDonnell Douglas MD-82/83	20 Lockheed L-1011 TriStar	
59 Boeing 727-100/200		
9 Boeing 767-200ER		

Photograph: Boeing 727-200ADV (author's collection)

TUNIS AIR

113 Ave. de la Liberte, 1012 Tunis
Tunisia
Tel. 288100

Three letter code	IATA No.	ICAO Callsign
TAR	199	Tunair

Tunis Air was founded in 1948 as a subsidiary of Air France by agreement with the Tunisian Government. Flight operations started in 1949 with DC-3s, initially from Tunis to Corsica and Algiers. In 1954 Tunis Air acquired its first DC-4 for flights to Paris. By 1957 the government had acquired a controlling 51% interest. Air France's shareholding has gradually reduced and is now only 5.6% with the government having a 42.5% holding. In 1961 the airline entered the jet age with the start of flights using SE 210 Caravelles. As a successor to the Caravelle was not available from France, the airline decided to buy Boeing 727s, and the first of these was added to the fleet in 1972. After the Caravelles had been taken out of service in late 1977, the smaller Boeing 737s were taken into service for the first time in 1980. European aircraft were purchased again, in 1982 with the Airbus A300 and the A320 in 1990. The present modern colours of Tunis Air were adopted when the first Airbus A320s were introduced.

Routes

Amsterdam, Athens, Bahrain, Baghdad, Brussels, Casablanca, Damascus, Dakar, Düsseldorf, Frankfurt, Geneva, Istanbul, Jeddah, Copenhagen, Cairo, London, Munich, Vienna, Zürich. Charter flights also to other destinations in Europe.

Fleet	Ordered
1 Airbus A300B4	4 Airbus A320
7 Airbus A320	
5 Boeing 737-200ADV	
8 Boeing 727-200ADV	
2 Boeing 737-500	

Photograph: McDonnell Douglas MD-83 (Uwe Gleisberg/Munich FJS)

TUR EUROPEAN AIRWAYS

Rihtim Cas Nesli Han 207/5
80030 Karaköy, Istanbul, Turkey
Tel. 1 2525497

Three letter code	IATA No.	ICAO Callsign
TCT	–	Avrupa

TUR was founded in 1988 and is owned by the Kavala group, one of the largest companies in Turkey in a joint venture, initially with Trans European Airlines of Belgium, which assisted in the early days with the lease of a Boeing 737. Charter operations started in April 1988 with two Boeing 727-200s, ex-Lufthansa aircraft. In 1990 MD-83s were added to the fleet, and another two Boeing 727-200s were added in 1991 and 1992. TUR flights are primarily used by immigrant workers and tourists from Western Europe. Its technical base and base airport is Istanbul.

Routes

Charter flights from Düsseldorf, Hamburg, Paris, London, Amsterdam and further cities to destinations in Turkey.

Fleet

2 McDonnell Douglas MD-83
4 Boeing 727-200

Photograph: de Havilland DHC-7-100 (Josef Krauthäuser/Innsbruck)

TYROLEAN AIRWAYS

Flughafen, 6026 Innsbruck
Austria
Tel. 0512 817770

Three letter code	IATA No.	ICAO Callsign
TYR	734	Tyrolean

Founded in 1958 as Aircraft Innsbruck, it operated until 1980 as a non-scheduled airline, when it acquired the rights to operate scheduled flights from Innsbruck to Vienna. Before starting flight operations in April 1980 with DHC-7s, the name was changed to Tyrolean Airways in 1979. In that same year further routes were opened to Zürich and Frankfurt. Tyrolean also operates from its Innsbruck base, as a holiday airline. Well over 400,000 passengers were carried in 1993. It also operates ad-hoc charters and air ambulance flights using its fleet of exclusively de Havilland Canada aircraft. In 1994 the domestic arm of Austrian Airlines, Austrian Air Services, was being integrated with Tyrolean following Austrian taking a 42.85% stake in the regional airline.

Routes

Scheduled services for other airlines and its own routes in Austria, to Zürich and Frankfurt, Düsseldorf, Amsterdam, Stuttgart, Munich. Charter flights to destinations in Italy and Greece.

Fleet	Ordered
2 de Havilland DHC-7	3 de Havilland DHC-8-100
8 de Havilland DHC-8-100	2 de Havilland DHC-8-300
4 de Havilland DHC-8-300	

Photograph: Boeing 747-400 (author's collection)

UNITED AIRLINES

P.O. Box 66100 Chicago, IL 60666
USA
Tel. 708 952 4000

Three letter code	IATA No.	ICAO Callsign
UAL	16	United

United Airlines Inc. of Chicago was founded on 1st July, 1931 as the new holding company of the former Boeing Air Transport, Varney Air Lines, National Air Transport and Pacific Air Transport. All four had started operations in either 1926 and 1927. United flew with Boeing 247s and compelled Douglas to design the DC-1/2, as no other airline was able to buy this model at the time. All the Boeing 247s produced went to United, because their orders were so extensive. As the DCs proved to be superior to the Boeing 247s, United decided to buy the DC-3s, and had more than 100 of them in use in the forties. After the war DC-4s and DC-6s were used, mainly on the airline's route from New York to Chicago. In 1946 Hawaii was served for the first time, and in 1959 the airline's first jet aircraft, a DC-8, was commissioned. United was the only US airline to order twenty Caravelles for short and medium-distance routes. There were no follow-up orders, however, and Boeing 727s were bought. On 1st June 1961 Capital Airlines, one of the largest airlines at that time, was taken over, making united the largest airline in the free world, a place which was only taken from the airline by American in the late eighties. Route rights were acquired in the Pacific, as were Lockheed TriStars, from PanAm in 1986. At the same time aircraft were bought from Boeing in order to replace the fleet. In June 1986, United set up feeder agreements with three US regional carriers, Air Wisconsin, Aspen Airways and West Air and they operate under the name United Express. United has been flying to Europe since 1990; in autumn 1993 it became a Lufthansa partner. The present colours were introduced at the beginning of 1993. United is the launch customer for the Boeing 777.

Routes

United's most important hubs are San Francisco, Chicago, Denver and Washington-Dulles with flights to over 150 destinations in the USA, to Hong Kong, Tokyo, Sydney, Auckland, Bangkok, Melbourne, Manila, Osaka, Seoul, Taipei, Frankfurt, Cancun, London, Mexico City, Beijing, Singapore, Munich, Zürich

Fleet

		Ordered
102 Boeing 727-200	26 Boeing 767-300ER	66 Boeing 737
69 Boeing 737-200	10 Boeing 747SP	23 Boeing 747-400
103 Boeing 737-300	27 Boeing 747-100/200	5 Boeing 767-300ER
60 Boeing 737-500	23 Boeing 747-400	34 Boeing 777
90 Boeing 757-200	54 McDonnell Douglas DC-10/10/30	45 Airbus A320
19 Boeing 767-200	5 Airbus A320	

Photograph: Boeing 727-100C (Josef Krauthäuser collection)

UNITED PARCEL SERVICE

1400 North Hurstbourne Parkway,
Louisville Kentucky 40223, USA
Tel. 502 3296500

Three letter code	IATA No.	ICAO Callsign
UPS	–	UPS

UPS-United Parcel Service was founded in 1907, and today it is the largest company in the world in its area of business. In 1953 the two-day 'UPS-Air' service was set up. In 1982 UPS entered the overnight small package market and now serves more US points than any other carrier. Flights to Europe were introduced in October 1985.
It was only in 1987 that UPS established its own flight operations. Up to that point other airlines had been commissioned to carry out the flights. (Even today a large number of outside companies operate on behalf of UPS). There are also regular flights to the European hubs in London and Cologne, from where the parcels are sent on. UPS induced Boeing to build a cargo version of the 757-200 and was the first customer to receive them. Older Boeing 727s are being equipped with new, more powerful and more environmentally friendly engines. These modified aircraft were first used in 1993, mainly to Europe. Its US hub is at Louisville, Kentucky. During the first three months of 1994, the company reported a 20.3% growth in air volume over 1993's first quarter, to an average of 1.13 million pieces a day. It plans to add twenty-three aircraft to the fleet in 1994 to cope with rapidly growing express package business. The planned expansion will take the fleet to 219 jet-powered freighters in service or on order plus another 302 leased aircraft.

Routes

Regular services to the USA, to Mexico, to Hong Kong, Japan, Korea, London and Cologne.

Fleet

11 Boeing 747-100F
52 Boeing 727-100/200
55 Boeing 757-200PF
11 Fairchild-Swearingen Metro/Expediter
50 McDonnell Douglas DC-8-70

Ordered

30 Boeing 767-300F
15 Boeing 757-200PF

Photograph: Boeing 737-400 (author's collection)

US AIR

2345 Crystal Drive, Arlington
Virginia 22227, USA
Tel. 703 418 7000

Three letter code	IATA No.	ICAO Callsign
USA	37	US Air

Founded on 5th March 1937 as All-American Aviation, it initially provided postal services.It began services on 13th September 1937 with a unique 'pick-up' mail services using Stinson Reliants over a network of routes from Pittsburgh. These mail services were discontinued in 1949 and the airline changed its name to All American Airways on 7th March 1949, from when scheduled passenger services commenced from Pittsburgh via Washington to Atlantic City using DC-3s. Martin 2-0-2s and Convair 340/440s replaced the DC-3s, the name was changed in 1953 to Allegheny Airlines and new routes were opened, especially in the eastern United States. Lake Central Airways was taken over on 1st July 1968, followed on 7th April 1972 by Mohawk Airlines with its large network of routes and its BAC 1-11 aircraft. After deregulation, Pacific Southwest Airlines and the much larger Piedmont Airlines were taken over. On 28th October 1979 the airline's new name, US Air, was a sign of its new size. Its first services to London were in 1988, followed in 1990 by Frankfurt and Zürich. After the integration of Piedmont the airline took on new colours. Fokker 100s were introduced in 1989, enabling this aircraft to make a breakthrough on the American market. US Air took over the shuttle service from New York to Washington and Boston from Trump. In January 1993 British Airways made a $400 million investment and would like to invest more, subject to cost-cutting working to restore profitability. BA and US Air have an effective code-sharing arrangement providing BA with passengers fed to its US gateways by US Air and its regional partners in US Air Express. Some transatlantic services are now flown by US Air aircraft in BA colours. With 65 million passengers carried annually US Air is one of the largest airlines in the world.

Routes

Central hubs are Washington, Baltimore, Pittsburgh, Philadephia, Indianapolis, Dayton and Charlotte. 180 destinations are served including Nassau, San Juan, Bermuda, London, Frankfurt, Zürich, Montreal, Ottawa and Toronto.

Fleet

	Ordered
41 Fokker F-28	101 Boeing 737-300	32 Boeing 737
40 Fokker 100	54 Boeing 737-400	4 Boeing 737-400
73 McDonnell Douglas DC-9-31/32	8 Boeing 727-200/ADV	19 Boeing 757-200
37 McDonnell Douglas MD-81/82	22 Boeing 767-200	1 Boeing 767-200ER
81 Boeing 737-200	12 Boeing 757-200ER	1 Airbus A320-200
	8 Airbus A320-200	

Photograph: Ilyushin IL-114 (Martin Bach collection)

UZBEKISTAN AIRWAYS

Proletarskaya 41, 700100 Tashkent
Uzbekistan
Tel. 337357

Three letter code	IATA No.	ICAO Callsign
UZB	250	Uzbek

In 1992 the government of the newly formed government of Uzbekistan assumed the air sovereignty over its national territory. At the same time the aircraft of the former Tashkent directorate of Aeroflot became the property of Uzbekistan. The routes were partly taken over and continued. Particular attention was paid to the new routes via Tashkent to the Far East, and it was here that the airline with its particularly low priced tariffs entered into competition with established airlines. In order to be able to meet the sophisticated needs of travellers from Western countries, Uzbekistan leased two Airbus A310-300s. The first of these aircraft arrived in Tashkent in July 1993 and services started to London and Middle Eastern cities. Lufthansa provides technical assistance. It is the only airline operating in the country.

Routes

Amsterdam, Bangkok, Frankfurt, Zürich and another thirty destinations in the CIS and in Uzbekistan.

Fleet

2 Airbus A310-300
28 Antonov An-24
10 Ilyushin IL-62
13 Ilyushin IL-76
10 Ilyushin IL-86

23 Tupolev Tu-154
27 Yakovlev Yak-40

Ordered

10 Ilyushin IL-114

Photograph: Boeing 747-300 (author's collection)

VARIG

Av. Almirante Silvio de Noronha 365
CEP 20021 Rio de Janeiro, Brazil
Tel. 021 2975141

Three letter code	IATA No.	ICAO Callsign
VRG	42	Varig

Founded on 7th May 1927 with the technical assistance of the German Kondor Syndikat, Varig developed initially in the south of Brazil. Its first aircraft was a Dornier Wal flying boat which operated the first service on 3rd February 1928 on the Porto Algere-Rio Grande route taken over from Kondor. Lockheed 10A Electras were introduced in 1943 after Montevideo had become the first international destination the year earlier, followed later in the decade by a Buenos Aires service. After the Second World War, Varig acquired thirty-five C-47s (DC-3s) and expanded its network of routes considerably. In 1951 Aero Geral

was taken over as well as its routes to Montevideo and Buenos Aires. A scheduled service to New York was started on 2nd August 1955 using Lockheed Super Constellations. The switch was made to Caravelles on 2nd October 1959 and in late 1960 Boeing 707s came into service on this route. A further airline, REAL, was taken over in 1961. The much smaller Varig airline thus acquired new types of aircraft such as CV 990s, Lockheed L-188s and C-46s, plus a large network of routes. Its network was also expanded internationally by order of the government in 1965, when it was ordered to take over Panair do

Brasil. DC-10-30s came into service in May 1971, a further airline, Cruzeiro do Sol was bought in 1975 and finally, in 1981, Airbus A300s and Boeing 747-200s were acquired. Varig was one of the last passenger operators of the Lockheed Electra, which were used into the early 1990's on domestic routes. Boeing 767s, Boeing 747-400s and MD-11s are the latest aircraft in the Varig fleet. Cruzeiro was dissolved as an independent company in 1993 and completely integrated into Varig. Rio de Janeiro, with South America's most modern maintenance hangar, is Varig's base.

Routes

Varig has a dense network in South America, it flies to the USA, Canada, South Africa, Japan. In Europe Lisbon, Madrid, Rome, Zürich, Frankfurt, Amsterdam, London, Paris and Copenhagen are served.

Fleet

		Ordered
5 Boeing 747-300	17 Boeing 737-200	6 Boeing 737-300
3 Boeing 747-200	5 Boeing 727-100	6 Boeing 737-400
3 Boeing 747-400	6 McDonnell Douglas MD-11	
10 Boeing 767-200/300ER	10 McDonnell Douglas DC-10-30	
31 Boeing 737-300		

Photograph: Boeing 737-200ADV (author's collection)

VASP

Edifico Sede VASP 4 andar Congonhas
Airport Sao Paulo SPCEP 04695, Brazil
Tel. 0115337011

Three letter code	IATA No.	ICAO Callsign
VSP	343	VASP

Viacao Aerea Sao Paulo SA was founded on 4th November 1933 by the regional government of Sao Paulo and the Municipal Bank of Sao Paulo. Flight operations started on 16th April 1934, using two 3-seater Monospar ST-4s and in 1935 a scheduled route was opened between Rio de Janeiro and Sao Paulo using two Junkers Ju 52/3s acquired in 1935. When it took over the Brazilian-German Aerolloyd Iguassu on 28th October 1939, the network of routes included numerous destinations. VASP had six Saab Scanias in use from 1950 on, and later all the aircraft of this type ever built were in VASP's

service, a total of eighteen aircraft and the last of the type in service was retired in 1966. VASP obtained its first Vickers Viscounts in October 1958. Two airlines, Loide Aereo Nacional (LAN) and Navegacao Aerea Braziliero (NAB), were taken over in 1962 as part of the general nationalisation of air services in Brazil. The first jet aircraft was a BAC 1-11 in December 1967. Eight NAMC YS-11As were bought in late 1968 as replacement for the Vickers Viscounts and DC-4s. VASP evolved over the years into Brazil's second largest airline and continually modernised its fleet, adapting to the market situation. The first four

Boeing 737s were used in July 1969. In the late seventies the Brazillian-built Embraer 110 Bandeirante regional aircraft came briefly into service until the entire fleet was changed over to jet aircraft only. The three Airbus A300s in the fleet are used on the high density Sao Paulo routes to Rio de Janeiro and Brasilia as well as on other routes. VASP has been in a severe financial crisis for some time, which it is seeking to overcome by means of reorganisation.

Routes

Dense network of scheduled routes in Brazil to more than thirty destinations such as Belem, Belo Horizonte, Brasilia, Campo Grande, Florianapolis, Iguacu, Maceio, Manaus, Porto Alegre, Recife, Rio de Janeiro, Sao Paulo, Vitoria.

Fleet

3 Airbus A300B2
2 Boeing 737-300
17 Boeing 737-200
4 McDonnell Douglas MD-11

Photograph: McDonnell Douglas DC-10-30 (Josef Krauthäuser/Frankfurt)

VIASA

Torre Viasa, Avenida Sur 25, Los Caobos
Caracas 105, Venezuela
Tel. 2 5729522

Three letter code	IATA No.	ICAO Callsign
VIA	164	Viasa

VIASA (Venezolana Internacional de Aviacion SA) was established at the instigation of the government on 21st November 1960 and incorporated on 1st January 1961 as a new internationally operating national airline. The government held 75% of the shares and Avensa, the remainder. The international flights of the two airlines Avensa and Aeropostal were taken over by VIASA on 1st April 1961 when the latter started flight operations with a service from Caracas to Amsterdam via Paris and London using a KLM DC-8. The new airline was built up and expanded in co-operation with KLM. On 8th August 1961 a Convair 880 took off for the first time on the new route from Caracas to New York which was the carrier's official inaugural flight using its own aircraft. Constellations and DC-6s of Avensa and Aeropostal were used on other services. Further VIASA aircraft were DC-8s delivered in 1965, a Boeing 747 was acquired in 1972 and in 1973 DC-10-30s. MD-11s will replace the DC-10s in the 1990s for long-haul routes to Europe while the Airbuses serve North and South America. VIASA is now wholly-owned by the Venezuelan Government.

Routes

VIASA flies to the European destinations of Amsterdam, Frankfurt, Madrid, Paris, London, Lisbon, Zürich and Rome. In the US there are flights to Miami and New York, with additional destinations in the Caribbean.

Fleet

5 McDonnell Douglas DC-10-30
5 Boeing 727-200ADV
2 Airbus A300B4

Ordered

3 McDonnell Douglas MD-11

Photograph: Tupolev Tu 134A (Josef Krauthäuser/Ho Chi Minh City)

VIETNAM AIRLINES

Gialem Airport, Hanoi
Socialist Republic of Vietnam
Tel. 26611

Three letter code	IATA No.	ICAO Callsign
HVN	738	Vietnam Airlines

After the end of the Vietnam war and the coming together of North and South Vietnam, a new airline also came into existence in 1976, Hang Khong Vietnam. It took over the aircraft and staff of the former CAAV and partly those of Air Vietnam. However the fleet was very quickly changed over to Soviet standard, as spare parts could not be obtained for Western aircraft. Air Vietnam had been 92.75% owned by the old government in 1975, shortly before the fall of Vietnam. It had been formed to take over the services of Air France in the area. In the early and mid-1980s Tu-134A operated several weekly services from Hanoi to Ho Chi Minh City (ex-Saigon), Phnom Penh, Bangkok, and Vietiane. It was only when the country opened up politically towards the West and towards the US that it was possible in 1990 to place an order for Western aircraft. As a replacement for the IL-18s two ATR-72s were ordered. A slow expansion of the network of routes is planned for the nineties. In 1990 some Tu-134s were bought from Interflug stocks, the name was changed to Vietnam Airlines and new colours were introduced. The fact that the country had opened up politically made it possible for Air France to acquire a stake in Vietnam Airlines; Air France provided A320s for international flights and took over training and service from late 1993 on. It is planned to phase out the Russian-built airliners over the next two years in favour of Western aircraft; already Boeing 767s are being wet-leased.

Routes

Hanoi, Bangkok, Phnom Penh, Ho Chi Minh City, Singapore, Hong Kong, Vientiane as well as some destinations in Vietnam.

Fleet

2 Yakovlev Yak-40
3 Antonov An-24
1 Ilyushin IL-18
13 Tupolev Tu-134
2 ATR-72

5 Airbus A320
1 Boeing 767-200

Photograph: Airbus A340-300 (Virgin)

VIRGIN ATLANTIC

Ashdown House, High Street, Crawley
West Sussex RH10 1DQ, United Kingdom
Tel. 0293 562345

Three letter code	IATA No.	ICAO Callsign
VIR	932	Virgin

Virgin Atlantic can trace its history back to British Atlantic Airways, set up in 1982 with Richard Branson involved. It proposed to operate services between Britain and the Falklands and then between Gatwick and New York. However the British CAA declined to approve a licence and subsequently Branson decided to set up his own operation, Virgin Atlantic, through the Virgin Group. The collapse of the low fare airline Laker Airways encouraged Branson to establish an airline along the same lines, as there was obviously a need for a 'cheap airline' from London. Virgin Atlantic obtained a licence for London-New York (Newark) in March 1984, and the first flight was on 22nd June 1984. In

November a daily connecting flight to Maastricht in Holland using BAC 1-11s was started. This flight later changed over to Vickers Viscounts and was discontinued in 1990. In June 1987, Virgin introduced a successful service to Dublin from Luton using a Viscount. 1988 saw the launch of its first charter flights to Orlando on 26th May and a Luton-Maastricht service, in addition to the Gatwick operation, started on 17th June. With imaginative advertising, this airline offering only cheap flights attracted more sophisticated passengers. New routes to New York (JFK) and Los Angeles were awarded to Virgin following the British Airways/British Caledonian merger. Approval for a new service

to Tokyo was granted in August 1988 for scheduled flights to begin on 1st May 1989. Steady expansion continues with the launch of London Heathrow services (to where Virgin has transferred all its long-haul routes apart from to Boston) to Hong Kong on 21st February 1994 and to San Francisco from May 1994. It set up a franchise with Athens-based South East European Airlines to operate Athens-London feeder services from 29th March 1993 and on 10th January 1994, a Dublin-London City service through CityJet of Dublin, both airlines with their aircraft in Virgin colours. The first Airbus A340s were delivered in Spring 1994, and the first Boeing 747-400 in May 1994.

Routes

From London (Gatwick and Heathrow) to Los Angeles, San Francisco, Miami, New York, JFK, New York/Newark, Moscow, Tokyo,Hong Kong.

Fleet		Ordered
1 Boeing 747-100	1 Boeing 737-400	2 Airbus A340
1 Boeing 747-400	2 Airbus A340	1 Boeing 747-400
7 Boeing 747-200		

Photograph: Boeing 737-300 (André Dietzel/Frankfurt)

VIVA AIR

Camiro de la Escoliera 4, 07012 Palma de Mallorca, Spain
Tel. 71713208

Three letter code	IATA No.	ICAO Callsign
VIV	728	Viva

Viva Air, initially a German-Spanish charter airline belonging to Iberia and Lufthansa, was founded on 24th February 1988 and started its first flight from Nuremberg to Palma de Mallorca on 15th April 1988. The airline started the first season with three Boeing 737-300s, and two more Boeing 737s were acquired in 1989. In addition to the purely charter business, Viva Air flew supplementary flights for Iberia. In 1993 the leased DC-9s were taken out of service and further Boeing 737s were acquired. Viva Air is now 98% owned by Iberia and also has its own independent scheduled domestic services, operating them instead of Iberia. It has two scheduled services to the UK, into London Gatwick from Malaga and Madrid. A third, from Santiago de Campostela in north-west Spain started at the end of March 1994 but, after less than two weeks, Iberia took over the operation because of a shortage of aircraft at Viva Air.

Routes

Barcelona, Frankfurt, London, Malaga, Madrid, Manchester, Munich, Palma de Mallorca, Paris, Salzburg, Vienna, Zürich and further destinations with charter services.

Fleet

9 Boeing 737-300

Photograph: de Havilland DHC-7 (Heinz Kolper/Skolvaer)

WIDERØE

P.O. Box 247, 8001 Bodø
Norway
Tel. 13500

Three letter code	IATA No.	ICAO Callsign
WIF	701	Widerøe

Viggo Widerøe founded his Widerøe's Flyveselskap A/S on 19th February 1934. First he obtained a licence to open a route from Oslo to Hangesund. On behalf of DNL, the established airline of the time and the predecessor of SAS, he opened a postal service in 1936 to Kirkenes in the north of Norway. After the Second World War Widerøe started charter and supply flights again. It took over the Narvik-based Polarfly in 1950. Widerøe made a particular contribution to the opening up of northern Norway. The first DHC-6 Twin Otters were received in 1968 which was the year scheduled services using Twin Otters were introduced on local routes. With the support of the government a network of routes from Bodø and Trondheim was built up, and this was followed over the years by around 30-40 smaller airfields, all of them standardised with standardised landing aids and a runway 800-1000 m long. In this way the necessary infrastructure was created in this inaccessible area criss-crossed with fjords. Towns like Kirkenes and Hammerfest had only been accessible by ship until flights started international scheduled flights were launched to Copenhagen. Fred Olsen, SAS and Braathens S A F E have stakes in Widerøe, the oldest Norwegian airline still in existence.

Routes

Alta, Andenes, Batsfjord, Bervelag, Bodø, Bromnoysund, Hammerfest, Kirkenes, Leknes, Moirana, Mosjoen, Namsos, Narvik, Rost, Skolvaer, Stokmarknes, Tromsøe, Trondheim, Vadso, Vardøe.

Fleet	Ordered
12 de Havilland DHC-6 8 de Havilland DHC-7 6 de Havilland DHC-8	9 de Havilland DHC-8

Photograph: McDonnell Douglas DC-10-30 (André Dietzel/Munich FJS)

WORLD AIRWAYS

13873 Park Center Road,
Herndon, Virginia 22071, USA
Tel. 703 8349200

Three letter code	IATA No.	ICAO Callsign
WOA	468	World

World Airways was founded on 29th March 1948 and started charter flights with a Boeing 314 flying boat from the east coast of the United States. One year later the flights were moved from water to land; Curtiss C-46s were used. In 1950 Edward Daly acquired an 81% interest in the airline and made it into one of the large, well-known supplemental charter airlines in the next few years. From 1960 onwards World Airways took over an increasing number of flights for the MAC, and DC-4s, DC-6s and Lockheed 1049 Constellations were bought or leased. The first Boeing 707s were acquired in 1963, and regular flights to and from Europe were introduced using these aircraft, as well as services to the Caribbean and South America. Boeing 727s were ordered in July 1966. In May 1973 charter flights to London from Oakland started using Boeing 747s. CAB approval for low-cost, coast-to-coast scheduled services was granted in early 1979. World commenced linking Newark and Baltimore/Washington with Los Angeles and Oakland on April 1979 and the bargain fares sparked a transcontinental price war. Operations were abruptly halted in June 1979 when the US Government ordered the grounding of DC-10s. Transcontinental flights restarted in February 1980. Scheduled flights were further expanded with the introduction of the DC-10s, and the Hawaii-Los Angeles-Baltimore-London-Frankfurt flights were the lowest priced charter flights to these destinations for many years. After restructuring in 1988 World Airways withdrew from scheduled flights. Since then World has been flying charters and leases aircraft out to other airlines, but passenger operations re-started in March 1993 and scheduled round-the-world cargo services are planned.

Routes

Charter flights all over the world.

Fleet	Ordered
7 McDonnell Douglas DC-10-30 4 McDonnell Douglas MD-11	3 McDonnell Douglas MD-11

Photograph: Boeing 757-200 (Uwe Gleisberg/Hong Kong)

XIAMEN AIRLINES

Gaoqi Airport 361009 Xiamen
People's Republic of China
Tel. 592 622961

Three letter code	IATA No.	ICAO Callsign
CXA	–	Xiamen Airlines

Xiamen Airlines was founded in 1991 by China Southern Airlines and is virtually a subsidiary but with its own aircraft fleet and operating area. Flight operations were begun in 1991 with partly leased Boeing aircraft. There are services to the south and east of the People's Republic. In late 1992 a route to Hong Kong was opened.

Routes

Dense network of over fortyscheduled routes complementing China Southern in the south and east of the People's Republic of China, Hong Kong.

Fleet

4 Boeing 737-200ADV
4 Boeing 737-500
3 Boeing 757-200

Photograph: McDonnell Douglas DC-10-30 (author's collection)

ZAMBIA AIRWAYS

Ndeka House, Haile Selassie Ave.
P.O. Box 30272, Lusaka, Zambia
Tel. 01 228274

Three letter code	IATA No.	ICAO Callsign
ZAC	169	Zambia

Zambia Airways Corporation was founded in 1964 as a subsidiary of Central African Airways, itself founded in 1946, to take over that company's operations in the newly independednt state of Zambia (formerly Northern Rhodesia). Flight operations started on 1st July 1964, using two DC-3s and some de Havilland Beavers. After the dissolution of CAA, the airline became an independent, wholly government-owned concern on 1st September 1967. Two BAC-1-11s came into service in January 1968 and were introduced on regional routes to Malawi, Kenya, Zaire and Tanzania, and on 1st November a

scheduled route to London via Nairobi and Rome was opened using DC-8s leased from Alitalia. Technical and Managerial assistance had initially been provided in the late 1960s by Alitalia and from 1974 by Aer Lingus. The BAC-1-11s were replaced by Boeing 737s in 1983, and Zambia commissioned its first DC-10 on 31st July 1984. When ATR-42s were acquired, the older HS-748s were taken out of service in 1989, the same year as another DC-10 was leased. An MD-11 has been ordered, continuing the replacement of the small fleet.

Routes

Bombay, Dar-Es-Salaam, Entebbe, Frankfurt, Harare, Jeddah, Johannesburg, London, Mauritius, Monrovia, Nairobi, New York, Rome, Windhoek and around ten domestic destinations from Lusaka.

Fleet	Ordered
2 ATR-42	1 McDonnell Douglas MD-11
1 McDonnell Douglas DC-10-30	
1 McDonnell Douglas DC-8-71	
2 Boeing 737-200ADV	

Photograph: McDonnell Douglas MD-83

ZAS AIRLINE OF EGYPT

c/o Novotel, 21 Fahmyst.
Cairo Airport, Egypt
Tel. 2907840

Three letter code	IATA No.	ICAO Callsign
ZAS	708	ZAS Airline

Zarkani Aviation Services (ZAS) is a privately owned Egyptian company formed by the Zarkani Group in June 1982. In August 1982 ZAS obtained a licence as a cargo carrier. Flight operations began on 23rd November, 1982 with a flight from London to Cairo via Amsterdam. Gradually the airline started to operate passenger charter flights in addition to the cargo business. Initially pilgrims were flown to Mecca, then in September 1987 ZAS obtained a licence for worldwide charter flights with passengers to Egypt. Flights were operated from Cairo to Zürich among other destinations, and scheduled domestic flights started in late 1988 after an MD-82 had been acquired in March 1988 on lease. This was joined also by a leased DC-9. Domestic routes are served and the main international service was between Cairo and Amsterdam. Seasonal peaks are bridged by leasing other aircraft, e.g. Airbus 300/310s, but the heart of the fleet is the MD-83/87. The Boeing 707s and JetStars were put up for sale in March 1991. ZAS also uses the title Airline of Egypt.

Routes

Domestic Egyptian connections between Cairo, Aswan, Luxor, Hurgada and Alexandria. Charter flights to Cologne, Frankfurt, Zürich, Paris, Munich among others.

Fleet

2 Boeing 707-300C
2 McDonnell Douglas MD-83
3 McDonnell Douglas MD-87
3 Lockheed JetStar

Airline Three letter codes (IATA codes in parentheses)

AAA = Ansett (AN)
AAG = Air Atlantique
AAH = Aloha Airlines (AQ)
AAL = American Airlines (AA)
AAN = Oasis International (OB)
AAR = Asiana (OZ)
AAS = Austrian Air Services (SO)
ABB = Air Belgium (AJ)
ABL = Air BC (ZX)
ABR = Hunting Cargo Airlines (AG)
ABW = Albanian Airlines (7Y)
ABX = Airborne Express (GB)
ACA = Air Canada (AC)
ACF = Air Charter (SF)
ACU = Aero Cancun
ADP = Aeronaves del Peru
ADR = Adria Airways (JP)
AEA = Air Europa (KX)
AEF = Aero Lloyd (YP)
AES = ACES Colombia (VX)
AFE = Airfast Indonesia
AFG = Ariana Afghan Airlines (FG)
AFL = Aeroflot Russian Airlines (SU)
AFM = Affretair
AFR = Air France (AF)
AGN = Air Gabon (GN)
AGS = Air Gambia
AGU = Air Guadeloupe (OG)
AGV = Air Glaciers
AHK = Air Hongkong (LD)
AHR = Air Holland (GG)
AHY = Azerbaijan Airlines (J2)
AIC = Air India (AI)
AIE = Air Inuit (3H)
AIH = Airtours International (VZ)
AIZ = Arkia
AJM = Air Jamaica (JM)
AJT = Amerijet (JH)
ALK = Air Lanka (UL)
ALM = ALM Antillean Airlines (LM)
AMC = Air Malta (KM)
AMI = Air Maldives
AML = Air Malawi (QM)
AMM = Air 2000 (DP)
AMT = American Trans Air (TZ)
AMU = Amadeus Air
AMX = Aeromexico (AM)

AMY = Ambassador Airways
ANA = ANA-All Nippon Airways (NH)
ANG = Air Niugini (PX)
ANZ = Air New Zealand (NZ)
AOM = AOM French Airlines (IW)
AOR = Air Comores
APF = Aero Pacifico
API = Panama Air International
APT = LAP Colombia
APW = Arrow Air (JW)
ARG = Aerolineas Argentinas (AR)
ARN = Air Nova (QK)
ARU = Air Aruba (FQ)
ASA = Alaska Airlines (AS)
ASD = Air Sinai (4D)
ASE = ASA-Delta Connection (EV)
ASU = Aerosur
ASW = Air Southwest
ATC = Air Tanzania (TC)
ATI = ATI Linee Aeree Nazionale (BM)
ATL = Air Atlantic (9A)
ATT = Aer Turas Teoranta
AUA = Austrian Airlines (OS)
AUC = Austrian Airtransport
AUI = Air Ukraine International (PS)
AUR = Aurigny Air Services
AUT = Austral (AU)
AUY = Aerolineas Uruguayas
AVA = Avianca Columbia (AV)
AVE = Avensa (VE)
AVN = Air Vanuatu (NF)
AWA = Ansett W. A. (MV)
AWE = America West Airlines (HP)
AWI = Air Wisconsin-United Express
AWT = Air West
AYC = Aviaco (AO)
AZA = Alitalia (AZ)
AZE = Arcus Air Logistic (ZE)
AZM = Aerocozumel (AZ)
AZR = Air Zaire (QC)
AZW = Air Zimbabwe (UM)
BAF = British World Airways
BAG = Deutsche BA (DI)
BAL = Britannia Airwyas (BY)

BAR = Bradley Air Service
BAW = British Airways (BA)
BBB = Balair CTA
BBC = Biman Bangladesh (BG)
BCS = European Air Transport
BEE = Norwegian Air Shuttle (BS)
BEN = Business Air
BER = Air Berlin (AB)
BFC = Basler Airlines
BHS = Bahamasair (UP)
BHY = Birgenair (KT)
BIA = Baltic International (TI)
BKP = Bangkok Airways (PG)
BLI = Belair
BMA = British Midland (BD)
BOI = Aboitiz Airtransport
BOT = Air Botswana (BP)
BOU = Bouraq Indonesia (BO)
BRA = Braathens S.A.F.E. (BU)
BRY = Brymon European Airways (BC)
BUR = Businessair
BWA = BWIA International (BW)
BZH = Brit Air (DB)
CAA = Carnival Air Lines (KW)
CAL = China Airlines (CI)
CAV = Calm Air
CAW = Comair (MN)
CAY = Cayman Airways (KX)
CBE = Aerocarribe (QA)
CBF = China Northern Airlines (CJ)
CCA = Air China (CA)
CDN = Canadian (CP)
CES = China Eastern Airlines (MU)
CFG = Condor Flugdienst (DE)
CFP = Faucett Peru (CF)
CGW = Air Great Wall
CHK = Chalks International (OP)
CHP = Aviacsa (6A)
CJG = Zhejiang Airlines
CKS = Kalitta American International (CB)
CKT = Caledonian Airways
CLC = Classic Air
CLH = Lufthansa Cityline (CL)
CLX = Cargolux (CV)
CMM = Canada 3000 (2T)
CMP = Copa Panama (CM)

CNB = Air Colombus (BO)
CNF = Conifair Aviation
CNW = China Northwest Airlines (WH)
COA = Continental Airlines (CO)
COM = Comair (OH)
CPA = Cathay Pacific (CX)
CRL = Corsair (SS)
CRN = Aero Caribbean
CRQ = Air Creebec (YN)
CRX = Crossair (LX)
CSA = CSA (OK)
CSC = Sichuan Airlines (3U)
CSH = Shanghai Airlines (SF)
CSN = China Southern Airlines (CZ)
CTH = China General Aviation
CTN = Croatia Airlines (OU)
CUB = Cubana (CU)
CWU = Wuhan Air Lines
CXA = Xiamen Airlines (MF)
CXJ = Xinjiang Airlines (XO)
CXN = China Southwest Airlines (SZ)
CXP = Casino Express (XP)
CYH = Yunnan Airlines (3Q)
CYP = Cyprus Airways (CY)
DAH = Air Algerie (AH)
DAL = Delta Air Lines (DL)
DAT = DAT Belgian Regional
DHL = DHL Airways (ER)
DLA = Air Dolomiti (EN)
DMA = Maersk Air (DM)
DOA = Dominicana de Aviacion (DO)
DQI = Cimber Air (QI)
DRK = Druk Air (KB)
DSB = Air Senegal (DS)
DTA = TAAG Angola Airlines (DT)
DYA = Alyemda (DY)
EBA = EBA-Eurobelgian Airlines (BQ)
ECA = Eurocypria Airlines (UI)
EEB = Euroberlin (EE)
EIA = Evergreen International Airlines (EZ)
EIN = Air Lingus (EI)
ELL = Estonian Air (OV)
ELY = EL AL Israel Airlines (LY)
ENR = Ensor Airlines
EPC = Conti Flug (DD)

ETH = Ethiopian Airlines (ET)
EUL = Euralair (RN)
EVA = Eva Air (BR)
EWW = Emery Worldwide (GJ)
EXC = Excalibur Airways
EXS = Channel Express (LS)
EYT = EAS-Europe Aero Service (EY)
FAB = First Air (7F)
FAJ = Fiji Air
FAT = Farner Air Transport
FAV = Finnaviation
FCN = Falcon Aviation (IH)
FDX = Federal Express (FM)
FEA = Far Eastern Air Transport
    = (EF)
FIN = Finnair (AY)
FJI = Air Pacific (FJ)
FLI = Atlantic Aiways
FOF = Fred Olsen Airtransport (FO)
FOX = Jetair
FRS = Flandre Air (IX)
FSH = Flash Airlines
FUA = Futura International Airways (FH)
FWL = Florida West Airlines (RF)
GAA = Bex-Delta Connection (HQ)
GAW = Gambia Airways
GBL = GB Airways (GT)
GBU = TAGB T. A. Guinea-Bissau (YZ)
GCB = Lina Congo (GC)
GFA = Gulf Air (GF)
GHA = Ghana Airways (GH)
GIA = Garuda Indonesia (GA)
GIB = Air Guinee (GI)
GMI = Germania
GNV = Grand Airways (QD)
GRL = Groenlandsfly (GL)
GRN = Greenair (WK)
GUG = Aviateca (GU)
GYA = Guyana Airways (GY)
HAL = Hawaiian Air (HA)
HAS = Hamburg Airlines (HX)
HDA = Dragonair (KA)
HJA = Air Haiti
HLA = Heavylift Cargo Airlines
HLF = Hapag-Lloyd Flug (HF)
HMS = Hemus Air (DU)

HNA = USAir Expres-Henson Airlines
HRH = Royal Tongan Airlines (WR)
HTC = Haiti Trans Air (TV)
HVN = Vietnam Airlines (VN)
HZL = Hazelton Airlines (ZL)
IAC = Indian Airlines (IC)
IBB = Binter Canarias (NT)
IBE = Iberia (IB)
ICE = Icelandair (FI)
IMX = Zimex Aviation (MF)
IRA = Iran Air (IR)
IRB = Iran Airtours
IRC = Iran Asseman Airlines
IRK = Kish Air (KN)
IRT = Interot Airways (IQ)
ISS = Meridiana (IG)
IST = Istanbul Airlines (IL)
ITF = Air Inter (IT)
IYE = Yemenia Airways (IY)
JAA = Japan Asia Airways (EG)
JAC = Japan Air Commuter (JN)
JAL = Japan Airlines (JL)
JAS = Japan Air System (JD)
JAZ = Japan Air Charter (JZ)
JEA = Jersey European Airways (JY)
KAC = Kuwait Airways (KU)
KAL = Korean Air (KE)
KBA = Ken Borek Airlines (4K)
KDA = Kendell Airlines
KEY = Key Air International
KGA = Kyrghyzstan Airlines (K2)
KIA = Kiwi International Air Lines (KP)
KIS = Contact Air
KLC = KLM-Cityhopper (HN)
KLM = KLM Royal Dutch Airlines (KL)
KOR = Air Koryo (JS)
KQA = Kenia Airways (KQ)
KRE = Aerosucre
KRT = Cretan Airlines
KZA = Kazakhstan Airlines
LAA = Libyan Arab Airlines (LN)
LAI = Lesotho Airways (QL)
LAM = Linhas Aereas Mocambique (TM)
LAN = LAN Chile (LA)
LAO = Lao Aviation (QV)

LAP = Lineas Aereas Paraguayas (PZ)
LAV = Aeropostal (LV)
LAZ = Balkan Bulgarian Airlines (LZ)
LCO = Ladeco (UC)
LDA = Lauda Air (NG)
LDE = LADE (LD)
LEI = Air UK-Leisure (UK)
LGL = Luxair (LG)
LHN = Express One International (EO)
LIA = Liat Caribbean Airlines (LI)
LIB = Air Liberte (VD)
LIC = LAC Colombia (LC)
LIL = Lithuanian Airlines (TE)
LIT = Air Littoral
LLB = Lloyd Aeroe Boliviano (LB)
LOG = Loganair (LC)
LOT = LOT Polish Airlines (LO)
LPR = LAPA (MJ)
LRC = Lacsa (LR)
LTE = LTE International Airways (XO)
LTL = Latavio Latvian Airlines (PV)
LTS = LTU-Süd International Airways
LTU = LTU International Airways (LT)
MAB = Millardair
MAG = Air Margarita
MAH = Malev Hungarian Airlines (MA)
MAM = Meta Aviotransport Macedonia
MAS = Malaysia Airlines (MH)
MAU = Air Mauritius (MK)
MDA = Mandarin Airlines (AE)
MDG = Air Madagascar (MD)
MDL = Mandala Airlines (RI)
MEA = Middle East Airlines (ME)
MEP = Midwest Express (YK)
MES = Northwest Airlink-Mesaba Airlines
MGL = Miat Mongolian Airlines
MGM = MGM Grand Air (MG)
MLD = Air Moldovia (9U)
MNA = Merpati (MZ)
MNX = Manx Airlines (JG)

MOA = Morris Air (KN)
MON = Monarch Airlines (ZB)
MPH = Martinair Holland (MP)
MRK = Markair (BF)
MRS = Air Marshall Islands (CW)
MRT = Air Mauritanie (MR)
MSE = Mesa Airlines (YV)
MSR = Egypt Air (MS)
MTM = MTM Aviation
MTQ = Air Martinique
MXA = Mexicana (MX)
NAM = Air Manitoba (7N)
NCA = Niipon Cargo Airlines (KZ)
NEE = Northwest Airlink-Northeast
NFD = Eurowings (NS)
NGA = Nigeria Airways
NMB = Air Namibia (SW)
NOP = Novair
NOV = Avianova (RD)
NSE = Setena (ZT)
NWA = Northwest Airlines (NW)
NWT = NWT Air (NV)
NZM = Mount Cook Airlines (NM)
OAL = Olympic Airways (OA)
OAS = Oman Aviation (WY)
OHY = Onur Air (8Q)
OIR = Slov Air
OKJ = Okada Air
OLT = Ostfriesische Luft-transport (OL)
ONT = Air Ontario (GX)
OWS = Cargosur
OXO = Millon Air
PAL = Philippines (PR)
PAO = Polynesian Airlines (PH)
PAS = Pelita Air Service (EP)
PBU = Air Burundi
PDX = Paradise island Airlines (BK)
PEG = Pelangi Air (9P)
PGA = Portugalia (NI)
PGT = Pegasus Airlines
PIA = Pakistan International Airlines (PK)
PJE = Private Jet Expeditions (5J)
PLI = Aero Peru (PL)
PMK = Palair Macedonia (3D)
PUA = Pluna (PU)
QFA = Qantas (QF)

QNK = Kabo Air (9H)
QSC = ASA African Safari
QXE = Horizon Air (QX)
RAM = Royal Air Maroc (AT)
RAT = Ratioflug
RBA = Royal Brunei (BI)
RIA = Rich International Airways (JN)
RJA = Royal Jordanian (RJ)
RKA = Air Afrique (RK)
RME = Armenian Airlines (R3)
RMV = Romavia (VQ)
RNA = Royal Nepal Airlines (RA)
ROA = Reno Air (QQ)
RON = Air Nauru (ON)
ROT = Tarom (RO)
RQX = Air Engadina (RQ)
RSN = Royal Swazi National Airways
RTL = Rheintalflug (WG)
RVV = Reeve Aleutian Airways (RV)
RWD = Air Rwanda (RY)
RYR = Ryanair (FR)
SAA = South African Airways (SA)
SAB = Sabena (SN)
SAM = Sam Columbia (MM)
SAS = Scandinavian (SK)
SAT = Sata Air Acores
SAY = Suckling Airways (CB)
SBY = Berliner Spezialflug (FC)
SBZ = Scibe Airlift Zaire (ZM)
SCH = Schreiner Airways (AW)
SCX = Sun Country Airlines (SY)
SER = Aero California (JR)
SET = SAETA (EH)
SEY = Air Seychelles (HM)
SFR = Safeair (FA)
SGL = Senegal Air
SHA = Sahsa Honduras (SH)
SHK = Shorouk Air (7Q)
SIA = Singapore Airlines (SQ)
SJM = Southern Air Transport (SJ)
SKW = Skywest-Delta Connection (OO)
SLK = Silkair (MI)
SLL = Saarland Airlines (QW)
SLM = Surinam Airways
SLR = Sobelair

SOA = Skoda Air	THA = Thai Airways International (TG)	ULA = Zuliana de Aviacion
SOL = Solomon Airlines (IE)		ULD = LANSA
SPP = Spanair (JK)	THY = THY Turkish Airlines (TK)	UPA = Air Foyle (GS)
SRR = Star Air	TKE = Flitestar (GM)	UPS = United Parcel Service (5X)
SSR = Sempati Air (SG)	TLE = Air Toulouse	USA = US Air (US)
SUD = Sudan Airways (SD)	TMA = TMA of Lebanon (TL)	USS = USAir Shuttle (TB)
SUE = Aerosur	TMD = Transmed Airlines	UYC = Cameroon Airlines (UY)
SVA = Saudia (SV)	TNA = Trans Asia Airways	UZB = Uzbekistan Airways (HY)
SWA = Southwest Airlines (WN)	TOW = Tower Air (FF)	VBW = Air Burkina
SWR = Swissair (SR)	TPA = TAMPA Columbia (QT)	VDA = Volga Dnepr Cargo Airlines (VI)
SXS = Sunexpress (XQ)	TPC = Air Caledonie (TY)	
SYR = Syrian Arab Airlines (RB)	TRA = Transavia Airlines (HV)	VDT = Vayudoot (PF)
TAB = Taba (TT)	TRK = Air Truck	VIA = Viasa (VA)
TAE = Tame (EQ)	TRX = Air Terrex	VIR = Virgin Atlantic Airways (VS)
TAI = TACA International Airlines (TA)	TSC = Air Transat (TS)	VIV = Viva Air (FV)
	TSO = Trans Aero (4J)	VRG = Varig (RG)
TAJ = Tunisavia	TSW = TEA Basel (BH)	VSP = VASP (VP)
TAK = Transkei Airways	TTR = Tatra Air (QS)	VTA = Air Tahiti (VT)
TAL = Talair (GV)	TUI = Tuninter (UG)	VUN = Air Ivoire (VU)
TAM = TAM Linha Aerea Regional (KK)	TUN = Air Tungaru (VK)	WDL = WDL Aviation
	TVO = Transavio	WIA = Winair
TAP = TAP Air Portugal (TP)	TWA = Trans World Airlines (TW)	WIF = Wideroe (WF)
TAR = Tunis Air (TU)	TWE = Transwede (TQ)	WLO = Willowair
TAT = TAT European Airlines (IJ)	TYR = Tyrolean Airways (VO)	WOA = World Airways (WO)
TBA = Transbrasil (TR)	UAE = Emirates (EK)	WWM = American Eagle-Wings West
TBL = The Berline (BZ)	UAL = United Airlines (UA)	
TCT = TUR European Airways (YI)	UBA = Myanma Airways (UB)	YRR = Scenic Airlines (YR)
	UCA = USAir Express-Commutair	YVK = Cyprus Turkish Airlines
TCV = TACV Cabo Verdes (VR)	UGA = Uganda Airlines (QU)	ZAC = Zambia Airways (QZ)
TEI = TEA Italia	UKA = Air UK (UK)	ZAN = Zantop International (VK)
TEJ = TAESA (GD)	UKR = Air Ukraine (GU)	ZAS = ZAS Airline of Egypt (ZA)

International Aircraft Registration Prefixes

AP	Pakistan		**HS**	Thailand
A2	Botswana		**HZ**	Saudi Arabia
A3	Tonga Islands		**H4**	Solomon Islands
A40	Oman		**I**	Italy
A5	Bhutan		**JA**	Japan
A6	United Arab Emirates		**JY**	Jordan
A7	Qatar		**J2**	Djibouti
A9C	Bahrain		**J3**	Grenada
B	China, Peoples Republic, and Taiwan		**J5**	Guinea Bissau
C	Canada		**J6**	St. Lucia
CC	Chile		**J7**	Dominica
CCCP	former Soviet Union		**J8**	St. Vincent and Grenadines
CN	Morocco		**LN**	Norway
CP	Bolivia		**LV**	Argentina
CS	Portugal		**LX**	Luxembourg
CU	Cuba		**LY**	Lithuania
CX	Uruguay		**LZ**	Bulgaria
C2	Nauru		**MI**	Marshall Islands
C3	Andorra		**MT**	Mongolia
C5	Gambia		**N**	USA
C6	Bahamas		**OB**	Peru
C9	Mozambique		**OD**	Lebanon
D	Germany		**OE**	Austria
DQ	Fiji		**OH**	Finland
D2	Angola		**OK**	Czech Republic
D4	Cape Verde		**OM**	Slovak Republic
D6	Comores		**OO**	Belgium
EC	Spain		**OY**	Denmark
EI	Ireland		**P**	North Korea
EK	Armenia		**PH**	Netherlands
EL	Liberia		**PJ**	Netherlands Antilles
EP	Iran		**PK**	Indonesia
ER	Moldovia		**PP**	Brazil
ES	Estonia		**PZ**	Surinam
ET	Ethiopia		**P2**	Papua New Giunea
EW	Belarus		**P4**	Aruba
EX	Kyrghyztan		**RA**	Russia
EY	Tadjikistan		**RDPL**	Laos
EZ	Turkmenistan		**RF**	Russia
F	France		**RP**	Philippines
F-O	France Overseas		**SE**	Sweden
G	Great Britain		**SP**	Poland
HA	Hungary		**ST**	Sudan
HB	Switzerland (and Lichtenstein)		**SU**	Egypt
HC	Ecuador		**SX**	Greece
HH	Haiti		**S2**	Bangladesh
HI	Dominican Republic		**S5**	Slovenia
HK	Colombia		**S7**	Seychelles
HL	South Korea		**S9**	Sao Tome
HP	Panama		**TC**	Turkey
HR	Honduras		**TF**	Iceland

TG	Guatemala	ZK	New Zealand
TI	Costa Rica	ZP	Paraguay
TJ	Cameroon	ZS, ZU	South Africa
TL	Central African Republic	Z3	Macedonia
TN	Congo	3A	Monaco
TR	Gabon	3B	Mauritius
TS	Tunisia	3C	Equatorial Guinea
TT	Chad	3D	Swaziland
TU	Côte d'Ivoire	3X	Guinea
TY	Benin	4K	Azerbaijan
TZ	Mali	4L	Georgia
T2	Tuvalu	4R	Sri Lanka
T3	Kiribati	4U	United Nations
T7	San Marino	4X	Israel
T9	Bosnia-Herzogovina	5A	Libya
UK	Uzbekistan	5B	Cyprus
UN	Kazakhstan	5H	Tanzania
UR	Ukraine	5N	Nigeria
VH	Australia	5R	Madagascar
VN	Vietnam	5T	Mauretania
VP-F	Falkland Islands	5U	Niger
VP-LA	Anguilla	5V	Togo
VP-LM	Montserrat	5W	West-Samoa
VP-LV	British Virgin Islands	5X	Uganda
VQ-T	Turks and Caicos Islands	5Y	Kenya
VR-B	Bermuda	6O	Somalia
VR-C	Cayman Islands	6V	Senegal
VR-H	Hong Kong	6Y	Jamaica
VT	India	7O	Yemen
V2	Antigua and Barbuda	7P	Lesotho
V3	Belize	7Q	Malawi
V4	St. Kitts and Nevis Islands	7T	Algeria
V5	Namibia	8P	Barbados
V6	Micronesia	8Q	Maldives
V7	Marshall Islands	8R	Guyana
V8	Brunei	9A	Croatia
XA, XB	Mexico	9G	Ghana
XT	Burkina Faso	9H	Malta
XU	Cambodia	9J	Zambia
XY	Myanmar	9K	Kuwait
YA	Afghanistan	9L	Sierra Leone
YI	Iraq	9M	Malaysia
YK	Syria	9N	Nepal
YL	Lithuania	9Q, 9T	Zaire
YN	Nicaragua	9U	Burundi
YR	Romania	9V	Singapore
YS	El Salvador	9XR	Rwanda
YU	Serbia-Macedonia	9Y	Trinidad and Tobago
YV	Venezuela		
Z, Z2	Zimbabwe		
ZA	Albania		

Place	Name	Passenger Boarding (Millions)
1	American Airlines	86,007
2	Delta Air Lines	83,117
3	United Airlines	66,696
4	Aeroflot	62,627
5	USAir	54,655
6	Northwest Airlines	43,052
7	Continental Airlines	38,791
8	ANA All Nippon	34,992
9	Air France (group)	32,708
10	Lufthansa	27,900
11	Southwest Airlines	27,839
12	British Airways	25,373
13	Japan Airlines	24,005
14	Iberia	23,172
15	TWA Trans World	22,438
16	Alitalia	19,689
17	Korean Air	15,249
18	America West Airlines	15,173
19	SAS Scandinavian	14,514
20	Saudia	11,575
21	Malaysia Airlines	10,976
22	Air Canada	9,900
23	KLM	9,183
24	Thai International	8,952
25	Singapore Airlines	8,512

Other Airline and Airliner Books

from Midland Counties Publications

Midland Counties Publications is probably the world's leading mail-order supplier of aviation books of all kinds. We have many years experience of world-wide business, thousands of satisfied customers and extensive stocks. We pay careful attention to packaging and are very happy to accept telephone or faxed orders to be charged to MasterCard or Visa accounts. Free illustrated catalogues on request.

Amongst the thousand of titles in stock are hundreds on all aspects of civil aviation, airlines and airliners – here are just a few:

abc Airline Liveries (Gunter Endres)	£7.95
Turbo-Prop Airliner Production List (Roach/Eastwood)	£10.95
Piston-Engined Airliner Production List (Roach/Eastwood)	£8.95
Flights to Hell (Allan Edwards) – worlds worst air disasters	£18.95
British Airports: Then & Now (Leo Marriott)	£12.99
The Ford Tri-Motor 1926-1992 (William T. Larkins)	£39.95
Skyliners – 117 colour photos of '50s/60s props in N. America	£17.95
Skyliners II – airliners from Europe and Latin America	£17.95
Jets: Airliners of the Golden Age (J. O. H. & A. Gesar)	£19.95
Aeroflot: An Airline and its Aircraft (R. E. G. Davis)	£24.95
Russian Propliners & Jetliners (Colin Ballantine)	£15.95
British Piston Aero Engines and their Aircraft (A. Lumsden)	£39.95
Golden Age: British Civil Aviation 1950-65 (C. Woodley)	£16.95
Faded Glory: Airline Colours of the Past (J. Merton)	£14.95
Flying the Big Jets (Stanley Stewart/3rd edition)	£16.95
Douglas Propliners, DC-1 to DC-7 (Arthur Pearcy)	£18.95
VC-10 (Phil Lo Bao/Airlines & Airliners 2)	£4.95
Vanguard (Phil Lo Bao/Airlines & Airliners 3)	£4.95
Airliners in Colour (Udo Schaeffer)	£15.95
The Spirit of Dan-Air (G. M. Simons)	£19.95
A History of the Bristol Britannia (David Littlefield)	£19.95
Aviation Disasters (David Gere) – airliner accidents since 1950	£17.50
Lockheed Constellation: A Pictorial History (Stringfellow/Bowers)	£18.95
Jetliners in Service since 1952 (John Stroud)	£30.00
Celebrating Concorde (Reginald Turnill)	£14.99
World Airliner Colours of Yesteryear (R. D. Halliday)	£13.95
Douglas DC-3 (A. J. Brown) – colour album	£8.99
Lockheed Constellation (A. J. Brown) – colour album	£8.99
Boeing 707 (A. J. Wright/Classic Civil Aircraft 2)	£12.95
de Havilland Comet (P. Birtles/Classic Civil Aircraft 3)	£12.95
Vickers Viscount (A. J. Wright/Classic Civil Aircraft 4)	£14.95
Douglas DC-9 (A. Pearcy/Airline Markings 9)	£8.95
From the Flightdeck 9: Toronto – Heathrow	£9.99

Post and packing: UK Please add 10% (minimum £1.50, maximum £3.00) orders over £40.00 sent post-free; **Overseas:** Please add 15% (minimum £2.00), or 10% of order over £150. MasterCard and Visa welcome.

Midland Counties Publications

24 The Hollow, Earl Shilton, Leicester, LE9 7NA.
Tel: 0455 233 747   Fax: 0455 841 805

SLED DRIVER
Flying the world's fastest jet

Brian Shul

No aircraft has ever captured the curiosity and fascination of the public like the SR-71 'Blackbird'. Nicknamed the 'Sled' by those who flew it, the aircraft was surrounded in secrecy from its inception. From 1966, the SR-71 was the fastest, highest flying jet aircraft in the world. For nearly a quarter of a century it performed a vital reconnaissance mission for the US with impunity, and when it was retired in 1990, all of its speed and altitude records were still untouched.

Now for the first time a 'Blackbird' pilot shares his experience of what it was like to fly this legend. Retired Major Brian Shul's engrossing words and captivating photography give an insight on all phases of flying, including the humbling experience of

simulator training, the physiological stresses of wearing a space suit for long hours, and the intensity and magic of flying 80,000 feet above the earth's surface at 2,000 miles an hour. This is truly one of the best aviation books we've seen in years - almost impossible to put down!

Hardback, 304 x 254 mm
152 pages
108 colour photographs
Available now
1 85780 002 8
£19.95

WRECKS AND RELICS
14th Edition

Ken Ellis

The latest version of this popular biennial reference, is greatly expanded with no less than 64 extra pages of text (the RAF in particular have retired a lot of aircraft lately!) and a further 16 pages of photos.

The book lists and traces the movements of thousands of aircraft held in museums, preserved with individuals, in use as gate guardians, instructional airframes, on fire dumps etc, in the United Kingdom and Ireland, and on RAF bases overseas.

Includes museums with opening times, BAPC member groups, BAPC/IAHC registers, and enormously useful indexes by both aircraft type and location. This new edition features detailed histories, the improved layout and referability of the 13th Edition.

Previous editions still in print:
10th edition (1986) 254pp   **£7.50**
12th edition (1990) 252pp   **£9.95**

Laminated Hardback
210 x 148 mm, 336 pages
with 152 photos.
Available now
1 85780 025 7
£12.95

WINGS OVER LINCOLNSHIRE
Peter Green, and Mike Hodgson

The rural county of Lincolnshire can perhaps lay claim to being England's premier aviation county. It is the home of the Royal Air Force College at Cranwell, and was host to thousands of Allied aircrew during the Second World War. The county's illustrious aviation heritage is now an attraction for many aviation enthusiasts and general tourists.

This new pictorial chronicles Lincolnshire's strong ties with the worlds of both civil and military aviation from before the First World War. The five sections begin with ballooning in the nineteenth century and continue through the First World War, the inter-war period, the Second World War and post-war to the present day Tornado and Sentry.

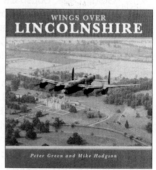

In addition to the aircraft, the personalities such as B C Hucks, Sir Alan Cobham and Alex Henshaw are included. The photographs come from local archives and private collections.

For the enthusiast, this is a fascinating gap-filler, and for the less committed, it is a useful introduction to Lincolnshire's diverse aviation history.

Softback
200 x 210 mm, 48 pages
143 photos
Available now
1 85780 024 9
£7.95

WAR PRIZES

Phil Butler
Foreword: Capt E.M.'Winkle' Brown, RN

Meticulously researched study of the many German, Italian, and Japanese aircraft taken to Allied countries or flown by the Allies during and after the Second World War, in essence greatly amplifying the scope of the author's earlier book 'Air Min', but with extensive new information, some long held myths debunked and an unrivalled selection of photographs, many previously unpublished. The coverage includes civilian aircraft and sailplanes as well as military types; post-war production of German designs and details of surviving air-craft in museums. Appendices include German and Japanese aircraft designation and marking systems.

UK chapters include such units as RAE Farnborough, 1426 (Enemy Aircraft) Flight, and many other squadrons, organisations and manu-facturers. The US chapters deal with aircraft flown by the USAAF at Wright Field, Freeman Field, and in Europe by 'Watson's Whizzers', the US Navy-led TAIC at Anacostia, TAIUs in Australia, the Philippines, and many other units in all theaters of war.

Hardback
282 x 213 mm, 320 pages
with 450 photos.
Available now
0 904597 86 5
£29.95

FOREIGN INVADERS
The Douglas Invader in Foreign Military and US Clandestine Service

Dan Hagedorn and Leif Hellström

The Douglas A-26 Invader is without doubt one of the most unsung of combat aircraft, with a long and chequered history. It served worldwide with many air forces even until the 1970s, and was also quite popular with the CIA for clandestine operations, including the notorious 'Bay of Pigs' invasion of Cuba.

This book focuses on the non-US military use of the Invader, covering service in twenty countries. Also covered in fascinating depth is use by a host of paramilitary forces and clandestine users, in over a dozen wars, conflicts and coups.

Here two immensely qualified and thorough authors present a deeply researched insight into all these operations, including a wealth of

rarely published information and refuting some long perpetuated 'facts'. This is supported by a fine collection of photographs, most previously unpublished.

This fine historical record, is an excellent reference for modellers (colour side views are included) and of interest to 'warbird' enthusiasts.

Hardback
282 x 213 mm, 200 pages
265 b/w photos + 8pp colour
Available now
1 85780 013 3
£22.95

OKB SUKHOI

Vladimir Antonov, Yefim Gordon, Nikolai Gordyukov, Vladimir Yakovlev & Vyacheslav Zenkin, with Jay Miller

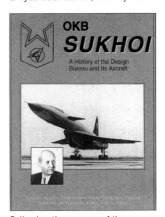

Following the success of the acclaimed 'OKB MiG', we are pleased to announce that another famous Soviet aircraft design bureau is thoroughly documented in this new book, which has been prepared with the co-operation of the Sukhoi bureau, and with extensive access to their records and photo files. There is a massive amount of fresh and unpublished information and illustration included in what must become a 'standard' reference on this important military aircraft designer. Each individual aircraft type is reviewed in detail, including prototypes, testbeds and projects. There are various three view and other drawings.

Hardback
280 x 212 mm, 248 pages
About 600 photos including colour section
Autumn 1994
1 85780 012 5
£29.95